The Ghost Ship of Brooklyn

The

GHOST SHIP

of

BROOKLYN

———— ★ ————

An Untold Story *of the*
American Revolution

ROBERT P. WATSON

DA CAPO PRESS

Da Capo Press
Hachette Book Group
1290 Avenue of the Americas
New York, NY 10104
www.dacapopress.com

Printed in the United States of America
First Edition: August 2017

Published by Da Capo Press, an imprint of Perseus Books, LLC, a subsidiary of Hachette Book Group, Inc.

The publisher is not responsible for websites (or their content) that are not owned by the publisher.

Print book interior design by Jack Lenzo

Library of Congress Cataloging-in-Publication Data has been applied for.

ISBNs: 978-0-306-82552-1 (hardcover), 978-0-306-82553-8 (ebook)

LSC-C

10   9   8   7   6   5   4   3   2   1

To all prisoners of war: your sacrifices
and service are not forgotten

Contents

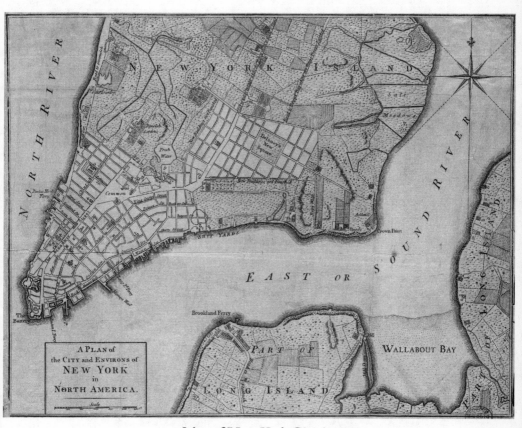

Map of New York City in 1770

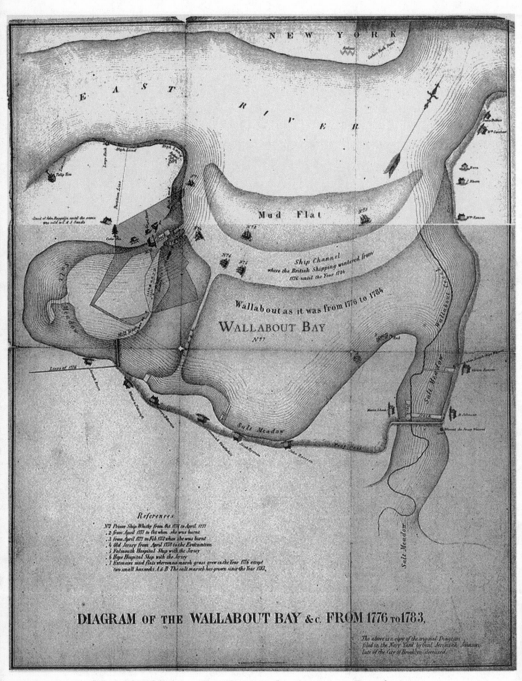

Map of Wallabout Bay During the American Revolution

Preface

The treatment of prisoners of war throughout history has been unimaginably horrific. Those soldiers and civilians unfortunate enough to be captured during times of conflict have been subjected to a bewildering array of abuses, including forced labor, starvation, torture, rape, and solitary confinement. Others were simply murdered. Tragically, every country, culture, and conflict has suffered such crimes. Some have been worse than others. The Aztecs, for instance, tied prisoners to stone slabs and cut out their hearts . . . while the prisoner was still alive. In the Second Sino-Japanese War, Imperial Japanese forces murdered tens—and possibly hundreds—of thousands of Chinese civilians in what became known as the "Nanking Massacre" or the "Rape of Nanking." The Chinese would later return the cruelty, beheading captured Japanese soldiers and using their heads as soccer balls. And during the Nazi reign, Dr. Josef Mengele, the infamous "Angel of Death," conducted savagely cruel medical experiments on concentration camp prisoners. Such incidents are all too common in the annals of history and are far too numerous to list.

On the other hand, there have been efforts by the international community, individual governments, and human rights groups to limit such barbarous behavior. One such example is the Geneva Convention, a series of international treaties and agreements on the status and treatment of prisoners of war, first developed in 1864. The subsequent record has been mixed. In the wake of history's bloodiest conflict, when approximately 3.3 million Soviet prisoners taken by the Axis powers died in captivity and Joseph Stalin and the Red Army, in turn, killed countless German prisoners and millions more of their own citizens, the world community came together in 1949 to ratify two new conventions. Sadly, none of this stopped the mistreatment of prisoners.

Americans have been among those prisoners who have suffered during conflicts. This includes the Civil War, when the Confederacy treated Northern prisoners with neglect, disdain, and brutality. Perhaps the most reprehensible example was when roughly thirteen thousand Union soldiers incarcerated at the notorious Andersonville Prison in Georgia died from malnutrition, poor sanitation, disease, exposure to the elements, and abuse at the hands of individuals who had, until only a few years prior, been their fellow countrymen. In the twentieth century, the crimes against American servicemen in Germany, Japan, Korea, and Vietnam were particularly loathsome and numerous.

The ensuing years have been plagued by campaigns of genocide around the world in Cambodia, Rwanda, Bosnia, Darfur, and elsewhere. As I write this preface, the headlines are dominated by news of public beheadings of prisoners by groups such as the self-proclaimed Islamic State and abuses directed at prisoners of war and political prisoners in China, Russia, parts of Africa, and much of the Middle East.

Yet, long before the Geneva Convention, concerns over the mistreatment of prisoners arose during the Revolutionary War, when some of the most odious and vile crimes in American history occurred at the hands of the British and were directed against American soldiers and sailors fighting for independence. While the stories of the Boston Massacre, Boston Tea Party, and Paul Revere's midnight ride are well known by any American schoolchild, the plight of American prisoners during the Revolution remains largely unknown. In particular, history has forgotten the struggles that occurred on an old, rotting prison ship moored off the coast of Brooklyn, despite the fact that as many as 11,500 prisoners may have died in her holds—a number roughly twice the total number of American lives lost in combat during the entirety of the war!

This little-known story is shocking and grisly, but the struggles of those who escaped and, against all odds, survived are nothing shy of inspiring and heroic. They are also important, for they compel us to rethink our inaccurate view of how the British prosecuted the war, to remember the sacrifices made by so many forgotten patriots, and to explore one of the worst tragedies in American military history, one involving a wretched and cursed ghost ship that the British believed would frighten patriots into submission. It did not. It had the opposite effect and unintentionally ended up helping the colonists win the war.

A note to the reader: The words of the prisoners aboard the hellish ship as well as the war records and letters of prison wardens and generals are all quoted verbatim in the following pages. Some of the spelling reflects the time period and varying degrees of literacy of the men and boys in the book.

The book would not have been possible without the assistance of several people. First, I would like to thank my incredible literary agent, Peter Bernstein. I am also fortunate to have Robert Pigeon as my editor. It has been a pleasure to work with such a talented editor as Bob and the entire team at Da Capo Press and Perseus Books— Lissa Warren, Justin Lovell, Skyler Lambert, Michael Clark, Sue Warga, Jack Lenzo, and too many others to mention.

I would like to acknowledge Jared Wellman, a librarian at Lynn University, for his help in tracking down old and obscure documents, and both Juan Tirado (who passed away in 2016 after a long and courageous struggle with cancer) and David Garcia for making photocopies of them for me. Nancy Katz and George Goldstein, M.D., read an early version of the manuscript and provided me with valuable feedback. Thanks also to Julie Stoner and Bruce Kirby of the Library of Congress, Joanna Lamaida of the Brooklyn Historical

Society, Dr. Daniel Rolph and Steven Smith of the Historical Society of Pennsylvania, Alicia Parks of the Museum of the American Revolution, the reference staff at the New York Public Library, and many other archivists and librarians for their help with accessing historic documents.

Mostly, however, I would like to thank my family—Claudia, Alessandro, and Isabella—for their constant support. Lastly, this book is dedicated to all the men and women who have suffered the misfortune of being a prisoner of war. Your sacrifices are not forgotten.

ROBERT P. WATSON
Boca Raton, Florida

"A Vast and Silent Army"

The various horrors of these hulks to tell—
These prison ships where Pain and Penance dwell.
Where Death in ten-fold vengeance holds his reign,
And injured ghosts, yet unavenged, complain:
This be my task.

—Philip Freneau, "The British Prison-Ship" (1781)

On a crisp winter's morn in the closing days of the year 431 B.C.E., the Athenian statesman Pericles climbed a high platform for the painful but honored task of eulogizing his brethren who fell in the Peloponnesian War.* The struggle against Sparta had started earlier that spring and would prove to be a long and bloody affair. Accordingly, this would be but one of many burials in Athens, though history would remember Pericles' funeral oration that day as one of the most important speeches of the ancient world.

It was customary in Athens for men lost in war to be honored at elaborate funerals. These ceremonies began a few days prior to the

---

* The long war lasted until Athens surrendered in the year 404 B.C.E.

burial, when the fallen soldiers' remains were placed on public display, providing an opportunity for family members, friends, and other Athenians to gather to pay their respects and make offerings. Coffins were then carried in carts to a scenic spot on the outskirts of the city for the burial, with one of the coffins remaining empty—a haunting symbol of the dead who were still missing. After the processional, the heroes were laid to rest in a large sepulcher. The grand ceremony concluded with comments from an individual of great esteem.

And so it was that day that the famed orator Pericles offered his remarks. The account was recorded that day and retold by Thucydides, the Athenian historian and general who wrote the history of the Peloponnesian War. According to Thucydides, Pericles opened with these now-famous lines: "Most of my predecessors in this place have commended him who made this speech part of the law, telling us that it is well that it should be delivered at the burial of those who fall in battle. For myself, I should have thought that the worth which had displayed itself in deeds would be sufficiently rewarded by honors also shown by deeds; such as you now see in this funeral."

Noting that the fallen were part of something larger than themselves, Pericles maintained, "It is for such a city, then, that these men nobly died in battle, thinking it right not to be deprived of her, just as each of their survivors should be willing to toil for her sake." The statesman did more than recognize the dead as heroes. In a comparatively brief eulogy, he heralded the special qualities of Athenians and enshrined the sacrifices within the larger context of the struggle for freedom.

Two millennia later, President Abraham Lincoln also stood atop a viewing stand for a similar purpose: to commemorate a new national cemetery at Gettysburg, Pennsylvania, the site of a bloody clash that had taken place in early July 1863. That pivotal battle of the American Civil War claimed a staggering 23,000 Union casualties, along with roughly the same number on the Confederate side. The death toll overwhelmed the small farming community and prompted the need for the creation of a stately public resting place.

Although Lincoln was not the featured speaker—he followed musical performances and a lofty, two-hour disquisition by Edward Everett, the president of Harvard and a famed orator—his remarks echoed those of Pericles. In a surprisingly brief address, Lincoln not only honored "a portion of that field, as a final resting place for those who here gave their lives that a nation might live," but placed the sacrifices into the larger context of "a new birth of freedom." Like Pericles, the Great Emancipator also poetically noted that the deeds of those who had fallen would never be forgotten and their service would consecrate the sacred spot far beyond any words he offered.

Both Pericles and Lincoln confessed that they were humbled by the task before them. Yet both used the occasion to call upon their countrymen to remember and honor the fallen by continuing their work. "It is for us the living, rather," admonished Lincoln, "to be dedicated here to the unfinished work which they who fought here have thus far so nobly advanced." Both orations remain as among the most celebrated speeches in history, even prompting Professor Everett, the Gettysburg keynoter, to sheepishly later admit in a letter to Lincoln, "I wish I could flatter myself that I had come as near to the central idea of the occasion in two hours as you did in two minutes." Indeed.

It is hard to imagine two more eloquent and fitting wartime eulogiums than those offered by Pericles and Lincoln, as it is hard for us today to imagine not honoring those who made the ultimate sacrifice for their country. Indeed, in ancient Greece the failure to commemorate those who died in war was seen as an unforgivable breach of honor and nothing less than an affront to patriotism. It was akin to a public rebuke, display of cowardice, or a dismissal of their deeds by another.

Yet, tragically, this was precisely the fate of countless thousands of men who died during the single bloodiest struggle of the entire American Revolution. For these wretched souls there was no grand homily, no public procession, no pomp or pageantry, no act of remembrance when their bodies were laid to rest. As one New Yorker living shortly after the tragedy lamented, for the prisoners aboard the ships "no degree of gratitude [has been] expressed, in written record or enduring memorial."* Rather, for the starved and tortured prisoners, the end was marked with their bodies' being dumped unceremoniously into shallow, unmarked graves on the Brooklyn shoreline. Apallingly, their sacrifices have largely been forgotten.

Belatedly, however, these prison ship martyrs from the Revolutionary War would get their Pericles, their Lincoln. None other than Walt Whitman, one of America's most significant poets, sought in the mid-nineteenth century to memorialize the prisoners aboard the monstrous ship. The Long Island native lived near the site of the worst struggle of the Revolution and, during his lifetime, the bones of Americans who had died on the prison ships still occasionally washed ashore or were unearthed by construction projects. It pained the celebrated poet greatly that the burial sites had been desecrated when workers dredged the shoreline to build a new naval facility, and he cursed the "thoughtless boys" in town who played in the martyrs' crypts, often using the skulls and bones they found in games.

Whitman wrote an article in the *Brooklyn Standard* hoping to raise public awareness for a suitable commemoration for what he described as "a vast and silent army" of ghosts scattered in shallow graves along Brooklyn's waterfront. On July 2, 1846, he also published a poem in the *Brooklyn Daily Eagle*. His intention was for the lyrics to be put to the melody of "The Star-Spangled Banner" and have the public gather by the site of the tragedy and sing the poem at the Independence Day celebration two days later. Whitman's first verse read,

> *O, God of Columbia! O, Shield of the Free!*
> *More grateful to you than the fanes of old story,*
> *Must the blood-bedewed soil, the red battle-ground be*
> *Where our fore-fathers championed America's glory!*

---

* There has since been a monument erected to their memory in Brooklyn.

Then how priceless the worth of the sanctified earth,
We are standing on now. Lo! The slope of its girth
Where the Martyrs were buried: Nor prayers, tears, or stones,
Marked their crumbled-in coffins, their white, holy bones!

Whitman was not the only one to attempt to commemorate the "vast and silent army" that died along Brooklyn's shoreline. There was another. In 1895 the noted attorney, scholar, and Brooklyn resident Dr. Charles E. West addressed a group of students at the Brooklyn Heights Seminary. Like the famed poet before him, West told his audience, "The horrors of the British prison ships of the Wallabout have never been revealed to the public eye." While the claim failed to acknowledge Whitman's earlier poems, Dr. West was correct in saying that the tragedy "for some unaccountable reason has been omitted from the leading American histories and very many ordinary well-informed people know practically nothing of the unparalleled cruelty of the British or the unflinching courage of the patriots who met martyr's deaths in defence of their country." West gave the address well over a century after the incident, and with the passing of years, the tragedy was again largely forgotten.

Here we are now, well over a century after West's speech and more than 230 years after the demise of the ghost ship of the Revolution. His complaint that "the muse of history sits silent by the tomb of the American martyrs, draped in mourning," still rings mostly true. Thankfully, there is today a lone obelisk known as the Prison Ship Martyrs' Monument that stands quietly on a small hilltop in Fort Greene Park in Brooklyn. It overlooks the reinterred remains of the prisoners and site of so much suffering so long ago.

But this solitary testament to the tragedy is overshadowed by the hustle and bustle of the city and so many other, more popular and frequented sites. Even the touching Soldiers' and Sailors' Monument at Trinity Church in New York City is rendered nearly inconsequential by the surrounding skyscrapers. Unfortunately, unlike Revolutionary sites in Boston, Philadelphia, and Williamsburg—with their many visible reminders, intact colonial buildings, and large historic districts—amid New York's skyline and onslaught of development few tangible connections to the prisoners' stories remain.

History remembers and celebrates Lexington and Concord, George Washington's surprise Christmas night attack against the Hessians at Trenton, and the triumphal American victory in 1781 over Lord Cornwallis at Yorktown. But the single bloodiest conflict of the Revolution does not appear in textbooks and has been discussed in only two scholarly books. It has yet to be made into a Hollywood film or musical score. The tragedy in the waters off Brooklyn is not featured in museums, taught in schools, or evoked today with either reverent pride or solemn remembrance during Independence Day ceremonies. In short, it has never captured the popular imagination.

We may have forgotten the story of Brooklyn's Wallabout Bay today, but prison ships were not always a mystery. Charles Dickens, for instance, in his classic book *Great Expectations*, features a ghostly prison ship. Dickens introduces the scene with a properly haunted location—a foggy churchyard next to a shrouded marsh during a dark night. Nearby, a search party is hunting an escaped prisoner still wearing irons on his legs. Dickens's character Pip has a frightening brush with the prisoner, a scene made all the more unnerving when the flickering light of the search party's torches reveals a "black hulk lying out a little way from the mud of the shore, like a wicked Noah's ark, cribbed and barred and moored by massive rusty chains." Dickens, a social critic and reformer, was likely inspired to include a prison ship in his novel because of their widespread and controversial use by the British. He most probably observed them, as prison ships were anchored off the towns of Portsmouth and Woolwich on the outskirts of London as well as at ports in the West Indies during Dickens's lifetime.

Yet most people have never heard of the Old Sugar House in New York City, Wallabout Bay, or the British prison ships of the

Revolution. Nevertheless, these places were the scenes of some of the most gruesome events in the nation's history and constitute the ugly secret of the Revolutionary War. Ironically, few aspects of the Revolutionary War were as thoroughly documented yet as quickly forgotten as the prison ships. Captured ships were listed, prisoners' names were registered, and deaths recorded.

In 1832 the U.S. Congress finally passed a measure allowing veterans of the Revolutionary War to petition for pensions. Sadly, most of those who fought were by then long gone. For those still alive, the legislation offered a much-needed yearly stipend to anyone who could prove at least six months of wartime service. Unfortunately, most of the elderly petitioners had little to no proof of their service—maybe an old uniform, a scar from a gunshot or bayonet wound, an enlistment certificate, or discharge papers. What all of them had, however, were memories. The petitioners who came forward shared stories with court clerks who documented them and encouraged veterans to record their experiences in order to prove their status as veterans. We can be thankful that many put quill to paper.

Others were motivated by their families to write memoirs. In particular, five men and boys—Christopher Hawkins, Thomas Dring, Thomas Andros, Ebenezer Fox, and Andrew Sherburne—somehow survived the most cursed of all the prison ships and wrote detailed narratives of the experience. Together, these remarkable and gripping accounts of battles, captures, imprisonment, and escapes or releases offer a firsthand telling of perhaps the most dreadful event of the Revolutionary period.

In the words of Thomas Dring, an officer from Rhode Island, "Among the varied events of the war of the American Revolution, there are few circumstances which have left a deeper impression on the public mind, than those connected with the cruel and vindictive treatment which was experienced by those of our unfortunate countrymen whom the fortune of war had placed on board the Prison-Ships of the enemy." Christopher Hawkins echoed Dring's account of the ships. A young boy captured by the British and imprisoned aboard the worst of the ships, he described the ordeal in the opening lines of his journal, saying, "Among the various modes adopted by the British, during the Revolution, for taming the American people into submission to the English yoke, none were more barbarous and more revolting to humanities than the cruelties inflicted by means of the prison ships."

The macabre and grisly chapter in American history they described occurred in the waters just off the coast of Brooklyn. From 1776 to the very end of the war in 1783, the British occupied New York City and Long Island and made them the staging ground for their military operations in America. The waterways throughout the city soon filled with supply vessels, transport craft, and warships, prompting the British command to use older ships to incarcerate American soldiers and sailors captured in battle. Civilians suspected of supporting the colonial cause or refusing to swear an oath of allegiance to the Crown were arrested. They joined countless thousands of soldiers from the Continental Army and sailors from warships, merchant craft, and privateers who were imprisoned belowdecks in the cramped, diseased holds of these floating dungeons. As thousands perished, the prison ships moored in a shallow and otherwise forgettable body of water known as Wallabout Bay quickly became massive, ghostly coffins.

The most notorious of these ships was the HMS *Jersey*. More than a thousand prisoners at a time were held aboard the ship. The deplorable conditions belowdecks resulted in a half dozen to one dozen men, on average, dying every day from smallpox, dysentery, typhoid, or yellow fever as well as from the effects of malnutrition, polluted water, and torture. This single ship accounted for the lion's share of the misery and deaths of American prisoners during the war, an amount described as "obscenely high" by one source. In fact, more Americans died on board the ghost ship of Brooklyn than died in combat during the entirety of the Revolutionary War—by a factor of two!

The tragedy of the *Jersey* and other horrid prison ships was irrefutably "the darkest in the history of our Revolutionary struggle." An attorney from Brooklyn tasked with preparing a report on the floating dungeons after the war concluded that although there are always "occasional acts of inhumanity and cowardly brutality, committed in the heat of battle," this particular catastrophe could never be "excused." On the contrary, he argued that the ordeal was a chilling example of the "temporary triumph of passion and vengeance over reason and humanity."

To be sure, the British command intended the *Jersey* to be a weapon of terror. The threat of imprisonment in her deadly bowels, they reasoned, would deter even the most ardent of patriots from fighting. And so they crammed thousands into the dark, dank hull and moored the ship far enough from shore to prevent the disease that soon permeated her rotting timbers from inflicting the city, yet close enough to be seen and smelled by all who passed by. However, the plan backfired. As prisoners aboard the dreaded ship escaped and as colonial pamphlets and newspapers such as the *Connecticut Courant*, *New York Journal*, *Pennsylvania Journal*, and others told their gruesome stories, the "Old *Jersey*" quickly emerged as a powerful symbol of British oppression and cruelty. Like the Boston Massacre, an event that crystalized support for the cause of liberty a decade earlier, the horrors that occurred on the *Jersey* turned loyalists into patriots and ended up inspiring the struggle for independence.

This is the story of an old warship that, because of the obscenely high death toll and inhumane conditions below her decks, was nicknamed "Hell Afloat" or simply "Hell." She earned the reputation.

—— 1 ——

Warship

Ungenerous Britons, you
Conspire to murder whom you can't subdue.

—Philip Freneau, "The British Prison-Ship" (1781)

The rivalry between Britain and Spain for supremacy of the seas had a long and bloody history. The two naval powers squared off time and again from the beginning of the Age of Exploration through the colonial period, including a bitter struggle during what was essentially the first modern world war—the War of Spanish Succession, fought in the early eighteenth century. The centrality of the seas to the rivalry was such that even the terms of the peace treaty, signed in the Dutch city of Utrecht, emphasized maritime trade and naval relations. In it, Spain agreed to a thirty-year trade deal that permitted Britain to ship a specified annual tonnage of goods to Spain's colonies along with a limited number of slaves.

But the history between the two naval powers proved too onerous for the treaty to hold. Neither nation trusted the other. The Spanish suspected the British of smuggling additional goods and slaves in violation of the treaty, while British captains did not take kindly to having limits placed by the Spanish monarch on what they could carry. Tensions increased and ultimately resulted in yet another conflict—the Anglo-Spanish War, fought from 1727 to 1729.

The negotiations leading to the Treaty of Seville, which ended that war, again affirmed British maritime trade, but in return gave the Spanish the right to stop and inspect British ships. In the ensuing years, both sides navigated the arrangement with great difficulty and distrust. Ultimately, this agreement, like the others before it, was destined to fail.

It happened on April 9, 1731, when the Spanish patrol boat *La Isabela* seized the British merchant craft *Rebecca* in waters off Havana. Spanish authorities suspected Captain Robert Jenkins and his crew of smuggling goods in violation of the treaty. During the argument that ensued between Jenkins and the commander of the Spanish ship, Julio León Fandiño, the British officer's left ear was cut off. Back in England, the incident was met with outrage and became an emotional and memorable symbol of Spanish interference with British shipping. Relations between the two powers eroded.

Then, in March 1738, Captain Jenkins was called before the House of Commons to testify about his ordeal and, in general, Spanish harassment of British shipping. Jenkins, still fuming over his lost ear, was only too happy to stir up anti-Spanish sentiment. Some accounts suggest that, to the horror of some members of Parliament (but to the delight of the war hawks), he held forth the severed ear, which he had preserved by having it pickled.* British politicians were already in the clutches of war fever, and Jenkins's passionate description of the humiliation he had endured produced cries in Parliament for retribution.

And so it happened. The following year Robert Walpole, the British prime minister, was pressured into declaring war on Spain. Yet he offered a portent of things to come. Speaking of the warmongers in his country, the prime minister warned, "They may ring their bells

---

* The historical record remains unclear as to whether Jenkins actually brought along his severed appendage, with some recent sources questioning the authenticity of the story.

now; they will be wringing their hands before long." The conflict that resulted was a senseless and tragic affair, which many years later the British essayist Thomas Carlyle dubbed "The War of Jenkins' Ear."

Britain immediately developed plans to attack Spanish colonies in North and South America, and the two powers were at war once again. To lead the assault, the British chose Admiral Edward Vernon, who had been a staunch defender of Captain Jenkins and an advocate of a muscular response to perceived Spanish abuses. Vernon was elevated to the position of vice admiral on July 9, 1739, and given six powerful ships of the line to attack Spanish commerce and forts on the other side of the Atlantic. Admiral Vernon launched his invasion by successfully sacking Porto Bello and other Spanish settlements in Panama. News spread of the victories, and Vernon was celebrated as a hero back in England.

In 1741 Britain's naval hero was ordered to destroy the remaining Spanish colonies in the New World and given a massive force to accomplish the mission. It included 29 ships of the line, 22 frigates, and 135 transport and supply vessels as well as more than 15,000 sailors and some 12,000 marines and soldiers. The fighting force also included roughly 3,600 colonial troops from America under Colonel William Gooch of Virginia. The admiral's main target was the Spanish stronghold at Cartagena, in present-day Colombia.

Despite the impressive size of his fleet, nearly everything that could have gone wrong ultimately did go wrong. In March, Vernon began the blockade and bombardment of Cartagena. However, poor planning and bickering among the British leadership resulted in the armada being inadequately provisioned. The admiral also suspected that his top general, Thomas Wentworth, was inept. Wentworth would soon prove Vernon right. At the same time, yellow fever, dysentery, and typhus struck the ships. Roughly five hundred British soldiers and sailors were already dead by the time the siege began, with another fifteen hundred too sick to fight.

A garrison of just three thousand men and six warships defended Cartagena. However, the celebrated warrior Vice Admiral Blas de

Lezo, who had lost an arm, leg, and eye in previous wars, led them. The wily de Lezo had designed a creative but risky plan for defending the city. Allowing the British to take smaller fortifications, the admiral ordered his men to fall back and inspired them to make a determined defense of the colonial city. For sixty-seven days, the British repeatedly attempted to take the city. A great number of cannonballs poured down on Cartagena while land forces attacked throughout the region. But the walled fortress held long enough for de Lezo's secret weapon to arrive.

When the rainy season came, it brought heavy tropical storms that drenched the British fleet and marine assault force. Jungle paths became impassable, and swarms of mosquitos ravaged the invaders, as did the resulting fevers. As the British attack ground to a stop because of the weather, the Spanish concentrated their fire on the main British warships with devastating accuracy.

Even though the Spanish lost all six of their ships and five small forts, the battle was calamitous for the British. It is estimated that Vernon suffered between 9,500 and 18,000 dead, with another 7,500 wounded and sick. The Royal Navy lost six ships, more than two dozen transports and supply craft, and fifteen hundred guns. Another seventeen warships were badly damaged. Admiral Vernon was forced to withdraw. Determined to achieve victory elsewhere and salvage the invasion, Vernon sailed to Cuba. But disease, jungle terrain, tactical miscalculations, and a determined guerrilla resistance once again decimated the British.

Vernon was forced to abandon Cuba. The proud Royal Navy was again embarrassed. Compounding the defeat was the fact that, with so many warships engaged in the grand invasion, British merchant craft were left unescorted. While the Royal Navy was otherwise preoccupied, Spanish privateers wreaked havoc on British shipping and trade in the Atlantic and West Indies. Back home, shame quickly turned to outrage, and in 1742 both Vernon and Wentworth were recalled to London. By the end of hostilities in May 1742, the majority of British sailors and soldiers in the expeditionary force had died from disease in the disastrous campaign. The government of Robert Walpole soon collapsed.

The War of Jenkins' Ear was not without other consequences for history. The captain of the marines serving on Admiral Vernon's flagship, HMS *Princess Caroline*, was Lawrence Washington, who would later name his home overlooking the Potomac River back in Virginia for his admiral. A few years later, the tuberculosis Captain Washington likely contracted during his service in Vernon's disastrous campaign worsened. After numerous failed efforts to treat the ailment, Lawrence was urged to seek relief in the warm environs of Barbados. Joining him on the trip in November and December 1751 was his teenage half brother, George. Sad to say, not even the tropical paradise could save Lawrence Washington; he succumbed to the disease in 1752. Ownership of Mount Vernon eventually passed to the younger Washington, who grew up wanting to emulate his older sibling by serving in uniform.

It was also during the Washington brothers' trip to Barbados that George contracted smallpox, but survived. As it turned out, his experience with the disease proved fortuitous when the scourge swept through the colonies during the Revolutionary War. The incident in Barbados had prompted the commander of the colonial army to have his men inoculated against the disease, thus avoiding a potentially devastating loss of colonial troops. These inoculations would also help save the lives of many of those suffering aboard the British prison ships when the disease tore through their holds.

There is another historical footnote from the conflict. One of the vessels involved in the War of Jenkins' Ear was the HMS *Jersey*. The powerful, sixty-gun warship was a key part of Admiral Vernon's fleet that attacked Cartagena. The campaign marked the new ship's first naval battle and the first of several doomed missions. The captain's log reveals that the ship suffered a second defeat after the disaster in the waters off Colombia. In June 1745 the *Jersey* was badly damaged, as described by her senior officer: "The braces, bowlines shot away several times, also the staysail halyards. The running rigging very much shattered. The main topsail yard shot . . . the foremast shot through about the collar of the mainstay, and another wound in the after part of the mast . . . the mainmast shot about two thirds up from the deck and divided [to] the starboard." The warship was nearly lost at sea. As the captain wrote of the desperate situation, "Ship making 11 inches of water an hour occasioned by two shots in the counter, under the water line."

These disastrous missions proved to be an ominous start for what would become one of history's most ill-fated ships. Like her namesakes before her—other British warships that ended up being captured, burned, or destroyed—the *Jersey* seemed to many to be cursed. Little did anyone know that the ship was headed for infamy during the American Revolution.

The British armada that fought in several campaigns included a series of warships commissioned by the Royal Navy in the early eighteenth century. The vessels were classified by, among other characteristics, the number of cannons they carried. "First rate" designations were for ships with one hundred guns, "second rate" ships carried roughly ninety guns, and "third rate" warships were fitted with seventy to eighty cannons. The *Jersey* was built for sixty guns, marking her as a "fourth rate" ship of the line. Though smaller than His Majesty's largest warships, the *Jersey* was nonetheless one of the most powerful and technologically advanced ships afloat when she was built. She was one of several ships of roughly the same size constructed in England that decade from an official regulation and rating scheme for warships developed in 1733.*

The *Jersey*'s armaments included twenty-four massive, 24-pound cannons on the gun deck, which functioned as the main firing platform of the ship. The warship also boasted twenty-six 9-pound

---

* This line of warships was very popular. A total of fifteen "fourth rate" ships carrying sixty guns were built in England in the 1730s. Another twelve carrying fifty guns were also constructed.

cannons on the upper deck, eight small 6-pounders on the quarter-deck—near the stern of the ship—and two small guns on the forecastle by the ship's bow. During times of war the ship often mounted anywhere from four to fourteen additional guns and was crewed by fully 450 officers, sailors, and marines.

Built in Plymouth Dockyard during a time of peace, the *Jersey* was launched on June 14, 1736. A marvel to behold, the ship was 144 feet in length (as measured on the gun deck) with a beam of over forty-one feet. Weighing more than one thousand tons, she was powerful yet sleek and, for the standards of the day, rather fast. Her keel extended nearly seventeen feet below the surface, allowing the ship ample storage space for powder, cannonballs, and supplies for her large crew and lengthy deployments.

By 1770, however, the *Jersey* had seen better days, having sustained considerable damage in several unsuccessful engagements. Thus, while serving in the waters of Britain's North American colonies before the Revolutionary War, the old ship that seemed to her crew to be cursed was converted to serve as a supply and hospital ship. This involved "hulking" the once-proud warship by removing her cannons, bridge, masts, sails, and even the figurehead on the bow. In the words of an unfortunate colonial who would soon call the ship home, "At the commencement of the American Revolution, being an old vessel, and proving to be much decayed, she was entirely dismantled, and soon after was moored in the East River at New York, and converted into a store-ship."

There she sat, anchored off the New York coast from April 1778 until the bitter end of the long conflict. Faced with a growing population of colonial prisoners during the Revolutionary War and not wanting to build prisons, British commanders made the decision to convert old warships to prison ships. Thus was the fate of the *Jersey* during the winter of 1779–80. She became a floating dungeon, as described by one of her prisoners: "Without ornament, an old, unsightly hulk, whose dark and filthy external appearance fitly represented the death and despair that reigned within."

2

"The Glorious Cause"

Better the greedy wave should swallow all,
Better to meet the death-conducting ball,
Better to sleep on ocean's oozy bed,
At once destroy'd and number'd with the dead;
Than thus to perish in the face of day,
Where twice ten thousand deaths one death delay.

—Philip Freneau, "The British Prison-Ship" (1781)

Contrary to the image of eighteenth-century Britain that is often presented in history books, the proud notion of "Rule, Britannia" was being challenged by provincial unrest throughout the empire. Rebellion in Scotland, discontent in Ireland, discord throughout the kingdom, and even periodic rioting at home posed problems for the Crown. It was about to get worse. The spark of revolution would soon follow in the American colonies, fanned by the Stamp Act of 1765, the Boston Massacre of 1770, the 1773 Boston Tea Party, and other events.

Lord North, the British prime minister at the time of the "uprising" (as the British viewed America's war for independence), initially sought to avoid armed conflict by attempting to reach compromise with the colonists. A similar hope was shared among many colonists in America who considered themselves British. Most celebrated their monarch and used English goods, even though they acted, dressed, and spoke in ways unlike their rulers across the Atlantic. However, after several miscalculations and amid escalating tensions, Lord North pursued a more aggressive course. Likewise, in 1775 King George III issued a Proclamation for Suppressing Rebellion and Sedition, labeling his royal subjects as "traitors." He also dispatched General Thomas Gage to Lexington and Concord to quell the rebellion and arrest the colonial "troublemakers." And war came.

Engagements fought at the start of the war in the spring and summer of 1775 went better than expected for the outnumbered colonial forces and "Minute Men" volunteers. Lexington, Concord, and Bunker Hill were positive steps, and the Americans also scored a major coup the next year when cannons captured at Fort Ticonderoga in northern New York by General Henry Knox were rushed to Boston. The British occupiers of the city awoke the next day to the sight of guns atop Dorchester Heights ready to fire down upon them. They wisely and sheepishly evacuated the key city on March 17, 1776.

The British had greatly underestimated American resolve at the outset of the war, suffering from a disastrous cocktail of arrogance and unpreparedness. Such was certainly the case for one British officer in Boston, who wrote of the colonials just prior to the start of the fighting, "It is a Masquerade Scene to see grave sober Citizens, Barbers and Tailors, who never looked fierce before in their Lives, but at their Wives, Children or Apprentices, strutting about in their Sunday wigs in stiff Buckles with their Muskets on their Shoulders, struggling to put on a Martial Countenance." Overconfident indeed. Of the prospective enemy, the officer concluded, "If ever you saw a Goose assume an Air of Consequence, you may catch some idea of the foolish, awkward, puffed-up stare of our Tradesmen."

It was nothing less than scorn and contempt from the world's mightiest army. The idea of a "citizen army" seemed downright silly to professional soldiers and the time-honored British officer corps. It was time to put an end to the rebellion, and to do that the British needed a military staging ground in the colonies. New York City was the obvious choice of locations.

General William Howe sailed for the city in the summer of 1776 with more than 32,000 troops, including 8,000 of the dreaded Hessian mercenaries.* An armada of thirty warships, hundreds of transport and support vessels, and 10,000 sailors under the command of Howe's brother, Admiral Richard "Black Dick" Howe, so named because of his "swarthy" complexion and dark countenance, accompanied the army. At the time it was the largest military venture ever sent overseas by Britain. An expeditionary force of this size would have been intimidating even to the strongest European powers, not to mention to a ragtag band of poorly trained farmers and ill-equipped blacksmiths. And that was precisely what was waiting for them in New York.

General Washington guessed correctly that the British would come to New York City. After taking Boston, he marched ten thousand troops and roughly nine thousand militiamen to the city in April and dug in. One of the many problems he faced was that there were simply too many points of entry on the waterways in and around the city to prevent the British from landing *somewhere*. But a show of force might dissuade the British from attacking the city—or at least Washington would make them pay dearly for the real estate. The army spent May and June preparing for the massive invasion. Earthworks were erected in Brooklyn, artillery batteries were positioned on Manhattan, and a fort was built on the northern end of the island and named for the general. And then they waited.

The coming battle was critical for other reasons as well. Washington knew he lacked experience leading a large army and managing a major war. His time in uniform was quite limited, and his first commands two decades earlier had been defined by costly, rookie

---

* As many as thirty thousand German soldiers, many of them from Hesse-Cassel, were contracted by the British to fight in the war.

mistakes.* The Virginian also had rivals eyeing his job, including Charles Lee, Israel Putnam, and even John Hancock. The general was forced to watch his back as questions about his fitness for command swirled.

Unlike his rivals, Washington had not stated his interest in command, although he arrived in Philadelphia for the key meeting of the Continental Congress in the full dress uniform of the Virginia militia, unmistakably signaling his ambition. When offered the position as commander on June 15, 1775, the new general quickly accepted but noted the challenge before him: "Tho' I am truly sensible of the high honour done me in this appointment, yet I feel distress from the consciousness that my abilities and Military experience may not be equal to the extensive and important Trust. However, as the Congress desires, I will enter upon the momentous duty and, exert every power I Possess in their service for the Support of the Glorious Cause."

Washington's troops were inadequately trained, poorly provisioned, and about to be seriously outnumbered and outgunned in New York. Perhaps only half of them were, in his words, "fit for duty." One soldier described his peers as "without clothes and shoes and covers to lie on." Patches were sewn on top of patches on already-old garments. For others, clothing was so scarce that a barracks was constructed at the temporary base expressly for the purpose of sheltering the naked. Short on food, men had resorted, according to their commander, to eating "every type of horse food but hay." More than three thousand were ill and a few hundred were either missing or on furlough that summer. The situation was grave.

The army that waited for the British was not much of one. Still, Washington issued orders to his men designed to prop up their waning confidence, announcing, "The time is now near at hand, which must probably determine whether Americans are to be freemen or slaves; whether they are to have any property they can call their own;

---

* Washington's mistakes while in command during the Jumonville Affair and the Fort Necessity campaign in 1754 contributed to the start of the French and Indian War.

whether their homes and farms are to be pillaged and destroyed. The fate of the unborn millions will now depend, under God, on the conduct and courage of this army."

The enemy arrived in July and established a beachhead on Staten Island. General Howe had license to attempt to negotiate a surrender or truce with the "rebels." But Washington would hear nothing of it, responding, "Those who have committed no fault want no pardon." Accordingly, Howe ordered his brother to ferry twenty thousand troops across the Narrows from Staten Island to Long Island and Brooklyn, with the main force landing at Gravesend Bay. The first major battle of the war was about to begin, and many of the men fighting would soon find themselves aboard prison ships.

The first shots were fired at dawn on August 27, 1776, near Upper New York Bay on the far western end of Long Island by a small detachment of Americans charged with defending the main road across the island. Consisting mostly of militiamen, the group was inadequately trained and poorly equipped. To their horror, the sound of a snare drum broke the morning silence; it was followed by the sight of a few hundred British regulars. The encounter was over as soon as it started. Most of the Americans ran. Those who fought, including their commander—Major Edward Burd—were taken prisoner. The British continued on to Brooklyn but split their forces in a diversionary move, sending some units west along the coast and others east by Jamaica Bay. The ploy worked.

The colonials retreated but regrouped about one mile up the road. Two officers there, Colonel Samuel Holden Parsons of Connecticut and Colonel Samuel Atlee of Pennsylvania, sent word back to General Washington that the invasion had begun, then rallied the men to dig in. But they were grossly overmatched. Two full brigades of British regulars, artillery companies, and the Royal Highland Regiment made quick work of the Americans. But this was just a distraction.

Two massive armies, one led by General Howe himself, were moving in from other directions.

General Washington placed the main line of his defenses at Brooklyn Heights under the command of his trusted friend General Nathanael Greene. Two other lines of defense were established in the city, one led by General John Sullivan, the other by General Lord Stirling. Unfortunately for the defenders, Greene became very ill and was replaced by General Israel Putnam of Connecticut. Unfamiliar with the city or terrain, Putnam failed to defend his left flank at a place called Jamaica Pass. The mistake would prove costly.

General Howe was tipped off about the gap in the enemy's defenses by locals loyal to the Crown, one of many instances when loyalists in the city conspired to undermine Washington's efforts. Under cover of darkness on the night of August 26, Howe maneuvered a force of ten thousand to Brooklyn and then along the undefended pass. The Americans were awakened at sunrise by cannon fire on their exposed left and rear. The Battle of Brooklyn was under way.*

The Hessians struck the center of the American line while five thousand British troops hit the defenders on the right flank. The British were everywhere. Amid the chaos, the center line of defense crumbled and the Hessians poured into the colonial ranks. The lines on the flanks were soon overrun as well, sending the Americans fleeing for their lives. Howe's ruse worked. Washington's men were surrounded, on the run, and cut off from escape. It happened so quickly that two American commanders—Sullivan and Stirling—were captured along with many captains, majors, and colonels.

In the disorganized retreat, some units fled into marshlands. In the words of one British officer, "The Hessians and our brave Highlanders gave no quarters . . . it was a fine sight to see with what alacrity they dispatched the rebels with their bayonets, after we had

---

* The battle is also known as the Battle of Long Island and the Battle of Brooklyn Heights.

surrounded them so they could not resist. Multitudes were drowned and suffocated in morasses—a proper punishment for all Rebels." The Hessians, who proved to be as effective and merciless as their reputations, bayoneted many of those who attempted to surrender. The writings of one British soldier provide a disturbing insight into their motivation. The Germanic mercenaries had been told before the battle that "the Rebels had resolved to give no quarters to them in particular, which made them fight desperately and put all to death that fell into their hands." Even though the warning was not true, the mercenaries believed it was a matter of "kill or be killed."

Accounts of the chaotic battle describe numerous instances of surrendering Americans being savagely beaten or murdered. One report comes from Lieutenant Jonathan Gillet of Connecticut, who said he and his men begged to be given quarter but were attacked: "I never shall forget the Roberys, blows and Insults I met with as well as hunger." While some of his men were killed, others were beaten with the butts of Hessian muskets. Gillet was spared but was robbed of his clothing and possessions when he surrendered.

A rifleman from Pennsylvania named Thomas Foster had an even more harrowing experience. When he was captured, the Hessians stripped him and put a rope around his neck. Foster was dragged to a nearby tree and hanged. Strangling and close to death, he was saved when the rope was cut by a knife at the last moment. Foster looked up to see the Hessians laughing. Their cruel game continued: once again, he was strung up by the neck, then cut down at the final moment before death. Another account was provided by Major Nicholas Fish, whose unit was beaten at Brooklyn. Fish recorded that many of his men were shot in the head as they tried to surrender.

But at least Gillet, Foster, and Fish lived. Numerous reports by civilians and prisoners in the city mention that many of the Americans they buried had their heads split open. The consensus was that they were "massacred" by the Hessians after surrendering. Elsewhere around the battlefield, the bodies of colonials hung lifelessly from trees with long bayonets protruding from their torsos.

The drubbing the colonials were getting at Brooklyn would have been even worse had it not been for Major Mordecai Gist and 250 brave volunteers from Maryland. Gist and his men held their ground and then counterattacked the main British advance. The courageous act helped divert the attention of the attackers and bought Washington's army valuable time to retreat. Watching the heroics from atop a nearby hill, an anxious Washington observed, "Good God, what brave fellows I must this day lose."

The American army was beaten badly. Washington, who was nearly captured, was forced to pull back to Brooklyn Heights on August 29. The Continental Army was decimated and morale was low but, fortunately for the Americans, the evening brought a lull in the fighting. Facing the prospect of having his entire army killed or captured the next morning, Washington used Howe's hesitation to evacuate his forces across the East River to Manhattan. A headstrong but capable fisherman from Massachusetts aided Washington. Colonel John Glover was tasked by his general to ferry thousands of men across the river in darkness and under the noses of the British, a feat he would soon repeat when Washington ordered his army across the Delaware River for his famous Christmas night attack on Trenton. The man Washington described as "a tough, little terrier" and his Marblehead fishermen and sailors worked through the night. Aided by a thick fog and favorable winds, they managed in nine hours to transport nine thousand exhausted and panicked troops along with supplies and cannons to safety. Washington's ingenuity and quick thinking allowed the Continental Army to live to fight another day. Fittingly, the general was the last man to leave Brooklyn.

The next day, General Howe stirred his forces from their sleep to finish off the Americans while Admiral Howe sailed thirty warships up the river. They were too late.

Washington, however, had little time to celebrate his escape, and his badly beaten troops had little time to recover. On September 15,

General Howe launched a massive amphibious invasion of Manhattan from the East River. Once again, the Americans were overrun. Howe captured hundreds more volunteers and soldiers, including another twenty officers. Washington was in full retreat for a second time in the city.

Again and again over the ensuing days, Washington found himself checkmated by Howe, who was aided by hundreds of loyalists throughout the city who provided him with valuable intelligence on every move made by the Continental Army. Admiral Howe's fleet responded by launching amphibious landings throughout the city, while General Howe pursued Washington on land. Washington had no choice but to abandon the important city, although he stationed a force of roughly three thousand at Fort Washington and ordered them to hold the last American position in New York City. Desperate to save what remained of his army, Washington then fled northward to White Plains.

On October 28, General Howe arrived at White Plains and attacked Washington's position. The embattled Americans managed to fight to a stalemate, then put distance between themselves and the British by crossing the Croton River and marching to North Castle. It was another humbling retreat. This time, however, Washington caught a break. Howe did not pursue his foe. His massive army headed back to Fort Washington and attacked the final American garrison in the city on November 16. By midday it was apparent the fort would fall and the commanding officer, Colonel Robert Magaw from Pennsylvania, made the difficult decision to surrender. The decision was fraught with peril, as Magaw and his men knew that many of their brothers in arms had been murdered while attempting to surrender. The lives of the defenders of Fort Washington were spared, but the British captured another 2,800 of Washington's best soldiers.

New York City was lost and the British could now isolate New England from Pennsylvania and the southern colonies. They also gained

an important harbor and base from which to wage war both northward and southward. The signs of war were everywhere. Buildings
were pockmarked by musket and cannon fire. Barricades, redoubts,
and camps were being erected throughout the city and adjacent communities on Long Island. General Howe also declared martial law in
the city, forcing residents to sign oaths of loyalty to the Crown or be
arrested. Many chose to flee the city for nearby Connecticut.

But the Howe brothers had their own problems. A staggering
thirty-two thousand soldiers needed housing, and there simply was
not enough food to feed everyone. Consequently, British troops were
quartered in any and all available homes and, because supplies were
very slow to arrive from England and subject to attack from American
privateers, royal quartermasters contracted with local farmers for cattle, eggs, and produce. When that proved inadequate to feed a hungry
army, they simply stole what they needed. The result was that both the
troops and local residents often went hungry. Prisoners starved.

The deteriorating conditions in the city and lack of housing were
compounded when many hundreds of loyalists from surrounding villages and other states arrived in the city, announcing they were war
"refugees." The quality of life in the city further deteriorated as the
British army confiscated essential materials. Civilians were forced to
scavenge and loot the towns and countryside in order to live. All public services ceased to function, bringing about shortages of medicine
and other essentials. Pools of waste soon accumulated and disease
swept through the city. A grisly account of another factor was recorded by Ambrose Searle, an aide to Admiral Howe, who described
"the Stench of the dead Bodies of the Rebels" in the woods and fields
around the city.

The turmoil and carnage were made all the worse by a shortage
of public buildings and homes. Around midnight on the evening of
September 21, as the patriots were abandoning the city, a fire tore
through the western part of the city and into the southern tip of
Manhattan. The blaze burned hundreds of structures—nearly one-
third of the city. General Howe attributed the inferno to anti-British

arsonists or General Washington's spies, and the resulting crackdown on the city's residents was harsh. It set the tone for the military occupation of the city for the remainder of the war. Many residents were intimidated into saying they were loyalists or simply had to keep quiet in order to be spared.

The entire campaign to seize New York City had lasted less than five months and cost the British only a few dozen dead and a few hundred wounded, whereas the Americans suffered thousands dead, wounded, or captured, including three generals, seven colonels, two majors, and nineteen captains.

As for General Washington, he finally managed to elude the Howe brothers. His army, greatly diminished in number, fled south through New Jersey and crossed the Delaware River into Pennsylvania, where they would camp during the cold winter of 1776–77.* Coming just weeks after the signing of the Declaration of Independence, the inglorious loss of New York City dealt a severe blow to the war effort. The city would remain in Redcoat hands for the remainder of the conflict.

The seizure of New York City and deterioration of the conditions in the area were observed by the crew of the HMS *Jersey*, an old British warship anchored not far from the fighting. The converted hospital and supply ship was about to enter the war . . . but in a vastly different way.

---

* It was from this encampment that Washington would cross the Delaware River and launch his daring Christmastime attack against the Hessian base at Trenton. The success of the battle would temporarily bolster his army, his command, and the larger war effort.

City of Prisons

If in this wreck or ruin, they
Can yet be thought to claim a tear,
O smite your gentle breast, and say
The friends of freedom slumber here!

—Philip Freneau, "The British Prison-Ship" (1781)

Few prisoners had been captured by either side prior to the Battle of Brooklyn. But after a summer and fall of fighting in and around New York City, General Howe found himself in possession of roughly four thousand American prisoners and did not know what to do with them. To put the growing prisoner dilemma in context, the British had captured only about thirty men at Bunker Hill the year prior. Most of the four thousand now in British possession were captured at Brooklyn and after the fall of Fort Washington. In the weeks to come, another one thousand private citizens of New York were arrested by the British on suspicion of supporting the patriots' cause. The numbers continued to rise, and New York soon became a "city of prisons."

British commanders were not prepared for so many prisoners; nor was New York City. In the year 1770, census numbers put the population of Brooklyn at only about thirty-six hundred people. It was a village of single-story, wooden homes and much of the surrounding area was made up of fields farmed by Dutch settlers. There was also a sizable slave population in King's County. In fact, the area had the highest slaves-per-capita ratio in the northern half of America. Under British rule, any attempts to abolish slavery and any slave uprisings in the region were suppressed, leaving the Dutch farmers to benefit from the shameful institution. As a result, most of the region's farmers remained steadfastly loyal to the British.

There were now far more people in New York City than available housing, especially after the destructive fire that swept through parts of the city. The region had only two proper jails—New Bridewell Jail and the New Jail, which was popularly known as "the Provost." The British were disinterested in devoting precious resources and personnel to building prisons, and after the decisive victories in and around New York City, it appeared the war would soon be over. Thus the decision was made by British officials to confiscate large buildings for use as temporary detention facilities for prisoners. This included the cavernous "sugar houses" of the region, such as Livingston's Sugar House on Liberty Street (formerly Crown Street), Van Cortland's Sugar House near Trinity Church, and the Rhinelander Sugar House on Duane Street. Unfortunately, many of these warehouses were demolished in the 1840s and 1850s, but descriptions of the deplorable conditions remain.

Even with the reallocation of the two jails and sugar houses there were still far too many prisoners without housing. The British were so in need of space that they even used King's College and City Hall on Wall Street as prisons.* Of course, none of the buildings were designed in a way that was conducive to housing a prison population, from the perspective of either security or adequate lodging for the inmates. But the situation was desperate; additional facilities were needed.

---

* King's College is now Columbia University.

The first buildings in the city to be used as prisons were the Presbyterian Church on Cedar and Wall Streets and the Dutch Reformed churches in the city, including the Middle Dutch Church on Nassau Street and the Old North Dutch Church on William Street. The latter church was forced to accommodate eight hundred prisoners even though it was designed for a fraction of that amount of parishioners. Pews were removed to make room for the swelling prison population and were later used as firewood that winter. But there was still inadequate space for the prisoners. Additional churches were commandeered, including the French Church on Pine and Nassau Streets, the Quaker Meeting House, the venerable Trinity Church, the Scotch Church on Cedar Street, and one known as the "Brick Church" on Park. Prisoners were crammed into these houses of worship with little regard for the well-being of either the churches or the prisoners.

It was war, and the British had been shocked by the determined opposition at Lexington, Concord, and Bunker Hill in 1775. For instance, on the march back to Boston after the fighting at Concord on April 19, the long line of British troops came under constant assault by American farmers and townsfolk, who fired at them from behind trees and out of barn doors as they passed by. Therefore, contrary to images in popular culture of British forces conducting the war by genteel means, they now intended to inflict massive hardships on the upstart Americans. This included prisoners in New York City. The temporary detention facilities would not simply house but punish colonials considered to be disloyal to the Crown.

The British had long since run out of patience and were now playing for keeps. Case in point: Admiral Samuel Graves, the Royal Navy officer commanding forces in Boston, advocated "burning and laying waste the whole country!" Graves attacked civilians and, in October 1775, destroyed the town of Falmouth, Maine. British commanders did not consider the Americans to be honorable foes. Therefore, the men suffering in squalor in old sugar houses and cramped churches were not classified as prisoners of war; they were seen as "rebels."

The same bitter feelings were present in England, where public sentiment soured on their brethren in America. The result was twofold: as stated by a British officer who captured Americans at Brooklyn, "Rebels taken in arms forfeit their lives by the laws of all Countries. The keeping of all the Rebel prisoners taken in arms, without any immediate hope of release, and in a state of uncertainty with respect to their fate, would certainly strike great terror into their army." Indeed, the British began to see imprisonment as a psychological weapon of terror, and as the war dragged on and on, the brutal treatment of prisoners worsened, especially on an old, rotting prison ship.

When the prisoners were first processed at the sugar houses, churches, and other makeshift prisons, they were stripped of their clothing and possessions and given old garments to wear. One such instance involved Alexander Graydon, who described the Hessians stealing his belongings and those of his comrades. He also recalled the taunts, complaining, "The term rebel, with the epithet *damned* before it, was the mildest we received." They were also threatened with hangings and subjected to beatings. Graydon expected to die.

A Pennsylvanian named Isaac van Horne shared a similar story: "[Our] side arms, watches, shoe-buckles, and even the clothes on our backs were wrestled from us." A fellow Keystone Stater, Lieutenant Samuel Lindsay, had been shot in the leg during the defense of Brooklyn but, despite his injury, was brutally beaten by the Hessians with blows to the head from the "butt end of a musket." He was nearly blinded and almost died.

With little planning and less concern, the British incarcerated soldiers by the hundreds in these cramped spaces. The American prisoners had no room to sleep, little food, and brackish water. The result was that they were soon afflicted by disease and the facilities overrun by pests. Prisoners started dying in alarming numbers. One eyewitness referred to the makeshift prisons as "dreadful." A British report admitted as much: "A number of people . . . crowded together in so small a compass almost like herrings in a barrel, most of them very dirty and not a small number sick of some disease, the Itch, Pox, Fever, or Flux." It went on to note that everywhere could be found "a complication of stinks enough to drive a person whose sense of smelling was very delicate and his lungs of the finest contexture, into a consumption in the space of twenty-four hours." Indeed, every horror plagued the prisoners—putrid food, polluted water, disease, lice, no hygiene or fresh air, and no proper burial.

The worst was the starvation. With food and supplies inadequate for His Majesty's army, American prisoners at the beginning of the war received rations only twice a week, consisting of one-half pound of biscuit, one-half pound of pork, one-half pint of peas, one-half cup of rice, and half an ounce of butter. Under such conditions, some prisoners resorted to eating old shoes. A prisoner named Samuel Young, captured at the beginning of the fighting in New York, remembered being incarcerated in a large stable in the city with five hundred other men. He described having food literally thrown at them, "in a confused manner, as if to so many hogs." The food consisted of "a quantity of old biscuit, broken, and in crumbs, mostly molded, and some of it crawling with maggots, which they were obliged to scramble for." They had no choice but to eat the rotten food if they wanted to live and, Young recalled, "they were obliged to eat [it] raw."

The allowance of water was such that it was barely enough to keep a man alive, and the prisoners were not provided with soap for bathing. The prisoners were also subjected to public humiliation, paraded through the streets of New York as a spectacle. Curious spectators lined the streets to hurl insults and rotten food at the men.

Yet another hardship was the weather. The heat of summer was difficult but, with a lack of blankets and coats, many prisoners froze during the abnormally cold winter of 1776–77. Snow accumulated inside the churches, sugar houses, and hulked ships through broken windows, covering those prisoners too weak or ill to move. Survivors of that first winter remembered the outcome: "Each morning, several frozen corpses were dragged out, thrown into wagons like logs, carted away, and then pitched into a large hole or trench to be covered up like dead animals." Another prisoner recalled, "The distress of the prisoners cannot be communicated by words. Twenty or thirty die every day. They lie in heaps unburied." Adding insult to injury, the naked bodies were often eaten by hungry swine. "What numbers of my countrymen have died by cold and hunger," a prisoner bemoaned, or "perished for want of the common necessities of life!" For him, the treatment by the British was such that he decided, "Rather than experience again their barbarity and insults, may I fall by the sword of the Hessians."

Not only was General Howe responsible for the atrocities committed under his command, but he was present for much of it and even condoned the violent treatment of prisoners. But Howe impacted the fate of American prisoners, including those eventually housed on the most notorious prison ship in history, in another way. He appointed as prison commissaries men with a lust for blood. These commissaries were in charge of overseeing the prisons, ordering food and supplies, and negotiating prisoner exchanges. A few of them would soon become infamous throughout the former colonies for their barbarity.

Howe selected Joshua Loring, a Tory from Boston, to be the head commissary. Loring approached his job with dispassionate efficiency and shared his general's view that any royal subject who challenged the Crown was a rebel, not a soldier, and therefore not deserving of humane treatment. He cared not as to where and how the prisoners would be housed. But Loring faced the immediate problem of a lack of prisons in New York City. He opposed confiscating barns and other such facilities because they were needed for agriculture. The massive British army, after all, needed to eat. Believing the war would end quickly, he also failed to plan for the long-term housing of prisoners.

Howe, it seems, permitted Loring much discretion, preferring instead to devote his attention to the commissary's attractive blond wife. A number of theories exist, but many of them suggest Howe and Elizabeth "Betsey" Loring were having an affair and that Joshua Loring turned a blind eye to the romance in order to keep his job, which he used to line his pockets.

Loring's scheme was simple: funds for a prisoner's rations, albeit minimal, continued until the prisoner was deceased. Loring appears to have delayed and underreported incidents of prisoner deaths in order to skim money from the prison accounts. He was getting rich; Howe could do as he pleased with Mrs. Loring, and it seems he did. For instance, when the general went to Philadelphia, he took Mrs. Loring with him, and the two were highly visible and affectionate at public social events. The joke back in London soon became, "Loring fingered the cash, while the general enjoyed the madam." There were similar jokes in America, including a well-known poem by Francis Hopkins, one of the signers of the Declaration of Independence:

> *Sir William he,*
> *smug as a flea.*
> *Lay all this time a snoring,*
> *nor dreamed of harm*
> *as he lay warm,*
> *in bed with Mrs. Loring.*

Judge Thomas Jones, a royalist who blamed Howe for the loss of the American colonies, went so far as to level the poetic charge, "As Cleopatra of old lost Marc Antony the world, so did this illustrious courtesan lose Sir William Howe, the honour, the laurels, and the glory, of putting an end to one of the most obstinate rebellions that ever existed."*

Irrespective of the affair, Loring treated the prisoners in New York City horribly. Yet, as bad as Loring was, the warden of the Provost

---

* After Howe was recalled by London in 1778, Elizabeth and her two children moved back to England, but her husband stayed in New York. The Lorings were reunited after the war and had additional children, leaving history to ponder the full nature of the affair.

was worse. His name was William Cunningham. Born in Ireland, Cunningham came to America in 1774 aboard the ship *Needham* as part of a business venture, which involved luring the Irish to New York with false promises and then selling his countrymen as indentured servants. However, Cunningham's racket caught up with him. His passengers were discovered to be so malnourished and ill that the authorities seized the ship in New York harbor and freed them. The corrupt Cunningham managed to flee to Boston, where he met General Thomas Gage, the British commander, at the outset of the war. Apparently impressed by Cunningham's sadistic ways, Gage appointed him as the warden of the Provost. Once back in New York City, Cunningham seemed only too happy to exact revenge on the people who had chased him out of the city.

The notorious, multiple-story prison was made of dark stone and located on the common by Chatham Street. It held a half dozen cells on each floor, and large rooms in the cellar contained "necessary tubs" overflowing with human waste. The prison, like others, was severely overcrowded. Because it served as a detention center for spies, officers, and other high-value inmates, Cunningham installed extra security measures such as posting British and Hessian guards throughout the facility and at the door at all times, putting iron grates over the deep-set windows, erecting a high wooden fence around the grounds, and using extra chains on his inmates.

Each prisoner brought to the Provost was personally processed by Cunningham, who noted the man's name, age, height, and rank. Officers were, as was the custom of the time, housed separately from enlisted men. The warden had an array of bizarre policies designed to inflict more cruelty on the inmates, including a rule that prisoners could turn over only once at night and it had to be "from right to left." That such a rule was unenforceable was irrelevant. It was another form of control and abuse. Like Loring, Cunningham made money off the prisoners, selling the rations of already deplorable prison food for money. He would then buy a fraction of the rations for his inmates. When families sent food and clothing to their loved ones, the "ignorant, drunken

Irish master," as one prisoner called him, would delight in selling it or destroying it. The warden was also known for forcing his prisoners to parade in chains in public, bellowing in a drunken stupor to crowds of loyalists, "This is the damned rebel, so-and-so!"

A number of other accounts from the war are equally disturbing. One said of Cunningham that his "cruelty and wickedness are almost inconceivable." Another described him in the following way: "His hatred of the Americans found vent in torture by searing irons and secret scourges to those who fell under the bane of his displeasure. The prisoners were crowded together so closely that many fell ill from partial asphyxiation, and starved to death for want of the food which he sold to enrich himself."

One of the prisoners in particularly dire straits was an old man from the city named Elias Baylis. Baylis was blind and had been transferred from one of the churches being used as a temporary prison to the Provost, where Cunningham beat him repeatedly and savagely. After two months there the old man was very close to death. Cunningham finally agreed to release Baylis, knowing the old man would not survive. Sure enough, Baylis died while being rowed across the East River on his way to freedom.

Another story of Cunningham's inhumanity comes from a colonial officer named Birdsall. During the Battle of Brooklyn the British captured an American ship filled with flour intended for George Washington's army. It was Birdsall who devised the plan to recapture the ship and requested permission to lead the mission. After handpicking a few reliable volunteers to join him, Captain Birdsall snuck onto the ship and managed to free it. But after liberating the ship, Birdsall and his men were caught by the British and sent to the Provost.

There Birdsall met Cunningham, whom he called the "monster in human shape." The monster would walk the hallways of the infamous prison at all hours with his black servant threatening "to hang and kill prisoners." To curses of "sons of bitches, god-damned ye," he would beat and flail them with his whip. At mealtimes Cunningham "threw food at them and kicked over the water and food bowls."

Once when Captain Birdsall requested paper and ink to write to his family, Cunningham screamed, "Damned rebel!" then drew his sword and stabbed Birdsall through the shoulder. As punishment for making the request, Birdsall was put in solitary confinement with no medical attention. Birdsall ended up spending several months in the Provost until, half dead from starvation, he was exchanged.

Baylis and Birdsall were not unique in being singled out by Cunningham for punishment. Once when the warden discovered that a guard had let a teenager from Boston named Peter Edes out of prison because he was a civilian and not a soldier, Cunningham exploded in rage. He screamed at the guard, "Damn them, let them die and rot; you have no authority to let them out," and ordered that the guard be punished. Cunningham's cruelty extended beyond his own guards to the wives and family members of dying prisoners, whom he turned away when they asked permission to see their loved ones. On one occasion when the wife of a prisoner arrived at the Provost in tears, begging to see her husband, Cunningham had her stripped and punished "unmercifully."

It was the dastardly Cunningham, on orders from General Howe, who put to death George Washington's famous spy Nathan Hale, executing him on September 22, 1776, in New York City. The story is well known: Hale had volunteered on September 10 to gather intelligence behind enemy lines in advance of the Battle of Harlem Heights. But after the massive fire in the city, the British were on the watch for sympathizers and spies. The young officer was captured while sailing back across Long Island Sound. Later, when secret documents were found on his person, the British discovered the purpose of his mission. After being interrogated by General Howe, Hale was sent to Cunningham to be put to death.

From the gallows the twenty-one-year-old allegedly declared, "I only regret that I have but one life to give for my country."* Little

---

* Howe recorded in his orderly book the following entry: "A spy from the enemy by his own full confession, apprehended last night, was executed this day at 11 o'clock in front of the Artillery Park."

is known about the spy's final days because the cruel prison warden burned many of the letters Hale had written for loved ones, saying, "The rebels should not know that they had a man in their army who could die with such firmness."

Cunningham's reign of terror included murdering prisoners in his care in New York City. These private executions, without trial, were conducted for his pleasure and with him in attendance. At such gruesome spectacles, Cunningham would order prisoners gagged and dragged out of their cells "under the cover of midnight darkness" to the grounds behind the Provost. One prisoner estimated that the warden hanged 260 men from the prison, while other accounts suggest his bloodlust resulted in five or six prisoners a night being hanged.

Tragically, even more prisoners died of neglect and abuse. One witness claimed that as many as a dozen dead bodies a day were carried out of the building, most having succumbed to hunger, disease, or the cold. During summer, temperatures inside the prison soared and there was little fresh air. A prisoner named Dunlap wrote, "In the suffocating heat of summer, I saw every aperture of those strong walls filled with human heads, face above face, seeking a portion of the external air." Despite the dire situation, prisoners were allowed out into the fenced-in courtyard for only thirty minutes a day. The hot, crowded, unsanitary conditions of the Provost were also a breeding ground for maladies of every kind. Such was the case during the summer of 1777, when a particularly deadly fever tore through the prison, killing many.

George Washington was so disturbed by the reports of prisoners dying that he wrote to the Continental Congress with a request that they establish commissaries charged with inspecting British prisons, securing food for the American prisoners, and negotiating prisoner exchanges. His request was approved and funding was allocated from a "Secret Committee" of the Continental Congress. Washington appointed several capable men, including John Beaty, Thomas Franklin, Lewis Pintard, and Abraham Skinner, as his commissaries.

One of them, Elias Boudinot, was appointed in April 1777. Like his peers, Boudinot was continually frustrated by the behavior of Loring, Cunningham, and other British wardens who often refused to provide access to the prisons and ships, exchange prisoners, or provide adequate food and clothing to those in their charge. Boudinot supplemented the meager funds available for prisoners with his own money and even collected donations from friends. Though his army was poorly provisioned and starving, General Washington also set aside clothing and rations for the prisoners. This was the case in spring of 1777, shortly after Boudinot was appointed commissary general of prisoners, when Washington noted in his journal, "I began to afford them some supplies of Provisions over and above what the Enemy afforded them, which was very small and very indifferent." These efforts, however, only pertained to prisoners from the Continental Army, not prisoners from militias or privateers; each state took care of their militiamen, and the privateers were often left to fend for themselves.

The efforts by Washington and Boudinot helped, but only a little, and only as Loring and Cunningham would allow. Boudinot recalled, "The Complaints of the very cruel treatment our Prisoners met with in the Enemy's lines rose to such a Height that in the Fall of this Year, 1777, the General [Washington] wrote to General Howe or Clinton reciting their complaints and proposing to send an Officer into New York to examine into the truth of them. This was agreed to, and a regular pass-port returned accordingly. The General ordered me on this service." Boudinot traveled on his own boat to visit the prisons and floating dungeons around the city on February 3, 1778. What he saw was appalling.

Accompanied at all times by a British officer, Boudinot toured the Provost, sugar houses, churches, and even the prison ships. He requested access to American prisoners, saying, "I therefore hoped they would each of them in their turn report to me faithfully and candidly the Treatment they severally had received,—that my design was to obtain them the proper redress." But he discovered that the prisoners were fearful of the guards and wardens, and therefore hesitant to come forward with complaints.

It took several efforts, but Boudinot eventually learned that what he had suspected was true: "That they had received the most cruel Treatment from the Provost Marshal, being locked up in the Dungeon on the most trifling pretenses, such as asking for more water to drink on a hot day than usual." The American commissary was particularly alarmed to find that "a Captain Vandyke had been confined eighteen months for being concerned in setting fire to the City." Vandyke was locked in the cellar dungeon on charges of setting the fire, despite the fact that Boudinot discovered he had been incarcerated before the fire was set. This detail did not change Cunningham's mind.

General Washington read Boudinot's reports with concern and repeatedly requested that he check on the condition of prisoners. Washington also sent letters to General Howe complaining that "many of the cruelties exercised towards prisoners, are said to proceed from the inhumanity of Mr. Cunningham." Howe replied to the grievances of Washington and the Continental Congress by denying the incidents of abuse, the crowded conditions, and the high death toll. Not only was Howe disinterested in improving the conditions, but he expanded Cunningham's powers. The brutality worsened.

Using churches, sugar houses, and other public buildings in New York City as prisons did not solve the problem. There were simply too many prisoners for the available spaces. Additional prisons were established at Flatbush, Flatlands, Gravesend, and New Utrecht. As the war continued, more prisoners were brought to the city from battlefields in New York, Pennsylvania, and New England; from fighting in the South; and from the West Indies and French ships seized by the Royal Navy. At the same time, civilians continued to be arrested and accused of disloyalty to the Crown.

The Royal Navy also started to capture American merchant vessels, fishing boats, and the privateers that harassed British ships.

Because the Royal Navy needed more sailors, it planned to press these seamen into joining their ranks. But those refusing to fight for the enemy were sent to prison in New York. The British were using every available space, but the prisoners kept coming. The prisoner dilemma had long before reached crisis levels, but Howe still refused to build proper facilities.

General Howe and Commissary Loring chose another approach. Prisoners were transferred to large transport vessels. After sailing to America at the beginning of the war, several old ships such as the *Pacific*, *Lord Rochford*, *Mentor*, and *Argo* remained anchored off Staten Island, Gravesend Bay, and other waterways around the city. Ultimately, the decision was made to sail or tow them to Wallabout Bay on the shores of Brooklyn.* There they would be hulked and used as floating dungeons.

Though it seemed as if conditions in the prisons could not get worse, they did. According to an old report on the prison ships, "Great, however, as were the sufferings of those incarcerated within the prisons of the city, they were exceeded, if possible, by those of the unfortunate naval prisoners who languished in the prison ships of the 'Wallebought.'" The inmates placed aboard the prison ships were about to meet a commissary who would make their time aboard the *Jersey* a living hell. His name was David Sproat.

---

* Today the location is between Williamsburg and the Manhattan Bridge.

— 4 —

Privateers

Americans, a just resentment show,
And let your minds with indignation glow;
While the warm blood shall swell each glowing vein,
Let fierce resentment in your bosoms reign;
Can you forget the vengeful Briton's ire,
Your fields in ruin and your domes on fire.

—Philip Freneau, "The British Prison-Ship" (1781)

The Royal Navy was the undisputed "Mistress of the Seas." And because of that, British leaders and commanders again greatly underestimated the colonists—this time on the high seas. Britain's supremacy in naval warfare extended across the Atlantic to America, where, even though the land war against her rebellious colonies was off to a sluggish start in 1775, the Royal Navy intended to quickly and easily subdue the colonials. This was surprising given the fact that at the start of the war Britain had only twenty-four warships in all of North America, a number wholly insufficient for securing the long eastern seaboard. Even though Admiral Samuel Graves received five additional warships after the difficulties at Bunker Hill, the Royal Navy simultaneously ordered three vessels in its North American squadron back home.

The small fleet under Admiral Graves patrolled from Maine to East Florida and operated out of a number of ports including Boston, Charleston, Philadelphia, and Providence at the beginning of the war. Remarkably, Admiral Graves also left New York's numerous waterways undefended, guarded only by the ten-gun *Kingfisher*. While such overconfidence and folly may not have mattered at the start of the war—the Continental Navy was almost nonexistent—things were about to change.

At the outset of the war, individual colonies outfitted their own ships and crews. These vessels were too small to engage large British warships, so the prudent decision was made by the Americans to avoid direct one-on-one engagements with the powerful Royal Navy whenever possible. Meanwhile, a Continental Navy was being built. A "Committee of Three" was organized in the Continental Congress on October 13, 1775, for the purpose of ordering two small warships (ten and fourteen guns). A week later, four additional members of Congress joined the committee and began work to launch two larger ships (twenty and thirty-six guns). Momentum built, and by December the Congress was appropriating funds for thirteen warships including larger, more powerful frigates. A Marine Committee was finally organized to develop and oversee the new and growing navy; it consisted of one member from each of the colonies. This was followed in November 1776 by the establishment of a Continental Navy Board. The result was that the Americans managed to launch several ships in the first two years of the war.

But even with the growing navy, American warships were not able to challenge British control of the seas. American ships were generally unsuccessful in breaking British naval blockades and striking their naval bases in New York and Halifax. One of the consequences of America's limited naval might would soon prove to be very costly: they were unable to penetrate the waters off Brooklyn to liberate the thousands of men incarcerated on British prison ships in Wallabout Bay.

There were some noteworthy naval successes, however. The lighter American warships were fast and able to both intercept transports and harass merchant shipping. One such example occurred in June 1776 when American warships captured several British transports and roughly five hundred soldiers and sailors. While it did not strike a major blow to British shipping, it did slow the resupply effort. Having prisoners also gave the Americans the means to promote prisoner exchanges or threaten retaliation for the abysmal conditions in the British prisons and aboard the hulks.

But Britain would eventually dispatch roughly seventy massive men-of-war, the largest and most powerful warships on the seas, to prowl the American coastline, blockade ports, enforce their rule, and attack defenseless merchant craft. These warships wreaked havoc on American coastal communities and shipping. American military and political leaders wisely decided to respond with privateers. It was a strategy born of necessity.

Privateering had a long history dating to medieval times and had been used by nearly every European power. It seemed a natural fit for the colonies—America had very few experienced naval officers, but it did have an abundance of skilled mariners and an inexhaustible supply of small merchant and fishing vessels. Accordingly, patriotic citizens were encouraged to arm small merchant vessels and take to the seas to harass British commercial and transport ships. The government in effect "licensed" private ships to wage war on the British.

Congress established formal legislation on privateering on March 23, 1776, to give some legitimacy to the unsavory endeavor. Privateers were commissioned through the issuance of letters of marque and given uniform rules of conduct. For instance, the owners of privateers were required to post bonds and guarantee their proper conduct and adherence to rules established by the government. Several states followed suit with their own licensure by marque. The result was that roughly a hundred privateers were commissioned in the first two years of war, mostly in New England.

The privateers were enticed by the promise of keeping the treasures they plundered from British merchant ships, and the pay for privateers was often better than that in the navy. Numerous ship owners and crew members became quite wealthy during the war by selling their prize for profit to fellow citizens who, because of British blockades, were suffering from severe shortages of most everything.

Most privateers were small, fast schooners with only a handful of guns, but their ranks also included the formidable twenty-six-gun *Caesar*, which operated out of Boston. While these ships were typically not able to confront a Royal Navy man-of-war or frigate, they inflicted serious damage to British shipping by attacking unarmed or lightly armed merchant and resupply ships. For example, according to the English publication *Remembrancer*, in 1776 alone an astonishing 342 British ships were seized by the Americans, of which only 18 were released and just 44 were recaptured. During the war, privateers captured a remarkable 2,283 ships and seized millions of pounds of gunpowder and ammunition. Records are incomplete, but one estimate of the total number of privateers to fight in the war put the number at 1,697, sailing with a total of 14,872 guns. Ultimately, privateers disrupted Britain's ability to ship supplies by sea and thereby helped to win the war.[*]

Another consequence of privateering was that the Royal Navy was forced to reallocate warships to escort and protect merchant convoys sailing the Atlantic. The price of the war soon became unacceptably high for many ship owners and merchants back in England.

Even though Britain had long used privateers in their wars against Spain and France, principally to undermine their foes' trade and shipping in the West Indies, the Royal Navy viewed American privateers as no better than pirates. As one early account of the war

---

[*] Edgar Stanton Maclay's *A History of American Privateers* (1899) estimates the total number of ships sailing as privateers at 136 in 1776, 73 in 1777, 115 in 1778, 167 in 1779, 228 in 1780, 449 in 1781, and 323 in 1782.

noted, "Nearly all wars carried on by [Britain] were based upon the principle that England must rule the seas, and whoever interferes with that principle is their bitter foe." As a result, the British were not just fighting the privateers; they took pride in their navy and sought to severely punish anyone daring to challenge their supremacy on the seas. The Royal Navy began aggressively hunting American privateers, who stood little chance of eluding powerful British warships.

Crews of privateers who were taken prisoner were treated as pirates or outlaws, not as soldiers or sailors. While both the promise of great riches and the lure of adventure attracted these teenagers and young men from coastal fishing villages up and down the coast, for many it would end up being their final voyage. The abundance of privateers also meant that they soon accounted for the majority of prisoners incarcerated on the old British hulks. Many sons of Providence and other coastal communities would end up perishing aboard the ship known simply as Hell. Against all odds, a few of the sailors imprisoned belowdecks on the wretched *Jersey* managed to record their stories, leaving behind detailed accounts of their ordeals. This is their story.

Patriots

The briny wave that Hudson's bosom fills,
Drained through her bottom in a thousand rills.
Rotten and old, replete with sighs and groans,
Scarce on the waters she sustained her bones.
Here, doomed to toil, or founder in the tide,
At the moist pumps incessantly we plied.
Here, doomed to starve, like famished dogs, we tore
The scant allowance which our tyrants bore.

—Philip Freneau, "The British Prison-Ship" (1781)

Life for most colonists living on the coast was tied to the sea, and the allure of the vast, unknown ocean captivated many a young boy eager for adventure or a better life. Likewise, wars are always fought by the young—lacking education, land, and a future, and with little to lose but their lives. One of them was Christopher Hawkins, who was born in Rhode Island in 1764. In May 1777, the thirteen-year-old was working as an indentured apprentice to Aaron Mason, also of Providence. Such was life for all but the few fortunate enough to have financial means or an education—at a young age, boys would be apprenticed to a friend of the family or a skilled worker willing to take on a new charge. These relationships often lasted years and provided the craftsperson with inexpensive labor. In return, the apprentice received food, boarding, and training in a trade that would likely allow him to make a living.

Young Hawkins was headed for just such a life. But that same month Captain Moury Potter was taking to sea from New Bedford, Massachusetts, as a privateer. His schooner *Eagle* carried twelve small cannons, and he intended to hunt British merchant ships sailing between New York City and England. Captain Potter was in need of a crew, so Mason "loaned" his young apprentice out to the captain, likely for a small amount of money and a percentage of whatever goods were seized. Hawkins was now a sailor. But like many young boys who shipped out to sea despite lack of experience, he was excited about both the chance to be a part of the war and the prospects of making money by plundering British ships. At least that was the plan.

Unlike other privateers who hugged the American coastline, Captain Potter boldly sailed the *Eagle* all the way to England. It was a daring move designed to capture unsuspecting British merchant vessels near their home ports. But the journey proved to be anything but adventurous. The crew did not even see another ship on the long, dull passage. Hawkins and the other boys who composed the crew would have spent endless hours scrubbing the deck, tending to the sails and riggings, enduring bouts of seasickness, and drilling for the moment that they hoped would arrive. Days blurred into weeks on the open ocean before Hawkins and the crew of the *Eagle* finally spotted the English coast. They "remained a short time" off the coast, but no opportunity presented itself, and concerns among senior officers about getting caught by one of the many British warships in the waters prompted Captain Potter to sail back across the Atlantic.

The voyage back was nearly as uneventful. The *Eagle* did, however, encounter an unarmed schooner flying no colors. The officers knew not whether it was British or French. Hoping for the former, they showed their guns, and the *Eagle*'s first lieutenant boarded the vessel in order to take her as a prize. Unfortunately, the ship was French; after debating the matter, the officers, in the words of young Hawkins, "did not deem it prudent to superadd piracy to the crime of rebellion." The *Eagle* sailed back to New Bedford empty-handed, her crew hungry and, according to Hawkins, "in no pleasant mood." It was a bitterly disappointing start to his naval career.

Resupplied, the privateer soon set sail again. It was with mixed emotions that young Christopher Hawkins went back to sea. The same feeling was likely shared by his family and employer. But during one of the first nights out the *Eagle* encountered a large English merchant ship, described by Hawkins as "a brig deeply laden" with goods and bound for New York. Captain Potter ordered his crew to chase "Old John Bull."* The thirteen-year-old Hawkins worked quietly and nervously on the rigging as the *Eagle* trailed the larger ship under cover of darkness. The crew had drilled and drilled, and now it was time. Hawkins and other young crew members prepared for their first taste of naval combat.

Captain Potter sailed the *Eagle* into position for a broadside, but first fired a warning shot at the merchant vessel. The captain of the brig immediately appeared on the top deck and, using a device called a trumpet, shouted out, "What in God's name do you want of us?" Captain Potter responded through his trumpet, "Shorten sail, come under my lee, and send your boat on board me." The British captain gave excuses, claiming that because his small launch was lashed under his booms, he could not free it while at sail. It would take time to lower his sails, so he requested that the American privateer wait until morning, when his crew could free the small launch. The British captain stated he would "lie to" until dawn.

According to Hawkins, Captain Potter, whom he described as shockingly "inefficient," foolishly agreed to the trick. He even failed to post sentries through the night. At first light, Hawkins and the crew of

---

* "John Bull" is the personification of an Englishman, a term that originated from the main character of the 1712 book of the same title by John Arbuthnot.

the *Eagle* awoke anxious to claim their prize, only to find that the large brig had quietly snuck away under cover of darkness. It was an embarrassing start for their second voyage, but it was about to get worse.

Captain Potter decided to set sail for Sandy Hook on the Connecticut coast, hoping to overtake the same British brig from the previous night. Motivated by revenge, the crew worked to speed the light vessel through the waves. But as the *Eagle* sailed to intercept the wily British captain, a "severe gale" suddenly and unexpectedly hit from the northeast and caught the privateer at sea. For two days, large swells tossed the small schooner about and violent waves crashed across her deck. Hawkins and his mates "had to exert their utmost skill and energies to keep her from foundering." They bailed, brought down sails, and desperately tried not to be washed overboard. They were fighting for their lives.

Just as the storm abated, an alarming aberration from Poseidon suddenly appeared out of the shrouded mist and gray clouds. It was upon them before the *Eagle*'s crew had time to react. It was the HMS *Sphinx*, a British sloop-of-war carrying twenty guns. Captain Potter frantically called for all hands on deck and tried to hoist and set the sails in order to escape, but the hunter was now the hunted. In the short, one-sided battle that ensued, the *Sphinx* easily bested the inexperienced crew of the *Eagle*. British marines boarded the damaged privateer, and the commander of the *Sphinx* ordered Hawkins and his mates taken to the holds of the British ship at bayonet point. As the prisoners descended the ladders of the warship, they caught one last look at the *Eagle* as it slipped below the waves.

The prisoners were sailed to New York City to be incarcerated in the dreaded prison ships off the shoreline of Brooklyn. Thus began what Hawkins called "a new era" in his life.

Another Rhode Islander who became a privateer was Thomas Dring. Born in Newport in 1758, Dring, like many men from the colony, had some experience sailing. Also like many Americans, he had suffered financially during the war. In his early twenties, Dring was eager to fight and make money. The opportunity for both presented itself when he was invited by Captain Daniel Aborn of nearby Paw-tuxet to join the crew of a privateer appropriately named *Chance*.

The ship, owned by Messrs. Clarke and Nightingale of Providence, carried twelve 6-pound cannons and was crewed by sixty-five boys and men, nearly all of whom were from Providence. One of the crew was a boy of only twelve, named Palmer, a naive and nervous lad whom Dring took under his care as if he were a younger brother. The average age on board the privateers was typically not much older than young Palmer. Dring and his crewmates all knew young men who had become wealthy through privateering, but they had also heard stories of young sailors who were caught and sent to the dreaded Hell Ship. Like ghosts, these men were never heard of again. Such thoughts likely haunted the crew as they reported for duty on the *Chance*.

Dring was offered the position of master's mate, making him the fifth officer behind the captain, first and second lieutenants, and the sailing master. When the *Chance* set sail from Providence in May 1782, Dring's head, like that of young Hawkins a few years earlier, was filled with images of great treasure. The war was now in its final stages and British ships were sailing back home, prompting all aboard the *Chance* to believe the threat to them was minimal. But the British had not abandoned the war effort quite yet.

Just a few days from port, the *Chance* was caught at night by the twenty-six-gun British warship *Belisarius*. Many of the privateers, including those crewing the *Chance*, were seasoned sailors, but they lacked the discipline and cohesion of a British warship and had no experience in naval warfare. It was scarcely a battle. The *Chance* was hit and rendered dead in the water. Armed marines from the *Belisarius* easily boarded the decks of the *Chance* and overpowered the privateers. Any further resistance was futile, and Dring, young Palmer, and the other privateers nervously awaited their fate.

The marines ordered the Americans belowdecks, driving them down into the holds of their own ship at bayonet point. There they were forced to spend an anxiety-filled night under guard. The next morning the hatches were opened and they were forcibly taken to the holds of the warship and "put in irons."

The *Belisarius* was not finished with its hunting and proceeded to capture two more American vessels the next day, the twelve-gun *Samson*, sailing out of New London, Connecticut, and a merchant schooner from Warren, Rhode Island. The crews of both ships were forced belowdecks and chained next to Dring and his mates.

The *Belisarius* now carried 130 prisoners locked in her dark bowels. Only occasionally were the prisoners permitted to go to the upper deck, and then only a few at a time and only during daylight hours. It was a rough few days of imprisonment, especially for the frightened young boy Palmer. The prisoners were uncertain of their fate but soon realized the *Belisarius* had sailed to New York City and anchored just offshore. The warship signaled that it carried prisoners and, not long afterward, two large gondolas came alongside to ferry the prisoners to the most dreaded of all hulks, the prison ship *Jersey*.

Born in Norwich, Connecticut, in 1759, Thomas Andros was the youngest of three brothers. The family lacked the financial means to extend their youngest son's education beyond the primary years, and while the eldest brother would eventually assume responsibility for the family business and property, little to nothing in the way of opportunity awaited young Thomas. So when the war started, the teenager volunteered at first opportunity, joining a unit being formed in Cambridge. The terms of enlistment were such that new, young recruits at the time were expected to furnish their own equipment, including "a good effective Firearm . . . Bayonet . . . Haches [hatchet] or Tomahawk, a Cartridge Box and Blanket." Given his family's background, young Andros had only the most basic of weaponry, but he was in the war. A few months later, the Declaration of Independence would be signed.

The teenager was thrown into combat soon after enlisting and was a part of the important siege of Boston in the winter and spring of 1776. By March, Continental forces had liberated the city. Andros's celebration was short-lived, however, as his unit was immediately ordered to march to New York City. He spent a nerve-racking summer in the city building forts, earthworks, and other defenses while awaiting the arrival of a massive British force. Nothing could have prepared the teenager for the army of well over thirty thousand that arrived under the command of General William Howe.

Andros was a part of General George Washington's unsuccessful defense of the city. His unit was routed while attempting to defend Brooklyn and later fled with Washington's army as it pulled back through the city. On the evening of August 29 what remained of the army found themselves facing complete annihilation, their backs to the water, and so the general ordered them to cross the river into Manhattan. One can only imagine the fear and adrenaline that coursed through the teenager's body as, by the dim light of the moon, he boarded the small craft to sneak across the river. It worked, and Andros and his fellow militiamen eluded the British. But the Redcoats chased Washington's army out of the city and north several miles to White Plains, where Andros's unit was again ordered to dig in. They would meet General Howe there, on terrain that Washington hoped would be advantageous for his beaten army.

Again the British attacked, and Andros and his fellow militiamen were on the run once more. Several dozen more soldiers and militiamen were killed, wounded, or captured, but Andros managed to escape with his life.

Enlistment periods for military service were quite short at the time, and when his ended Andros was only too happy to return to his mother's home in Plainfield, Connecticut. Unfortunately, Andros did not record the terms and length of his enlistment. However, enlistment records for other teenagers in Massachusetts at the time Andros joined the war show that they were expected to serve until the "first day of December." He therefore likely returned home for the winter of 1776–77, having survived two of the most important and largest of the early battles of the war.

But the call of duty prompted Andros to reenlist, most likely in the spring or summer of 1777, though this time with the Connecticut militia rather than the Massachusetts militia. His unit was sent to Providence. Andros fought in the Battle of Rhode Island in late August 1778, another important engagement between two large armies. Regulars from Rhode Island, the first black unit (the 1st Rhode Island), the French fleet, and several armies of militiamen under General John Sullivan converged to drive the British out of the colony. The American forces were nearly successful but ultimately were pushed out of Newport. Nearby, the Americans, led by the famed general Nathanael Greene, attempted to hold Butts Hill and use it to launch a counterattack. The teenage Andros and his fellow Connecticut militiamen put up a determined stand against a combined army of British, Hessian, and loyalist forces. Eventually, however, the British prevailed.

Andros was only seventeen when he first enlisted. After several long years of fighting and several enlistments, multiple defeats on the battlefield, and the death of friends, he still believed in the ideals of liberty and self-government. He wanted to continue fighting even after completing another term of enlistment, this time for three years. He would soon have the chance.

An event changed his life while he was back home in Connecticut during the summer of 1781. The *Hannah*, a captured British merchant ship, was brought into the port of New London to much fanfare and curiosity. She was, as Andros recalled, a "very rich prize." The privateers who seized her were, according to Andros, now wealthy, which "infatuated great numbers of young men who flocked on board our private armed ships, fancying the same success would attend their adventures." Even though Andros had heard of the horrors that awaited captured sailors aboard the Hell Ship, the bounty from the *Hannah* overrode his better judgment. "Among these deluded and infatuated youth I was one," he admitted.

The young man put to sea with the crew of *The Fair American*, a newly built brig designed to prey on British merchant vessels. It carried sixteen guns, a longboat, and a stockade of muskets and other weapons for boarding enemy ships. Andros was twenty-one. He did not have long to wait.

Soon after setting sail, they spotted a British ship of roughly the same size. While pursuing their prize from the rear, *The Fair American* took fire from the British ship's stern "chaser" cannons but was able to catch the ship. The captain continued the pursuit, and Andros and his fellow mates adjusted the sails and readied themselves for battle. Pulling alongside her foe, *The Fair American* opened up with broadsides. The merchant ship did not stand a chance. It was a quick and complete victory. Not a man was lost aboard the privateer, but the British ship was hit so hard that she was dead in the water. The American captain sent an armed boarding party. Andros grabbed a musket and bayonet and joined them.

Andros and other armed sailors poured over the railing onto the damaged deck for hand-to-hand combat. It was a nerve-racking experience, but the small merchant crew quickly surrendered. Andros helped his fellow privateers fill the hull of *The Fair American* with the valuable cargo they plundered. There was much rejoicing among the crew of the privateer, as they all would be richly compensated with the great wealth they seized.

However, the captain of *The Fair American* made a mistake that would prove fatal for many members of the crew. American ships, whether privateers or merchant vessels, were instructed to avoid New York and the nearby coastline until they were at a longitude even to New Bedford. From there they could sail northward with prevailing winds for New England. Eager to get ashore and enjoy their prize, the captain failed to heed the orders and foolishly sailed directly toward Long Island, which by then was protected by several British warships.

On August 27, 1781, the British frigate *Solebay* caught the American privateer. *The Fair American* was a capable ship, but it was no match for the superior warship and was easily defeated in the short battle. Andros and his crewmates were taken to the city, where they learned they were to be detained aboard the most ill-famed ship of the war.

Ebenezer Fox was born, as he described, in 1763, "at the conclusion of the treaty of peace between England and France, at the termination of the long and harassing war, known as the 'Old French War.'" Because he was one of many children of a poor tailor who struggled to feed his family and because he was a large and physically strong boy, at the age of seven Ebenezer was apprenticed to a farmer near his family home in Roxbury, Massachusetts. The young boy recalled that for five long years, he "suffered many privations and endured much hardship . . . compared with that of many other boys of my age." Fox grew "dissatisfied" with his "situation" and, fascinated by the revolutionary events that were swirling throughout New England, he longed for adventure and opportunity. Even as a boy, he was angered by the stories of "injustice and wrongs" at the hands of the British and soon became swept up by the "spirit of disaffection [that] pervaded the land."

When news arrived of the first shots fired at Lexington and Concord on April 19, 1775, Fox knew what he wanted to do. Young Fox and a friend named John Kelley, who was a few years his senior, decided they would run away and join the war. It was a bold decision. A few days after the start of the war, Fox, with half a dollar in his pocket and the clothing on his back, set off with his friend to enlist with a military recruiter. The boys walked for days before arriving in Providence, where they discovered that it was easy to "find employment as sailors." Crews of privateers were being organized on a regular basis throughout New England's coastal communities. These vessels of fortune were typically crewed by teenage boys, who were paid but a meager wage and promised only a small share of the riches plundered. Still, for many of them such as Ebenezer Fox, it was the promise of adventure as much as the pittance they earned—a sum that far surpassed what they made as an apprentice—that brought boys in droves to Providence's harbor.

Fox and Kelley were hired by Captain Joseph Manchester as cabin boys and paid half the wages of a sailor. They were told the merchant ship was sailing for the West Indies to trade for molasses. It was probable the ship was also a privateer. It scarcely mattered, however, as the boys were in the fight. It was their first time at sea. Ebenezer Fox was only twelve years old.

Although the small craft did not seize any British ships, the captain managed to avoid the warships that prowled the waters off the coast during their first round-trip voyage. Their luck did not hold. During the second trip, they were caught by British warships. While trying to elude the warships, Captain Manchester mistakenly sailed the small schooner onto a sandbar not far from Providence. The British opened fire. With exploding spouts of water all around the ship, the crew jumped overboard and swam for shore. Fox was frozen with fear and indecision. Curiously, Captain Manchester, who chose to remain with his ship, ordered the cabin boy to "remain on board with him and be taken prisoner." Fox hesitated, not knowing what to do, but as the British tender neared the merchant vessel, Fox could stand the tension no longer and jumped into the water.

As he swam, Fox remembered, bullets "whistled around my head while in the water." He made it ashore and, with the British still firing at him, raced into a nearby cornfield. But, finding his "wet clothes an incumbrance," he "stripped them off and ran with all speed." At the end of the field, he found the other sailors hiding. One of them lent him a shirt, which covered the boy down to his feet. Ebenezer Fox managed to elude the British. The young boy walked all the way to Providence to his aunt's home.

Fox remembered that the event should have been seen by him "as judgments against any more attempts" to go to sea. He failed to heed the warning.

The Sherburnes hailed from England and, in a familiar story, they sailed to America in search of a better life, settling in Portsmouth, New Hampshire. The family later moved to Rye, New York, where Andrew, the fourth child in a family of five boys and eight girls, was born in 1765. It was the year the Stamp Act was imposed on the colonies. As a child, Andrew had a close call with death. Just shy of his third birthday, the infant fell into a spring and, had it not been for the quick thinking of one of his older sisters, would have drowned. It formed a lifelong fear of the water in the lad, something that should have kept him from joining a privateer a few years later, where he would cheat death again and again.

As was common among poor families with many children, Andrew was sent away to live with a relative, in his case an aunt in the town of Londonderry. He was only seven and would not see his family again for another four long years. Lonely, the boy became despondent until his life was changed at age nine when a woman from Ireland, described by Sherburne as "crippled from birth," moved in with his aunt to serve as his tutor. His new tutor was deeply religious and introduced Andrew to the Bible. Religion soon became the center of his life. But his new tutor's God was one of vengeance and little patience. Under her stern instruction, Andrew soon believed he was a sinner and that his separation from his family was God's punishment. The young boy also developed a conviction that he needed to atone for his sins . . . somehow.

An idea presented itself the next year, when Andrew was ten years old and the war began. As was the case with Ebenezer Fox, the fighting at Lexington and Concord prompted many boys in rural New York to enlist. Sherburne was one of them. "I wished myself old enough to take an active part in this contest," he later recalled. Two years later, at age twelve, he traveled to hear a preacher in the nearby town of Epsom and was deeply moved by the sermon. Sherburne walked home alone afterward filled with thoughts of redemption. Along the way, he had a revelation: it was time to join the war. This would redeem him and allow the boy to atone for his perceived sins.

Sherburne said good-bye to his aunt and tutor and traveled to Portsmouth to inform his family of his intentions. While there he saw men and boys enlisting and ships being built. He also heard about treasure captured by privateers during the war. An older brother had joined the navy, so the boy made up his mind. "I was filled with anxiety to become an actor in the war," he admitted. Sherburne immediately informed his family of his intention to join the crew of a privateer, but his father disapproved of privateers and told his son that he was also too young to fight.

Thinking himself "almost a man," Sherburne announced his intention to run away and join the crew of a privateer over his father's objections. Worried their son was serious, Mr. and Mrs. Sherburne reluctantly gave their approval for him to join the war as long as it was not serving on a privateer. The Continental Navy was a more reputable service than a privateer, and two of Sherburne's half uncles were sailors on the warship *Ranger*. Several boys from the area were also enlisting, so at age thirteen, Andrew Sherburne became a sailor on the *Ranger*. He and nearly thirty other young boys signed a contract with the captain of the ship; then they simply had to "pack up their clothes, take a cheese and a loaf of bread, and steer off."

Writing years later, Sherburne admitted that the "rash young adventurers did not count the cost, or think of looking at the dark side of the picture." He went looking for adventure, service, and redemption for some imaginary sin, and it would nearly cost him his life.

At twenty-five, Thomas Dring was the "old man" of the group of five wide-eyed young sailors. Andrew Sherburne was the only one with combat experience. Little did they know it, but Hawkins, Dring, Fox, Andros, and Sherburne were about to become a part of the bloodiest battle of the Revolutionary War.

Adventure on the High Seas

Dull flew the hours, 'till from the East displayed,
Sweet morn dispelled the horrors of the shade.
On every side, dire objects met the sight,
And pallid forms, and murders of the night.
The dead were past their pain; the living groan,
Nor dare to hope another morn their own.

—Philip Freneau, "The British Prison-Ship" (1781)

Twelve-year-old Ebenezer Fox returned home from his initial voyage, only to travel to Providence to enlist on a ship commanded by a Captain Thomas just four days later. This time he was away at sea for six months. Having given him up for dead, the boy's family was surprised and overjoyed by his return. Fox's father warned him against enlisting a third time, saying that his son had been lucky to avoid any "evil consequences" from his "imprudent" action. He pleaded with the young boy, "I hope you will abandon all such schemes in the future."

However, after a few months back home in Roxbury apprenticing for a wigmaker, the boy learned that the Massachusetts militia was recruiting local boys. The wigmaker, a Mr. Bosson, had fallen on hard times and was feeling pressure to join the militia. Instead, he offered Fox the chance to take his place. The young boy agreed, and the payment was arranged by Bosson to both Fox and the militia recruiter. The young boy was thrilled to be making four dollars a month, the "largest sum I ever before possessed," he would later recall. Fox had a three-month enlistment with a unit from Boston. It was September 1779 and he was not quite sixteen.

Fox made it through his enlistment with no more excitement than blisters on his feet from all the marching. After his discharge, the young boy desired to return to sea to make money. So in January 1780 he joined the crew of the *Protector*, a twenty-gun warship of the Massachusetts colony commanded by John Foster Williams. Fox and the other new recruits marched to the port singing a tune popular among sailors of the time:

> *All you that have bad masters*
> *And cannot get your due;*
> *Come, come, my brave boys,*
> *And join with our ship's crew!*

In February the warship set sail with 350 men. They sailed north into the cold waters of Newfoundland hunting British merchant ships and small warships. After several uneventful weeks, Captain Williams sailed south for the main British trade routes from the West Indies. Finally, after four months spent mostly at sea, through the fog on the morning of June 9, Fox and his mates finally saw a British ship. It was a warship boasting thirty-two guns. Captain Williams ordered the crew to fly the British Union Jack. The trick worked, and the British ship allowed the *Protector* to approach close enough that Fox counted the guns and could read the ship's name—the *Admiral Duff*.

Fox was assigned to the quarterdeck. He and his crewmates were told to stay hidden and quiet until Captain Williams gave the command. Nervously they waited for the coming battle. Williams hoisted a trumpet and asked the British captain the purpose of his cruise.

The *Admiral Duff* was sailing from Jamaica to London laden with sugar and tobacco. But then the British captain, becoming suspicious, responded with his own questions. It was at that moment that Captain Williams gave the command to fire. The crew brought down the British flag and hoisted the Stars and Stripes. Loaded cannons were rolled out through the gun ports. From the quarterdeck, Fox helped ready a 6-pounder. The order rang out: "Fire!" The *Protector* unleashed a broadside into the *Admiral Duff*. Although the British ship was larger, her crew was caught unprepared.

The fight raged for thirty minutes, with both ships exchanging fire. The *Admiral Duff*, her sails and rigging nearly destroyed, attempted to sail away, but the Americans gave chase, pulling alongside the damaged ship to continue the fight. Fox was standing next to Captain Williams on the quarterdeck when a musket ball dinged loudly on the commander's trumpet. Fox exhaled when he realized his captain was unharmed and marveled at his calm during the battle. It inspired courage in the young boy. But at that moment a great explosion rang out. A storm of small iron balls and sharp objects known as grapeshot poured onto the quarterdeck of the *Protector*, killing and wounding several of Fox's crewmates. The scene was one of mayhem on both ships; the British were putting up a determined fight.

From the deck of the *Protector*, marines armed with muskets returned fire, sending volley after volley onto the upper deck of the *Admiral Duff*. Few men remained on the deck of the British warship. The battle was turning decidedly in favor of the Americans. Then finally one of the *Protector*'s cannonballs struck a powder supply in the stern of the *Admiral Duff*, igniting a great and terrible explosion that blew the back half of the ship into the sky. The battle was over. The *Protector* suffered massive damage but was still seaworthy.

The Americans surveyed the toll on the *Admiral Duff*, which Fox described as a "terrible slaughter among the enemy." For the first time in his life, the boy witnessed blood and death up close. Young Fox's first taste of combat ended in a grand victory, but he remembered being rendered momentarily deaf from the constant cannon fire and the explosion near him. The *Protector* sailed back to Boston for repairs.

Back home and contemplating his future, Fox watched a recruiting party that "paraded the streets under the American flag, accompanied by a band of martial music." Inspired by the spectacle and emboldened by the *Protector*'s victory, he decided to reenlist and set sail again in October 1780. On its next voyage the *Protector* enjoyed successful missions in the waters off Halifax, San Juan, and Charleston. Back home, enjoying the money he earned and his share of the plundered wares, Fox made the choice to go back to sea yet again. He also stopped worrying about getting captured or killed in combat, believing the prospect of any "evil" was likely "afar off" and that luck was with him. It was not.

A few days out at sea on Fox's next sailing, the lookout aboard the *Protector* spied two ships in the distance. It was soon apparent the ships were hunting them. The lookout announced they were both flying French flags, but Captain Williams informed the crew that their pursuers were likely British. He was right. As the ships neared, the French flags were taken down and replaced with the Union Jack. Williams ordered the *Protector* to make a run for it.

The *Protector*'s crew worked to catch the winds, but over the next few hours the two British warships closed the distance. Fox and his crewmates realized they were about to be caught. The sight of what was hunting them panicked the crew on the *Protector*. Closing fast was the forty-gun *Roebuck* and twenty-eight-gun *May-Day*. Sure enough, the British ships fired warning shots, then strategically separated, with one pulling alongside the starboard and the other off the port of the *Protector*. The British captains offered the Americans a choice—surrender or be fired on from both sides. Captain Williams wisely surrendered.

Fox remembered the fear he felt as the British boarded the *Protector* and yanked down the Stars and Stripes. To curses of "damned rebels," the victors proceeded to "strike or kick every [American] sailor." They then began confiscating the ship's supplies and the Americans' possessions. When the British found money on some of their new prisoners, they ordered all members of the *Protector*'s crew to strip naked and be searched. Fox had cleverly hidden money beneath the insole of his shoe and in the crown of his hat. However, when it was his turn to be searched, he was shaken and knocked around so violently that his hat fell off and the money was found. But his captors never found the money he hid in his shoe. Other members of the crew lost everything.

Young Ebenezer Fox's luck had run out. He and his crewmates were forcefully shoved down into the holds of the *Roebuck* and not permitted to go above deck for a full day and night. He soon learned he was being taken to New York.

One of the prisoners with a unique perspective on British prisons in both America and England—as well as on land and in ships—was Andrew Sherburne, the young boy from New York, convinced he was a sinner in need of redemption. Young Sherburne sought repentance by joining the crew of the Continental warship *Ranger*. He set sail in June 1779 on the eighteen-gun warship from Portsmouth as part of a three-ship squadron of frigates from Boston and Providence. The experience was rough for a landlubber. Sherburne and the other new members of the crew immediately became violently seasick. Nor did the naive boy understand the strange "dialect" and salty customs of the sailors. Like other teens at sea, he was also "ridiculed . . . insulted, and frequently obliged to fight" the older sailors. However, once he learned to fight and stand up for himself, the abuse abated.

Sherburne was soon assigned to wait upon the ship's boatswain, a man named Charles Roberts.* It was not the adventurous experience Sherburne wanted, but the job would soon end up saving his life.

---

* A boatswain manages the ship's crew and supplies.

The crew of the *Ranger* spent long days drilling and firing the cannons. In between these preparations Sherburne had to attend to the boatswain, serving him dinner and performing various chores. After "several weeks," they were cruising in the West Indies when the tedious routine was broken at seven one morning by a lookout screaming, "A sail, a sail on the lee-bow; another there, and there!" They had spotted a British fleet en route to Jamaica. As the thick morning fog dissipated, the lookout counted fifty sails through the spyglass. Hearts raced as the men were called to battle stations. They closed the distance to the convoy, and Sherburne soon saw three times as many sails, some of them atop armed escorts.

Undeterred, the *Ranger* boldly pursued the largest warship in the convoy, the twenty-two-gun *Holderness*, while the other two American ships chased the merchant vessels. Fortunately for Sherburne and his crew, their foe was slow and the crew not at full strength; the *Ranger* caught the rear guard of the convoy in only one hour. After weakening their foe from a distance, the *Ranger* repeatedly hit the *Holderness* with broadsides at close range until she struck colors. The marines on board the *Ranger* boarded their prize and found her hull filled with cotton, coffee, sugar, rum, and spices. In total, the small Continental squadron claimed ten ships. It had been a terrifying but exciting experience for young Sherburne.

The squadron sailed home in 1779 to a hero's welcome, and Sherburne was reunited with his brother, who was back from his service on a privateer. He also discovered he had a new baby sister. Sherburne's take from the prize was thirty-five gallons of rum, one ton of sugar, twenty pounds of cotton, and fifty dollars. He and his family were now wealthy.

Like so many other young privateers and sailors, the successful voyage did not quench Sherburne's appetite for adventure or, in his case, need for redemption. Sherburne tried his luck again, going back to sea in the fall of 1779 with the *Ranger* and the other two frigates. They captured a few small merchant ships and then sailed south past Florida. However, in May 1780, the squadron ran into gale winds.

During the storm, he and other young boys were sent up the masts to trim the sails. There, high above the ship, the wind and salty spray tore at the flesh while the rough seas tossed the boys about like rag dolls.

While the youngsters were busy at work and fighting for their lives, the weight of the sailors and ferocity of the storm snapped one of the wooden beams, sending several members of the crew crashing back to the deck and into the sea. Sherburne clutched the torn rigging and held on for dear life. Soon his wet hands lost their grip and he slipped momentarily, but somehow managed to catch hold of a rope. Sherburne dangled dangerously high above the violent waves. Miraculously, he eventually climbed safely down to the deck, exhausted, soaking wet, and trembling with fear. But it was about to get worse.

As they were sailing to Charleston to resupply and repair the damaged masts and sails, the small squadron encountered five larger British ships. The British gave chase, pursuing the three American frigates to Charleston harbor. The Americans found temporary shelter in the harbor, as the sandbars and the shallow depth prevented the larger British warships from entering the inlet. But the British warships blockaded any escape and then opened fire. During the battle, one of the British ships dispatched small launches with guns to establish a battery just offshore at James Island. The *Ranger* moved into position on the other side of the harbor to engage the battery, and after a ninety-minute exchange the battery was destroyed. Unfortunately, while trying to sail to another part of the harbor to avoid British fire, the *Ranger* became caught on a sandbar. During the time the ship was unable to navigate, several cannonballs struck her hull. In desperation, Sherburne and other crewmembers threw equipment overboard to lighten the ship and raise her draft, while others went overboard in rowboats in an effort to tow her free.

Watching the rowboats from his position on the upper deck, Sherburne heard a whistle and instinctively dove for cover behind one of the large guns—just in time. A cannonball exploded near him, sending shrapnel and wood flying across the deck. Sherburne escaped injury, but others standing beside him were not so fortunate. He recalled the feeling of absolute terror during the fight and attributed his miraculous survival to a higher power.

The American ships were sitting ducks in the harbor and were taking fire. They were also running low on ammunition. With the *Ranger* battered and Charleston under assault, it was decided to abandon the ship and help the poorly defended city. Sherburne and his crewmates grabbed weapons and went ashore, where they were immediately thrust into the middle of a heated battle. The British soon overwhelmed the city's defenders and the crews of the three frigates. The Americans surrendered on May 12, 1780, and were taken prisoner. During the surrender, Sherburne's life was likely saved when the British inexplicably allowed the petrified teen to accompany the officers from his ship. The officers were housed separately and given better rations. The other young boys on the *Ranger* were not so fortunate.

Not long after the surrender, a smallpox outbreak struck the city and swept through the ranks of the sailors. However, the officers had themselves and young Sherburne inoculated. Many of the sailors imprisoned in Charleston succumbed to the disease. Eventually the captain of the *Ranger* worked with negotiators from a cartel, and the British agreed to release the officers.* Sherburne's luck held when the captain and boatswain agreed to take him with them.

But Sherburne was not out of harm's way just yet. The small boat used by the officers to sail to Newport, Rhode Island, had meager rations and their water supply was "foul." Sherburne and a few of the officers soon became violently ill, so much so that when they arrived in Rhode Island they were quarantined by the port until they showed no further signs of disease or sickness. While biding their time, Sherburne was so desperate to wash away the filth and lice that covered his body that he waded into a small river. Not realizing just how weak he had become, he nearly drowned for a second time in his life

---

* A cartel was a group of mediators who represented the prisoners and their families in their negotiations with the Royal Navy.

(the first having been when he was a toddler) and had to be rescued by one of the officers.

The young sailor eventually made it back home, only to discover that his father had died and his brother had never returned from his last mission on a privateer. Andrew Sherburne was not yet fifteen.

It took the teen fully two months to recover his health, but Sherburne, like Thomas Dring, Christopher Hawkins, Thomas Andros, and Ebenezer Fox, did not learn his lesson. When a young captain out of Kennebunkport, Maine, who turned out to be more of a snake oil salesman than a mariner, approached Sherburne with the promise of "a short cruise" to "make your fortune," the lad enlisted with the privateer. Privateering "had now become the order of the day," he remembered, explaining his hasty decision. The newly built eight-gun schooner, *Greyhound*, was crewed by around twenty-five boys from New England, a few of them "not a dozen years old," several officers, and two captains. The ship sailed north toward Canada.

Soon after setting sail, the *Greyhound* was caught in a storm and Sherburne "very narrowly escaped being thrown off" the "pitching and rolling" ship. Later, while sailing on the St. Lawrence River, he observed his fellow privateers plundering civilian vessels and homes with no regard for whether they were loyalists or patriots. Homesick and regretting his decision, Sherburne confessed, "I endeavored to suppress all gloomy reflections and make the best of a bad bargain." It did not work.

The lawlessness of the privateers and his captain's increasingly erratic and reckless behavior raised concerns in the boy, who now requested to take leave of the ship. His request was denied, but Sherburne began planning to desert at first opportunity. Meanwhile, the *Greyhound* joined with another privateer and he was transferred to the other ship. There he encountered a captain named Arnold who was far worse than the commander of the *Greyhound*. Captain Arnold was mentally unstable and violent, and he had a perverse taste for young boys, causing the teen to fear for his life and spend most of his time aboard the privateer hiding, especially at night. Sherburne and the other boys were saved from the reign of terror when the captain disappeared while the ship was off the Canadian coast. The details were unknown to the crew, but it appeared that he stripped naked and jumped overboard. Of course, it is also possible one of the members of the crew killed or threw him overboard at night. The only clue remaining was his clothing, which was still on the ship.

Sherburne began to believe that both he and the ship were cursed. In a way they were. With no one to pilot or navigate the ship, it was dead in the water and was soon commandeered by an American privateer carrying twenty guns; rather than assist their fellow countrymen, its crew boarded the ship and looted what remained of the crew's supplies and provisions. Americans were now attacking Americans. It seemed as if the cruise could not get any worse, but soon more bad weather struck and the small privateer began taking on water. Floundering, the ship was captured by the British warship *Fairy*. It was likely the better of two bad fates that awaited the crew.

Sherburne and his crewmates were sailed all the way to England, where they were charged with "rebellion, piracy, and high treason on His Britannic Majesty's high seas." After giving his name, place of birth, age, father's occupation, and details about his privateer, Sherburne was sent to the Old Mill Prison in Plymouth.

The boy expected to die. There were few prisoner exchanges or releases at the time and one of the only ways out of prison was to join the Royal Navy, which he began contemplating. But Sherburne had contracted yet another disease and was too weak for the Royal Navy to accept him. He resigned himself to the inevitable. While he was awaiting death, an opportunity presented itself one night when the prisoners noticed that far fewer guards were patrolling the prison yard and walls than normal. The prisoners in Sherburne's cell had managed to remove the grate in their window in anticipation of just such an opportunity. Malnourished and skeletally thin, the boy was able to squeeze through the small opening, so his fellow prisoners sent Sherburne out the window.

Sherburne's memoir is not clear as to whether he was supposed to get help and rescue the other prisoners or simply make a run for freedom. The absence of detail indicates he was not able to rescue the other American sailors, but at least one of his friends in prison was soon released, suggesting that perhaps Sherburne did notify authorities to arrange for a prisoner release. Either way, while on the run Sherburne met a physician who treated him. The kind man contacted an American cartel and negotiated for them to take Sherburne home. It took fifteen months of travel, but the teen eventually made it home again. His family had long ago given him up for dead. After his incredible ordeal, he promised them he would never leave again.

But eventually Sherburne was enticed back to sea once more. This time it was with a friend from the Old Mill Prison in England. So many men from New England's coastal villages had enlisted in the war or on privateers or were dead or in prison that captains now had trouble crewing their vessels. And so it was that the captain and owners of the privateer *Scorpion* managed to find only eighteen men and boys to crew a ship requiring more than twice that number. The shortage was such that Sherburne was even offered the job of boatswain on the eight-gun vessel.

This voyage was doomed from the start. Only five days out from port a large British warship hunted them. The *Scorpion* escaped after the crew threw most everything overboard to lighten the ship for speed. After resupplying, they continued on their voyage to the West Indies, but did not capture any ships. Rather, the *Scorpion* was again chased by a British warship, this time off the coast of Guadeloupe. They eluded the warship, but were hunted off Montserrat and then a fourth time while on the way back to Virginia. After so many narrow escapes, the crew was exhausted, unnerved, and out of provisions.

While seeking shelter and supplies in Virginia, they were hunted again—this time by a much larger British warship. As it was about to overtake them, the winds slowed, and the *Scorpion*'s captain ordered what remained of the ship's guns and stores overboard. Sherburne and his crewmates also lowered their small launches and rowed for their lives, pulling the *Scorpion* away from their pursuer on the flat ocean. Sherburne remembered that they "rowed all day; we did not leave off even to eat." By nightfall the effort seemed to have paid off. There was no sign of the hunter on the dark horizon, allowing Sherburne and his exhausted mates a few hours to finally sleep. But as they did, out of the dark emerged the forty-gun *Amphion*. The Americans were outgunned and outmaneuvered, and the battle lasted only minutes. The *Scorpion* was destroyed.

So in November 1782 Sherburne found himself once again a prisoner. The thirteen surviving members of the *Scorpion* were taken belowdecks on the *Amphion*, where they joined a hundred prisoners from other privateers captured by the British ship. The conditions were deplorable and the prisoners lacked "sufficient room for each to stretch himself at the same time." But Sherburne's third trip to prison was about to be his worst. The men discovered that they were sailing to New York to be incarcerated aboard the *Jersey*. The Hell Ship, as Sherburne remembered, "had become notorious in consequence of the unparalleled mortality on board of her." He and his crewmates began to panic at the mere mention of the ship's name, recalling that their "prospects were more dubious than they had been before."

As the *Amphion* approached New York, some of the prisoners became nauseous and ill at the prospects of being put aboard the *Jersey*. Others attempted suicide or began planning an escape. In 1782, the crew of one American ship being detained by the British in Boston did just that. After discovering they were being taken to Brooklyn to be put aboard the most notorious ship of the war, the men mutinied rather than face the horrors of confinement on the *Jersey*. Remarkably, the prisoners succeeded in overpowering their captors and sailed their truce ship to Bermuda and to freedom. But a different fate awaited Sherburne and his crewmates.

Sherburne was still a teenager when he was put aboard *Jersey* in November 1782. The first thing he noticed about the ship was the "half-starved, emaciated, and imperious prisoners" who were "suffering almost without a parallel."

Floating Dungeons

Thus do our warriors, thus our heroes fall,
Imprison'd here, quick ruin meets them all.

—Philip Freneau, "The British Prison-Ship" (1781)

As was mentioned earlier, the British did not invent the practice of using old ships as floating dungeons during the Revolutionary War. Nor was the practice new for the Royal Navy. Earlier that century, Britain employed prison ships in their conflict with the Scots and incarcerated French sailors on derelict ships during the French and Indian War.* Indeed, the practice had a long, gruesome, and checkered history in Britain and around the world.

In the seventeenth and eighteenth centuries, the problem of prison overcrowding had risen to crisis levels in England, as did the crime rate, or at least public perceptions of criminal activity. In an effort to "get tough on crime," British politicians tacked on an endless array of offenses that were eligible for the death penalty, and capital punishment soon became something of a spectator sport. The regular

---

* Also known in Europe as the Seven Years' War.

public executions at Tyburn attracted large, unruly mobs that jeered and threw garbage at the condemned as they approached the gallows.* Despite the frequent executions, however, crime and arrests outpaced the hangings, and prisons grew ever more crowded.

At the same time, farmers displaced by the new mercantile order were moving to London in record numbers. Soon the streets filled with homeless beggars. Unemployment reached crisis levels. The situation was such that countless British citizens living in abject squalor volunteered to board ships to try their odds in America. In exchange for their passage, they agreed to live as indentured servants. For years, ships sailed from England to America loaded with indentured servants and the poor. Still, crime and prison overcrowding remained at crisis levels.

One of the men appointed to address the situation was William Eden, the first Baron Lord Auckland. From the 1770s through the early 1800s, Eden served in a number of positions, including as a member of Parliament, minister of the Northern Department, and minister of trade; he even visited America at the start of the Revolutionary War in a diplomatic capacity to attempt to negotiate a ceasefire. Eden also promoted an array of proposals allegedly designed to reform the English penal system and improve the treatment of prisoners. But they included such draconian measures as shipping prisoners to Australia and exchanging prisoners for the sailors held for ransom by the Barbary pirates of North Africa. Eden also convinced both the admiralty and Parliament to support his bill to incarcerate prisoners on old warships.

England was desperate for answers, and the compromise to the crisis was to utilize hulks to ease the overcrowding. In the words of Eden, "The fact is that our prisons are full and we have no way at present to dispose of the convicts but that what would be execrably bad; for all the proposals of Africa—desert islands—mines etc., means nothing more than a more lingering method of inflicting

---

* The nickname for the execution spot, named for its location: Tyburn Road.

capital punishment." Eden's Hulk Bill passed in the House of Commons in May 1776, just a few weeks before General George Washington and General William Howe would square off for control of New York City. Ironically, the result of both the bill and battle would be the incarceration of thousands of soldiers and sailors on hulks.

Old warships and support vessels were soon moored at Woolwich Dockyard on the Thames near London and berthed at Deptford, Plymouth, and other ports along England's southeastern coast as well as in Bermuda and the West Indies. Britain became so dependent on prison ships that they even hulked the legendary HMS *Discovery*, which had been captained by George Vancouver during his expedition to the Pacific and western coastline of North America. Of course, putting prisoners on derelict ships did not address the cause of crime. The abhorrent practice also brought with it disease, security risks, unsightliness (for people living nearby), and an alarmingly high death rate.

When the Revolutionary War started, the British used such ships as a way of temporarily dealing with the large population of American prisoners. Additionally, many people in Britain did not want prisoners from the American colonies shipped back to England. The practice was not uncommon, senior commanders believed the war would be a short one, and there was little interest in putting forth the effort to build prisons for the colonial "criminals" who dared oppose them. None of these transport ships were, however, intended to be a long-term solution to the prison dilemma. The ships were also needed to resupply the war effort.

When Parliament passed the Hulk Act in May 1776, word of the measure traveled across the Atlantic and arrived in New York around the time of the fighting in Brooklyn. General Howe immediately began hulking ships to be used as prisons. Prison ships in New York thus became an acceptable alternative to the gallows and a short-term compromise. And so, immediately after the fighting in Brooklyn during the summer of 1776, roughly four hundred prisoners were put aboard the transport ship *Pacific*, anchored off New York City.

As the sugar houses and churches of the city ran out of space to accommodate more prisoners, a few other transports such as the *Chatham*, *Glasgow*, *Grosvenor*, *Judith*, *Lord Rochford*, and *Mentor* were ordered to make room for prisoners. These transports had originally carried soldiers, cattle, and supplies across the Atlantic in the summer of 1776 and were now anchored at Gravesend Bay off Lower Manhattan. Once the British gained control of the entire city, the ships were moved to the East River, the Hudson River, and elsewhere. Similarly, when the war spread to the American South, the British used the HMS *Roebuck* to house prisoners in Norfolk, Virginia, and, in 1780, in Charleston, South Carolina.

One of the sites used as an anchorage for prison ships was Wallabout Bay, a small, shallow inlet shaped like a kidney off the East River.

The region had originally been home to the Iroquois, Algonquian, and other native peoples. Among the first Europeans to arrive in what would become New York were the French in the 1520s. The Dutch established settlements there as part of New Amsterdam and New Netherlands at the dawn of the seventeenth century. The first Europeans to settle along the shores of Wallabout Bay, however, were several families of French-speaking Walloons who arrived from Holland and the vicinity in the 1620s. It is believed that a trader-turned-politician named Joris Jansen Rapelje was first to build a house at Wallabout Bay. The small Dutch settlement he helped found was known as "Waal Bocht" or "Walloon's Bend." The name stuck.*

Hugging the northwest edge of Brooklyn, the bay's shoreline was cloaked with grasses and marshy meadows. Rolling, sandy bluffs rimmed the bay, and a few narrow footpaths led to the edge of the water. Small shrubs rather than trees lined the coast and, from the nearby village of Bushwick, an uninspiring creek named for the bay

---

* During the Revolutionary War, the bay was at times still called "Whallabocht" or "Wallebocht."

meandered through the marshlands and emptied into the brackish, stagnant waters. At the time of the Revolutionary War, it was a quiet and sparsely populated area. A few farmhouses owned by the Johnson, Remsen, and Tyerson families dotted the landscape. The bay, however, was not used by fishermen or boaters, as the mudflats along the soggy shoreline made it rather inaccessible. Clouds of mosquitos and other bugs also swarmed along the bay in summers, preying mercilessly on anyone unlucky enough to be there.

Today Wallabout Bay is nestled along a bend on the East River between the Manhattan Bridge to the west and Williamsburg Bridge to the northeast. It is directly opposite Corlears Hook and across the East River from Chinatown on Lower Manhattan.

The British selected the location in 1776 because they controlled Brooklyn and all of New York City. Moreover, the waters of Wallabout Bay were calm, yet the mudflats and marshes made it nearly impossible to boat, swim, walk, or crawl. Escape would be difficult. Wallabout Bay was chosen for another reason as well. Worried about the spread of contagion, the British moved the disease-infested prison ships out of New York harbor to the abandoned bay. Yet the bay and ships were still a visible reminder of what would happen should any colonist dare challenge His Majesty.

As the war dragged on far longer than the British had imagined, the hulks became the primary means of dealing with prisoners and Wallabout Bay emerged as the main location for the fleet of floating dungeons. During the course of the war there were as many as sixteen prison ships at Wallabout Bay. They held soldiers from the Continental Army, seamen from captured American merchant ships, nearby residents charged with disloyalty, and Dutch, French, and Spanish sailors. But the crews of captured American privateers constituted the main population on board the prison ships.

The first prison ship of the war to arrive at Wallabout Bay was the HMS *Whitby*. It was moored near Remsen's Mill on October 20,

1776, and hulked soon afterward. On orders from Commissary General Joshua Loring, the large transport ship took on its first prisoners in early December. The *Whitby* held roughly 250 prisoners, including soldiers from the Continental Army, most of whom were from Connecticut, and a few political detainees from New York City. Surviving accounts of the prison ship are alarming. According to one prisoner, "Bad provisions, bad water and scanted rations were dealt to the prisoners. No medical men attended the sick, disease reigned unrelieved, and hundreds died from pestilence, or worse, starved on board this floating prison."

A letter written by a prisoner named Timothy Parker only a few weeks after the ship was put into service states, "Our present situation is most wretched; more than 250 prisoners, some sick and without the least assistance from physician, drug, or medicine, and fed on two-thirds allowance of salt provisions . . . allowed to walk the main deck only between sunrise and sunset. Only two at a time allowed to come on deck to do what nature requires, and sometimes denied even that, and use tubs and buckets between decks, to the great offence of every delicate, cleanly person, as well as to great prejudice of all our healths." Parker concluded, "We have no prospect before our eyes but a kind of lingering inevitable death."

The letter also described another facet of life aboard the prison ships—that they were among the first places in America that were integrated, which offended some of the white prisoners. Parker remembered being "crowded promiscuously together without regard to color, person or office, in the small room of a ship's between decks." Another white prisoner complained of being "huddled together with negroes." There was not enough room onboard for all the prisoners to lie down at the same time, much less respect the segregationist norms of the time.

There are other disturbing accounts. Robert Sheffield of Stonington, Connecticut, managed to escape in June 1778 and offered a third-person description of the *Whitby*: "The steam of the hold was enough to scald the skin and take away the breath—the stench enough to poison the air all around. On his descending these dreary mansions of woe, and beholding the numerous spectacles of wretchedness and despair, his soul fainted within him." He was also shocked by the prisoners, saying, "Their sickly countenances and ghastly looks were truly horrible; some swearing and blaspheming; some crying; others delirious, raving, and storming; some groaning and dying—all panting for breath; some dead and corrupting." Most problematic was the air, which was "so foul at times that a lamp could not be kept burning, by reason of which the boys were not missed till then had been dead ten days." Sheffield was later recaptured and placed back aboard the ship.

Ichabod Perry, a seventeen-year-old private from Fairfield, Connecticut, lived through his incarceration on the *Whitby*. In his later years he penned an account of the ship for his children, claiming that one-third of the prisoners died from "no air" belowdecks. Perry shockingly maintained that he was once so starved he "could eat [his] own flesh without wincing." The young man ended up eating wood to stay alive.

Another Connecticut prisoner named David Thorp, from nearby Woodbury, remembered that four days a week he and the seven other men in his "mess" received only a little oatmeal with worms in it. The rations the other three days of the week consisted of two ounces of salted beef and a hard biscuit. Thorp and his fellow prisoners once went for three days without water.

Perry and Thorp were released in February 1777 during a prisoner exchange likely organized by Jonathan Trumbull, the governor of Connecticut. Although they could barely walk, the boys eventually made it home. The *Connecticut Gazette* documented the experiences of Perry, Thorp, and other home-state heroes who survived the *Whitby*. In an article published in February 1777, Lieutenant William Sterrett, who, like most of the prisoners, was captured in the fighting in Brooklyn on August 27, 1776, recalled that when he was being processed on board the ship his "clothing was stolen" and he "was abused by the soldiers." Those captives with wounds, he said, were "allowed to perish from neglect."

Not surprisingly, such newspaper accounts as this one, which likened the ship to Dante's hell, shocked the public. Later, when even more gripping newspaper reports appeared with alarming frequency about an even more notorious ship, they would help rally the patriots' cause.

That first winter, the *Whitby* was the only prison ship at Wallabout Bay. Yet so many prisoners died that, after only two months, the makeshift graveyard was full and a new site had to be dug nearby. One survivor recalled that "during two months in the spring the entire beach, between the ravine and Remsen's Dock, was filled with graves; and before the first day of May, the ravine itself was filled with the remains of hundreds who died from pestilence, or were starved to death in this dreadful prison." By May 1777, the beaches near the *Whitby* could accommodate no more bodies. The guards devised a new solution, which was described by James Little of Connecticut years later in his application for a war pension. In the morning, "dead bodies were hoisted on deck, a cannonball fastened to them, and they were thrown overboard with the shout of 'there goes another damned Yankee rebel.'"

That same month, two larger ships—the *Kitty* and a ship whose name has been lost to history—were towed to the bay to replace the *Whitby*, which was sold for scrap. Each one held roughly 250 prisoners. But the conditions on the replacement ships were just as bad, prompting some of the prisoners on a Sunday afternoon in October 1777 to set one of the ships ablaze. In the words of an eyewitness, the prisoners chose a quick death, "even by fire, to the lingering sufferings of pestilence and starvation." Another prisoner wrote, "So great was their suffering, that they were induced to set fire to the ships, which were burnt, hoping thus either to secure their liberty, or hasten their death." Many prisoners died in the fire, but some helped others escape out of portholes into the water.

But the act of desperation did nothing to stop the use of floating prisons. Nor did it alleviate the crowded conditions. On the contrary, after the fire "the prisoners, except a few, who, it was said, were burnt in the vessel, were removed to the remaining ship." Shortly after the October fire, two hospital ships were moored in Wallabout Bay near the remaining prison ship. Only four months later, the conditions were so bad on one of the hospital ships that it too was set on fire at night, also by the prisoners.

The war continued, and more patriots were captured. In 1778, another ship was towed into Wallabout Bay and was crammed with five hundred prisoners. By January 1780, so many prisoners had been captured that a small flotilla of vessels was brought from the North River to Wallabout Bay, including the *Prince of Wales*, the hospital ship *Falmouth*, the sloop *Hunter* (which was used as a hospital ship), the sloop *Scorpion*, the fire ship *Strombolo*, and the ironically named hospital ship *Good Hope*. Only two months after being anchored in the cursed waters off Brooklyn, the *Good Hope* burned as well.

Throughout the war, ships came and went; some were burned, others were called back to service, and some, such as the *Hunter*, *Scorpion*, and *Strombolo*, were sold for parts. Ever more ships were needed to accommodate the burgeoning prison population. Old transports no longer needed for the return trip across the Atlantic and warships past their prime such as the *Bristol, Chatham, Clyde, Glasgow, Providence, Scheldt*, and *Woodlands* were hulked in waters throughout New York. Even in the final months of the war, more of these floating dungeons were deployed to Wallabout Bay, including the transport ship *John* and two hospital ships, *Frederick* and *Perseverance*.

Prisons were soon a priority for His Majesty's commanders, and it would not be long before one prison ship in particular would serve another, more sinister objective. It would also be the largest prison ship in the ghostly fleet at Wallabout Bay, one that would remain until the bitter end of the war.

Dead Reckoning

No masts or sails these crowded ships adorn,
Dismal to view, neglected and forlorn;
Here mighty ills oppress'd the imprison'd throng,
Dull were our slumbers, and our nights were long—
From morn to eve, along the decks we lay,
Scorch'd into fevers by the solar ray.

—Philip Freneau, "The British Prison-Ship" (1781)

A veteran of naval wars in the South Atlantic, Mediterranean, and elsewhere, the HMS *Jersey* had been a powerful warship. In her prime, she carried sixty-four guns with a crew of roughly four hundred and had ample space for equipment and provisions for long deployments at sea. But after three decades of service, the old fourth-rate warship was decommissioned in 1769 and sailed across the Atlantic without armaments to serve as a troop and supply vessel in the American colonies.

Sometime in the 1770s before the start of the Revolutionary War, she was hulked in order to serve as a hospital ship, and by 1778 she was anchored in the East River near Tolmie's Dock off Manhattan.

The old wood planks of the *Jersey* had begun to rot. But the growing prison population during the war necessitated a change in the status of the old warship.

The earliest account of the vessel serving as a prison ship dates to December 1778. The first mention of the ship in an American newspaper was on September 1, 1779, when a paper in New London, Connecticut, wrote about the story of a prisoner named Stanton who was captured on June 5 and imprisoned onboard the *Jersey* for three or four weeks before being transferred to a nearby hospital ship.

In April 1780, the *Jersey* was towed to Wallabout Bay, where it was loaded with roughly four hundred prisoners. The number of prisoners on the old hulk, however, grew alarmingly, in part because the *Jersey* was designated as the receiving ship for all the hulks in the fleet. By 1781, 850 prisoners were on the ship. A year later, the ship held over 1,000 prisoners and had long since become a living hell for those trapped in her rotted, diseased holds. By 1783, reports indicate that 1,200 prisoners were somehow crammed below her decks. At one point in 1782, the ship was so grossly overcrowded that the *Jersey*'s captain ordered two hundred prisoners be moved to the transport ship *John*. Eventually the nearby transport and hospital ships became overcrowded, in large measure because of the number of sick prisoners from the *Jersey*. Astonishingly, war reports also show that fully half, and at times more than half, of the entire prison ship population of New York was incarcerated on the *Jersey*.

The ship was moored like a monstrous, condemned beast by heavy black chains. These old, rusting cables were affixed to the front and back of the ship at the midlevel deck, and angled down into the murky water. The *Jersey* sat roughly the length of a football field offshore in Wallabout Bay. Nearby, a few hospital ships clustered around her, spread out roughly two to three hundred yards to the southeast. There she sat as an ever-present reminder of what awaited anyone who dared challenge the might of the British.

The old, black hulk looked the part. She could no longer sail. Her rotted hull leaked, causing the prisoners to shiver in wetness during heavy rains, and the ship had to constantly be pumped to prevent her from filling with water. The *Jersey* was rudderless and had been stripped of all masts, sails, and structures except for a tall, bare flag-staff at the stern—"seldom used" except to send signals—and a derrick at the bow for hoisting provisions such as water, wood, and food up to the top deck. Long gone were the cannons on the middle and lower decks. In their place, prisoners crowded her three main decks as well as the quarterdeck and forecastle, which covered part of the upper gun deck near the stern of the ship. A small canvas awning sat on the upper deck at the stern for use as a tent by the guards.

A solitary accommodation ladder on the aft starboard side of the ship provided a way on and off the floating coffin for the crew. The derelict ship had a small gangway on the port side, midship, that angled down to a small, square wooden platform. It was from this point that rowboats and other small launches dropped off the condemned. There was only one other way off the ship, but that was reserved for the corpses wrapped in canvas or blankets. A guard remained stationed at the head of the ladder, a solitary sentinel to the purgatory that awaited the prisoners.

A barricade was constructed near the head of the ladder that extended outward in both directions to the side of the ship. It was roughly ten feet in height and contained a heavy door and small holes through which muskets could be fired. This barricade provided protection for the guards in the event of a prisoner uprising. The drill was for them to gather behind the barricade, seal the door, and fire at the prisoners from the safety of the gun holes. The real deterrent to mutiny, however, was the poor physical condition of the prisoners. Most were too weak from starvation and illness to fight. Nor could the old ship sail, so it made little sense to attempt to commandeer it, and it was next to impossible to walk or swim in the mud and swamps that rimmed Wallabout Bay.

All the portholes had been nailed shut. Iron bars in the shape of crosses eerily covered other possible exits, giving the ship a dismal, coffin-like appearance and sealing the wretched souls inside. The only openings were small notches in a twenty-inch square pattern drilled into the sides of the ship for ventilation. They ran roughly every ten feet along the ship. These were the only sources of light and air for the prisoners, but proved to be wholly inadequate for either. Indeed, the air became so foul at times that lamps did not burn and the men trapped belowdecks were left gasping for a breath during the long nights of confinement.

In short, the *Jersey* looked the part. A glimpse of the black, rotted hulk struck fear into the condemned being rowed out to the floating dungeon, as well as any passersby on shore.

Shortly before sunset each night, all prisoners were ordered below-decks and quieted. The hatchways were then sealed. The lucky ones gathered hammocks and bedding from storage in the spar deck and along the gangways on the middle deck. These hammocks were then hung on the middle deck, but the ship was so overcrowded that they had to be removed every morning and stored for the day. This routine was repeated every day. Prisoners occupied every available space, and the less fortunate ones bunked wherever they could find a few square feet on the old wooden floors. Worried that a fellow inmate might steal their personal possessions, some men chose to sleep on top of their bags and chests, which were stacked in rows in the gangways about ten feet from the sides of the ship. A few bunks in the stern port were designated for the sick and dying, although they were in-adequate in number to hold the throngs of ailing prisoners, most of whom simply died quickly or were transferred to hospital ships.

Because of concerns about fires being set or escape plans being hatched, candles and lanterns were not permitted at night, leaving prisoners confined in complete darkness. Nights amid the cramped spaces; stale, poisonous air; rats, and stifling heat were anything but a time for peaceful rest for the prisoners. Rather, the crowded decks soon became a chorus of "groans of the sick and dying" punctuated by sobbing and the "incoherent ravings of delirium." Many prisoners complained that crazed men in the grip of disease or mental anguish would pace about the ship and stumble over them in the pitch black. Others were haunted by the ghostly, skeletal images they saw lying next to them as darkness descended across the ship.

For the weakest among the prisoners it was even worse. A few large tubs were placed belowdecks and used as latrines. With the ship so severely overcrowded, these "receptacles of filth" often over-flowed onto the floors, and the stench near them was unbearable. Yet, with limited space, some men had no choice but to bunk beside the excrement.

The officers among the prisoners had it better. Far aft on the middle deck was the large gunroom. It had long ago ceased being used for weapons or ammunition, and was taken by the officers as their quarters. Since Thomas Dring of Rhode Island had served as a master's mate, he and his few fellow officers from the privateer *Chance* slept there. As for the crew of the *Jersey*, they occupied rooms at the stern. This included the steerage, which provided bunks for the guards and sailors. The ship's officers had a cabin under the quarter-deck in the back of the ship.

The ship had been stripped so that virtually no furnishings or facilities remained. There were, however, a handful of compartments on the ship. The middle deck contained the steward's room, which was near the stern and was where the prisoners received their daily ration of food. After receiving their rations, each assigned dining group, known by the military term "mess," gathered in the corridors of the gangways to eat. These dark, creaking gangways were roughly five feet in width and connected one part of the ship to another. Prisoners were permitted to walk along them on the spar deck, which was covered, the only place on the upper deck offering them protection from the sun and rain. But because the ship was so crowded, prisoners had to organize themselves into "platoons" that would face, walk, and turn in the same direction, thus allowing large numbers of men to exercise or move about the ship in a somewhat orderly manner.

The old ship had three main decks. Hatchways in the dead center of the ship led from one deck up or down to the next one. The two floors below the upper deck housed American prisoners, while European sailors were confined to the holds at the bottom of the ship, which the men referred to as the "lower dungeon." Most of the American prisoners never stepped foot on that wretched deck, nor did they want to. Thomas Dring was one of them. The officer recalled seeing French, Spanish, and Dutch sailors ascending the steps from the dungeon and observing their "dismal" condition.* Ebenezer Fox, the young boy who ran away after the battles of Lexington and Concord in order to join the war, noted that most of the Europeans soon gave up all hope. He described their plight: "The inhabitants of this lower region were the most miserable and disgusting looking objects that can be conceived. Daily washing in salt water, together with their extreme emancipation, caused their skin to appear like dried parchment. Many of them remained unwashed for weeks, their hair long and matted, and filled with vermin, their beards never cut except occasionally with a pair of shears. . . . Their clothes were mere rags, secured to their bodies in every way that ingenuity could devise."

In England, American prisoners were treated "with contempt" and given far less food than their French and Spanish counterparts. Yet life aboard the Hell Ship was worse for the French sailors and the few Spanish and Dutch prisoners on board. For example, a report from July 10, 1778, listed "about 350 men confined between decks, half Frenchmen." It also lists deaths aboard the ships, showing that the European prisoners suffered the highest rates.

Fox observed that the sailors "suffered even more" than the few soldiers on board because the British did not recognize the American navy as legitimate. Nor did they consider privateers to be anything but pirates. Therefore, reasoned the British command, they were not

---

* France and Spain had been covertly providing military aid to the Americans since 1776. France and Britain went to war in 1778. Spain joined the following year and the Dutch the year after that.

worthy of prisoner-of-war status and were the recipients of the foulest treatment on the old hulks. Fox complained that "British officers were willing to treat fellow-beings whose crime was love of liberty worse than the vilest animals."

Thomas Dring, who was confined on the *Jersey* during the summer of 1782, said he never met or heard of a single soldier imprisoned on the ship. The prison population during his incarceration included only sailors from the nations at war with Britain. The majority, Dring claimed, were young American privateers. Of them, he observed, "Most of these were young men, who had been induced by necessity or inclination to try the perils of the sea, and had, in many instances, been captured soon after leaving their homes, and during their first voyage."

In an attempt to cope with the abysmal conditions on the *Jersey*, officers among the prisoners formed a system of governance and developed bylaws based loosely on existing military and naval codes. The goals of the bylaws were to control the worst proclivities and temptations of the men, boost morale, and maintain a degree of military order. All new prisoners were read the rules by an officer, who then asked them to enter "a willing submission" to the code. This included promoting cleanliness, respecting the Sabbath, and prohibitions against bad language, drunkenness, theft, and smoking between decks on account of the risk of fire.

Typically, punishment was approved by consensus from the entire prison population, with the oldest officer presiding as judge. The most common violation on the *Jersey* was theft of personal property and food. Thomas Andros, the volunteer who fought with General Washington at Boston and Brooklyn, and for General Greene in Rhode Island, recalled the punishment as swift and severe, especially if the prisoner was caught stealing another's provisions or food. The Connecticut veteran said that most prisoners adhered to and enforced the rules, but desperation drove people to steal. Andros also recalled that, since so many of the prisoners like Christopher Hawkins and Andrew Sherburne were young boys barely into their teens, there was a rule that bigger and stronger prisoners were not permitted to "tyr-annize or abuse" their young or weak comrades.

As an officer, Thomas Dring was supposed to familiarize himself with the bylaws and enforce them. When he wrote his memoir of the war, the Rhode Islander still remembered many of the rules, in par-ticular one of them. Dring, like many of the prisoners, was addicted to smoking and found the restrictions on lighting up and the diffi-culty in obtaining tobacco to be a challenge, particularly at night. When the prisoners were permitted to gather on the upper deck during the day, Dring and other smokers would borrow fire from the cook through a small window in the bulkhead and indulge their favorite habit. Like others living in the eighteenth century, Dring believed the smoke helped to purify the putrid air, and he even at-tributed his survival to tobacco.

Welcome to Hell

But, what to them is morn's delightful ray?
Sad and distressful as the close of day.
O'er distant streams, appears the dewy green,
And leafy trees on mountain tops, are seen.
But they no groves nor grassy mountains tread,
Marked for a longer journey to the dead.

—Philip Freneau, "The British Prison-Ship" (1781)

When transferred to the *Jersey*, prisoners were typically released from the irons shackling their wrists and ankles and ordered into small launches. Marines stood watch nearby, guns at the ready. The nerve-racking process was overseen by the brutal commissary of British prison ships who frequently taunted his new charges, "I'll soon fix you, my lads."

From the prisoners' vantage point around the edge of the bay and in the predawn darkness, it would have been impossible to see the *Jersey*, but all would have known where they were headed. Like men condemned to carry the implements of their own executions, they were made to row the boats ferrying them to the old hulk. Arriving at Wallabout Bay in the shrouded moments before sunrise, the commissary would urge his new charges to "lean into the oars." Finally, through the foggy morning light they saw the outline of a large "black hulk."

Thomas Dring never forgot the "dreaded" feeling he and his fellow officers experienced as they approached the ship. There on the upper deck, they observed a "multitude of human beings" milling about slowly. All the prisoners looked close to death. As the small launches docked beside the ship, the commissary broke the still silence. Pointing upward to the high decks of the old warship, he bellowed in an "exulted manner . . . There, Rebels, *there* is the cage for you!"

One of the many terrors about the *Jersey* was the man in charge of prison ships. Joshua Loring, the prison commissary, and Captain William Cunningham, the warden of the infamous Provost, were not the only sadistic prison officials. Joining them was the commissary of the prison ships, David Sproat. Described as "notorious" and a man who "gloated" over the death of prisoners, he was said by Dring to be "universally detested for the cruelty of his conduct and the insolence of his manners." Subject to his brutality, Dring soon came to wish for a moment alone with Sproat in order to kill his tormentor.

Commissary Sproat was a Scot who sailed to Pennsylvania in 1760. He worked as a land speculator and trader who amassed "a pritty little fortune." Ever the opportunist, at the outset of the war he supplied the fledgling Continental Navy of John Paul Jones and was a business partner with fellow Pennsylvanians and patriots Robert Morris and James Wilson—that is, until he switched sides, presumably for financial gain. Like many other loyalists, Sproat considered himself a war "refugee" and joined a loyalist group headed by William Franklin, the deposed royal governor of New Jersey and son of the great scientist and Founder.*

---

* Benjamin Franklin was deeply upset by his illegitimate son's support for Britain, which ended their relationship.

Sproat moved to British-controlled New York City in January 1779 and, thanks to his business connections, was appointed to oversee naval prisoners on October 13 by Admiral Mariot Arbuthnot, at the time the commander of the Royal Navy in New York. The Scot would eventually assume control over all prisoners at the very end of the war after the longtime commissary, Joshua Loring, departed for London in November 1782.

Few reliable accounts of Sproat exist and they are divided about his service, but it is hard to come to any other conclusion than that he was ruthless and vicious in his administration of the prison ships.* Sproat routinely denied prisoners food, water, and medical attention, and even subjected prisoners to emotional torment and physical torture. He was also a shrewd propagandist who blamed prisoners' deaths on the hesitancy of General Washington and the Continental Congress to exchange prisoners. And, like other greedy commissaries, he was known to sell provisions meant for his charges and pocket the profits. Indeed, the record of Sproat's oversight of the *Jersey* is chilling, as the stories below reveal.

As a seasoned veteran of many battles, including General Washington's failed effort to hold New York City, Thomas Andros had seen more than his share of hardship, suffering, and death. Yet the Connecticut native was shocked by the conditions aboard the *Jersey*. Looking up at the old hulk from the loading platform while boarding, Andros described the unnerving sight of a "dark and filthy" vessel whose appearance "perfectly corresponded with the death and despair that reigned within." To Andros, it was the embodiment of hell. The prisoners were confined in the dark, dank bowels of a rotting ship infested with disease and vermin, where human excrement

---

* There are two accounts that are more sympathetic to Sproat, one of them being the book *David Sproat and Naval Prisoners in the War of Revolution* (1909) by James Lenox Banks, whose defense of the brutal commissary seems inspired by the fact that he was a descendant of Sproat.

piled up on the floors and maggots inhabited the meager rations of food they were served. Men entered Hell young and healthy; but, Andros warned, they departed the ship either gravely ill or in a makeshift coffin.

The ship, he recalled, "through age had become unfit for further actual service" and had been stripped of everything, including the rigging and even the lion figurehead that had once graced its bow. "Nothing remained but an old, unsightly rotten hulk . . . about twenty rods" from the shoreline.* The ghastly sight of skeletal prisoners shocked him. Pallid, bony hands jutted out through the bars on the portholes waving hats and signaling to "stay away."

Similar accounts of boarding the ship were recorded by Thomas Dring, who recalled that upon his arrival some prisoners issued warnings, but others asked for news of the war or hoped new prisoners were from their hometowns. One man issued a poetically foreboding message, saying it was "a lamentable thing to see so many young men in full strength, with the flush of health upon their countenances, about to enter that infernal place of abode." The man then gasped out of the air hole words that sent shivers down the spines of Dring and his crewmates: "Death has no relish for such skeleton carcasses as we are, but he will now have a feast upon you fresh comers."

As if that warning was not unnerving enough, from the rowboat docked by the *Jersey's* accommodation ladder new prisoners were greeted by a terrible stench that enveloped the landing platform. The vapor that wafted on the heavy morning air was, in Dring's words, "far more foul and loathsome than any thing which I had ever met . . . and produced a sensation of nausea far beyond my powers of description."

It was 1782, and Dring and the other officers from his crew were taken up the ladder on the larboard side of the *Jersey* and processed as prisoners. He knew what was in store for his crew. "It was my hard

---

* A rod is roughly 5½ feet in distance, meaning the ship was moored just over 100 feet from land. But another report puts the *Jersey* at about 100 yards from the shoreline.

fortune, in the course of the war," he told them, "to be twice confined on board the prison-ships of the enemy." Three years prior, he
had been captured and imprisoned on the *Good Hope*. Now he was
back in Wallabout Bay, a mere boat's length from where he had spent
more than four months before escaping overboard and swimming to
the coastline of New Jersey.

Dring had warned his shipmates of the Hell Ship's reputation.
The tales paralyzed the men with fear, especially a twelve-year-old
cabin boy named Palmer. From the accommodation ladder in the
faint light of dawn, the prisoners were assembled on the upper deck
in small groups by the barricade door. Each man stated his name,
rank (or his duty in the war, such as a seaman or sailor), hometown,
and other information to the guards, all of which was recorded for
the prison commissaries. The guards then conducted a quick inspection of their clothing, bags, and personal possessions. Much of it was
confiscated, but Dring and other officers were generally allowed to
keep the clothing they wore and one small bag of personal items.
From there, they were led through another door on the starboard side
of the old ship, down a ladder, and into the main hatchway.

Dring brought a small bag filled with items from the *Chance*
before it was captured. Oddly, the guards did not formally register
the few men from the *Chance* when they came aboard the *Jersey*. It
worked in Dring's favor. Having no record, Dring was able to escape
the added punishment doled out to repeat prisoners. Also, because he
had been held captive on a prison ship before, the master's mate had
known to put on extra layers of clothing when he was captured. The
layers could be removed during the "intolerable heat" of summers,
but he would need them in the freezing winters. Most of the prisoners were not so fortunate.

The boarding process was equally harrowing for Andrew Sherburne,
who, like Dring, was imprisoned on the *Jersey* in 1782. The young boy

from Portsmouth, New Hampshire, with a head filled with dreams of adventure had run off to enlist on a privateer but was now facing almost certain death. Sherburne remembered that "a large proportion of prisoners had been robbed of their clothing." He was one of them. Even officers from his ship were treated poorly and robbed, contrary to the protocol of the time.

Another prisoner was Christopher Hawkins, the Rhode Islander who, like Sherburne, had gone to sea at thirteen. After his captain blundered into a confrontation with a powerful British warship, Hawkins and his crewmates were captured and taken aboard the warship HMS *Sphinx* in 1777. In New York City they were temporarily detained on the old transport ship *Asia*, anchored in the East River. Because the British needed more sailors, American merchant crews and privateers were often offered a deal—release from the miserable conditions aboard a prison ship in exchange for service in His Majesty's navy. This was the deal offered to Andrew Sherburne's crew when they arrived at a prison in England, and such was the arrangement offered to Hawkins. After three weeks on the *Asia*, Hawkins agreed to the arrangement and was transferred to the HMS *Maidstone*, a twenty-eight-gun warship that prowled the American coast.

On board the *Maidstone*, young Hawkins—like Sherburne, who served his ship's boatswain—worked as a waiter and servant to one of the officers. He was relieved to be off the prison ship and, aside from being harassed as a "mere boy," Hawkins described his situation as "getting on quite comfortably in all respects." His only real torment was "the yearning wish" to go home to see his mother.

The teenager did what he was told and made no trouble aboard the British warship, to the extent that he "quieted the apprehensions" about the possibility he would attempt to escape. The officers soon seemed to forget that he was a colonial and privateer. Accordingly, Hawkins was permitted to go ashore when the ship was in port. He patiently waited for his opportunity, which came when the *Maidstone*

was back in New York City. Once ashore, the boy seized "an opportunity to make his escape, and return to North Providence." After
a precarious, "multiple-day trek through British lines," he arrived
home in November 1778. He had spent eighteen long months in the
Royal Navy, but was finally home with his mother.

Back in Rhode Island, Hawkins worked for a man named Oba-
diah Olney of Smithfield for just over two years. However, "a fit of
roaming again came over him." Against his mother's wishes, the
teenager went to Providence and, like the other boys in this book,
enlisted with the crew of another privateer. Hawkins was assured that
his chances of getting rich would be much better on a larger ship—in
this case a brig armed with sixteen cannons—and his chances of getting caught far less. In 1781, the ship sailed to Newport to begin its
marauding with Hawkins among the crew.

After just five days at sail with Captain Christopher Whipple,
two British cruisers caught the Providence privateer. Rather than getting rich, Hawkins again faced the "prospect of a long and gloomy
imprisonment." Worse yet, he and his crewmates learned they were
being taken to the most notorious ship in the Royal Navy, a hulk so
"far-famed" that the prospect before them "struck terror into every
heart." The teenager described his mood upon hearing the news as
"dark, gloomy and desponding."

Hawkins described the *Jersey* exactly as did Dring and Andros.
The ship, according to Hawkins, was "old and much decayed" and
"entirely dismantled," save for a naked flagstaff at the stern and the
bowsprit—the long wooden spar that extended from the front of the
ship. When taken belowdecks into what he described as a "miserable
dungeon," Hawkins discovered that the ship's "port holes were all
closed and strongly fastened." The other alarming realization was the
prevalence of so many sick and dying prisoners in the bowels of the
ship. Seeing the diseased prisoners, he "saw the reflection of his own
unhappy condition, and his own probable fate." One can only imagine the fear that gripped the boy as he prepared to spend the final
days of his brief life aboard the "floating Hell."

After a brief detainment, the guards escorted Thomas Dring and his crewmates into the hold. Even though he had been aboard the prison ship *Good Hope* three years earlier, the master's mate was not prepared for the sight before him. Men barely had room to sit, much less lie down, most wore tattered clothing and resembled walking skeletons, and many were in the grip of disease. Said Dring, "I found myself among the wretched and disgusting multitude." And then the hatch was shut above them and fastened down for the night.

Dring's immediate priority was finding a place to sit down and to hold tightly on to his bag, as he was worried someone would steal it. The stench and heat belowdecks were stifling, and the air felt thick and heavy in the trapped holds. On the side of the ship he spotted a faint "glimmering of light through the iron gratings of one of the air-ports." Clutching his bag, Dring worked his way toward the porthole, hoping to be able to sit down near the small opening and possibly bunk there. On the way, however, he repeatedly tripped over sleeping prisoners, who cursed him or moaned. Finally arriving at the small porthole, he discovered the area was crowded with prisoners who refused to allow him any space. Nor did they want to talk, other than inquiring about the state of the war. Most prisoners were too weak, had abandoned all hope, or simply kept to themselves. Not finding any of his mates from the privateer *Chance* or a decent place to bunk, Dring felt anxiety begin to wash over him.

But a pressing matter confronted him. When he finally found a place to sit, the Rhode Islander realized he was surrounded by men dying of smallpox. He had never had the disease and knew he would be vulnerable, but there were no inoculations on the prison ship. The officer remembered what happened next: "On looking about me, I soon found a man in the proper stage of the disease, and desired him to favor me with some of the matter for the purpose. . . . The only instrument which I could procure, for the purpose of inoculation, was a common pin. With this, having scarified the skin of my hand, between the thumb and forefinger, I applied the matter and bound up my hand." Dring had inoculated himself.

Dring's former shipmates finally found him and he informed them of his self-inoculation. He spent that first day helping his fellow officers inoculate themselves. He also took care to see that young Palmer, the frightened cabin boy from the *Chance*, received a small dose of the disease.

The other order of business was to form a "mess" in order to eat. Prisoners were served in these small groups at set times during the day, so it was vital that all new inmates either be assigned to a mess or find an available space in an established mess. If a prisoner was not assigned to a mess, he did not eat. It was that simple. There were no exceptions. But because Dring and other prisoners brought aboard from the British warship *Belisarius* were, for some reason, not formally registered onto the ship, they were not assigned a mess. Therefore, Dring and his mates did not eat that first day. Nor were they allotted a ration of water.

For a full day and night the men from the *Chance* remained painfully hungry and desperately thirsty, and began to worry how and when they would manage to eat. Fortunately, Dring had planned ahead. When captured, he had taken the precaution of putting a few biscuits into his bag. He had not eaten them while chained in the hold of the *Belisarius*, so now he quietly shared the meager morsels of food with the other officers and young Palmer. It was not much, but it momentarily propped up their spirits.

It was a nerve-racking and sleepless night. In the poorly lit and crowded ship Dring found no other shipmates beyond the few officers and Palmer, the cabin boy. Sleep eluded him. He recalled sitting in pitch blackness, being forced to "reflect on the horrors of the scene, and to consider the prospect before me." All around were the images of ghosts and the "dismal" sounds of dying prisoners. He remembered, "From every direction; a nauseous and putrid atmosphere filling my lungs at every breath; and a stifled and suffocating heat, which almost deprived me of sense, and even of life." Dring was overcome with the weight of despair.

Dawn brought a ghastly sight. Faces and bodies became visible in the dimly lit, dank holds of the ship, and Dring saw that he was surrounded by a pale throng of dying men with the look of famine and death upon their faces. He described it as "scenes of wretchedness, disease, and woe." He again looked around for other shipmates but could not find any. At last, at eight o'clock, the guards allowed the prisoners to climb the ladder to the top deck, where the master's mate finally found his friends. To his horror, he noticed, "How different did they appear . . . shrunken and decayed after only one day!"

The prisoners were given a few moments to enjoy the morning sun before being forced back into the dungeon-like holds. Rather than rekindle his energy, however, the daylight simply revealed the "motley crew of wretches with tattered garments and pallid visages . . . to be even more disgusting and loathsome" than he realized when first brought aboard the ship the day before.

Despite the situation, a sense of hope slowly returned. Dring "found that the wound had begun to fester; a sure symptom that the application had taken effect." The inoculation had worked—he contracted smallpox, but only lightly. Thankfully, he recorded, with "the blessing of Divine Providence, I soon recovered." Also, on the second day, the master's mate was able to get the officers and Palmer registered as a mess. Only a small "pittance of food" was offered to them, but at least they ate. Along with other famished prisoners, they now had to line up each morning and wait for their number to be called. A large boiling pot was available to "cook" their rations and soften the shoe-like consistency of the food so that it could be chewed without losing a tooth. Boiling their rations, Dring observed dryly, also cut the "putrid" smell of the rotting food and removed the insects that inhabited much of what was served.

The brief moment of hopefulness was fleeting, however. Later that day Palmer took ill. The symptoms of smallpox came on strong and fast. By night Palmer was delirious. In the pitch-black holds, Dring tried to comfort the boy, but there was nothing anyone could do. His constant appeals to the guards for a doctor went unheeded. Palmer's "convulsions" through the night tore at Dring, who felt guilty for inoculating the boy. He spent another sleepless night suffering through

Palmer's desperate "calling and imploring, in his delirium, for the assistance of his mother and other persons of his family." He remained by Palmer's side through the long, difficult night. But as the morning approached, the boy's cries became weaker.

Dring placed his hand over the cabin boy's mouth and did not feel any breathing. When the dawn's light struggled through the old iron grates that covered the portholes, the few officers from the *Chance* could finally see the "pallid and lifeless corpse" of their cabin boy, who was only twelve. In the morning, the prisoners were instructed to sew a blanket around the body and carry it and the corpses of others who had died overnight to the upper deck. Dring learned that the bodies were to be taken ashore for a quick and unceremonious burial. He requested to go ashore to bury Palmer, but was turned away because he had signs of smallpox.

After young Palmer, the next of Dring's crewmates to die were James Mitchell and his son-in-law, Thomas Sturmey, both of Providence. Both died at the same time. Dring had seen them only hours earlier but, because everyone now looked sick, he did not even know they were dying. The bodies were taken to the upper deck for burial. Dring raced up the ladder and saw the two corpses lying on the deck. He obtained blankets and wrapped them up for interment. Dring then asked permission to go ashore to bury the two sailors, as they had been his friends. The request was again denied, and he was forced to stand on the upper deck and watch for a second time as the "dead boat" was rowed ashore filled with bodies.

Those first few nights in Hell were also difficult for Thomas Andros, the veteran from Connecticut. He and his shipmates were "driven down" violently into the "darkness" of the crowded gun deck. His initial description echoed that of others: it was filled with men who looked like living skeletons. Although Andros had seen combat and men die, he said of the suffering on the ship that it "baffles all description. . . . On every side wretched, despondent shapes of men could be seen." In the dim traces of light from the hatch above, the young man also observed that there was no chance of escape. The area was "secured by iron gratings and an armed soldiery."

On board the warship sailing to Wallabout Bay, many of Andros's shipmates had become sick. They brought their maladies onto the *Jersey.* Thus, the fore of the gun deck where they were housed became a haven for disease. Not only was he frightened, but the sick and thirsty continually cried out for water through the night. Their requests were ignored by the guards, who, Andros recalled, seemed to take delight in torturing and tormenting the prisoners. Because prison ships had been burned earlier in the war, the guards on the *Jersey* did not permit the prisoners to have candles. Like Thomas Dring and Christopher Hawkins, Andros was forced to sit in the darkness listening to prisoners crying with grief and moaning in pain. Andros also spent a sleepless night contemplating his fate.

Unlike Dring, who vowed to fight and attempt to escape, Andros came to accept his judgment, believing he was being punished for a reason. During his night of soul-searching, Andros admitted to God that his motive for going to war was his own selfish "enterprise," rather than to "inflict a wound" against Britain by "striking at their commerce." He had also failed to heed the advice of "honorable men" who condemned privateering and told him not to enlist. Confessing that it was not "love of country or a desire to please my Maker, that prompted me to engage in this service," Andros resigned himself to the inevitable. God had condemned him.

"I was so overwhelmed with a sense of guilt," wrote Andros, "that I do not recollect that I even asked for pardon or deliverance at this time." The experience brought him to his knees. Andros spent his first night on the *Jersey* in prayer: "O Lord God thou art good but I am wicked. Thou hast done right in sending me to this doleful prison; it is just what I deserve." The *Jersey* was, in Andros's words, the "complete image and anticipation of Hell." Accordingly, amid the "horror" he was reminded of Milton's description of hell, which seemed to have been written with the prison ship in mind: "Sights of woe, regions of sorrow, doleful; Shades, where peace and rest can never dwell."* But his prayers were interrupted when one of the guards yelled down to the other newly arrived inmates, "Take heed to yourselves. There is a madman stalking through the ship with a knife in his hand." And then the hatches and doors were shut. It was pitch black in the hold.

---

* The lines are from the epic poem *Paradise Lost*, written in 1667 by famed English poet John Milton.

The Final Voyage

But, such a train of endless woes abound,
So many mischiefs in these hulks are found,
That, of them all, the memory to prolong,
Would swell too high the horrors of our song.

—Philip Freneau, "The British Prison-Ship" (1781)

Prisoners who boarded the *Jersey* were told by David Sproat, the cruel commissary of naval prisons, that this would be their final voyage. He was right. Most of them would not make it off the old hulk alive. Part of the reason was the food.

British soldiers during the Revolution were provided oatmeal, rice, peas, and a few ounces of butter or cheese each day. Meat was included whenever it was available. The rations, in terms of both quality and quantity, varied greatly during the war. Understandably, it was far worse for prisoners. It was a somewhat common practice among armies in the eighteenth century to provide prisoners with two-thirds of the normal ration of food allotted to their own soldiers. Yet this was not the case for privateers or on the prison ships. Three problems presented themselves. One was that there were severe food shortages during the war, to the extent that the British had trouble feeding their own soldiers, much less prisoners. The second was that they were not interested in providing fair rations to individuals whom they considered to be rebels not worthy of humane treatment. The third problem was the prison commissaries, men such as Joshua Loring, William Cunningham, and David Sproat who lined their own pockets at the expense of the prisoners and took cruel delight in torturing their charges.

Thomas Dring stated that he and his fellow prisoners could have lived on two-thirds of the normal ration, but the British rarely provided that much food and what was provided was "rancid." It was a problem of both quantity and quality, and Dring's health deteriorated precipitously as a result.

As mentioned earlier, the first order of business for prisoners boarding the *Jersey* was to organize in a mess. Regulations on the prison ship stated that food was distributed only by mess and that there be six men per mess. Therefore, Dring and his fellow officers organized as a mess. In the morning, they had to gather outside the steward's room at nine o'clock and wait for a bell to be rung. Each mess was then called by number, and one member of the mess had to line up to receive the ration, which was served by the steward and his assistants out of a small window in the bulkhead of the steward's room. If the men of the mess missed their number, they went hungry. There were no requests, no exceptions, and no differences among the messes in the food they received. Dring estimated that their mess of six men rarely received enough food for four.

Although rations were limited by and dependent on a fickle transatlantic supply chain, Britain's practice of purchasing or stealing food from American farmers, and chronic food shortages, there was a weekly schedule that the cook and steward of the *Jersey* followed.

Sunday: 1 pound of biscuits, 1 pound of pork, half pint of peas
Monday: 1 pound of biscuits, 1 pint of oatmeal, 2 ounces of butter

Tuesday: 1 pound of biscuits, 2 pounds of beef
Wednesday: 1½ pounds of flour, 2 ounces of suet*
Thursday: Same as Sunday
Friday: Same as Monday
Saturday: Same as Tuesday

Lest one think that such a "menu" was bearable, at times the British simply ran out of food and prisoners went hungry. The diaries of prisoners contain constant complaints of being forced to fast for a full day and night, or longer, a problem compounded by the fact that they were already severely malnourished and there were rarely any vegetables or fruit, much less fresh produce. As a result, scurvy and other dietary disorders ran rampant on the ship.

One of the few staples served on the *Jersey* was a ration the prisoners called "burgoo," which was a moldy oatmeal. Meat was available only sporadically. If the delivery of pork or beef to the *Jersey* arrived late, it was served in a hasty manner that did not offer prisoners time to cook it. They had to consume it raw. There were hogs living in a pen on the upper deck of the ship, but they were only for the British officers and, occasionally, the guards. Even the hogs ate better than the prisoners, prompting the men to try to steal the bran and slop fed to the pigs.

In his memoir, Ebenezer Fox described the routine, saying, "The prisoners received their mess at nine in the morning. All our food appeared to be damaged. The bread was mostly moldy and filled with worms. It required considerable rapping upon the deck, before these worms could be dislodged from their lurking places in a biscuit. As for the pork, we were cheated out of it more than half the time, and when it was obtained one would have judged from its motley hues, exhibiting the consistency and appearance of variegated soap. . . . The flavor was so unsavory that it would have been rejected."

* Suet is the hard, white fat on the loins and organs of sheep and cattle. Prisoners would prepare a pastry or mincemeat with it.

Indeed, the poor condition of the food was as problematic as the lack of food. Dring noted that the butter was not real; rather, it was a kind of sweet oil that "was so rancid, and even putrid, that the smell of it, accustomed as we were to every thing foul and nauseous, was more than we could endure." Instead, Dring and his fellow officers used their sweet oil as fuel for their lamps. However, the guards on the *Jersey* did not permit fires belowdecks after nine in the evening, and some days they had no access to fire to light their lamps. From time to time Dring gave the remainder of his ration of the "oil butter" to the Frenchmen in the lowest holds of the ship because they grumbled constantly of not having butter for their food.

Thomas Andros complained that insects infected the bread, observing, "I do not recollect seeing any which was not full of living vermin; but eat it, worms and all, we must, or starve." They had no choice. Other prisoners offered similar descriptions, saying the bread was "bad in the superlative degree" and the "moldy biscuits filled with worms." Andrew Sherburne was one of them, noting, "The bread had been so eaten by weevils, that one might easily crush it in the hand and blow it away. The beef was exceedingly salty, and scarcely a particle of fat could be seen upon it." Christopher Hawkins echoed his fellow teenagers and remembered always being hungry because the food was "of the worst description, and utterly unfit for a human being." This included biscuits "eaten by weevils, through and through," old bread that was "often covered with mould," and meat that was "discolored and putrefied by age, and through which myriads of maggots leaped about in play."

Every surviving account from prisoners on the *Jersey* describes the food in similar terms, saying it was "condemned," "rancid," "filthy," and the like. Moreover, the foul smell and appearance of the food made the men nauseous even before they ate it. Captain Alexander Coffin Jr., a naval officer imprisoned on the *Jersey* in 1782, summed it up: "There never were provisions served out to the prisoners that would have been eatable by men that were not literally in a starving situation."

Food was prepared in the forecastle or "galley." When there was meat or food to be cooked, it was boiled in two enormous copper kettles, one of them known as "the great copper" was used by the cook, the other one was available for the prisoners to use. These pots were several feet in diameter, enclosed in bricks, and located on the upper deck. A divider ran through the middle of them. On one side of the partition, peas and oatmeal were boiled in fresh water. The other side was for meat, which was fastened to strings and hooks and then boiled in salt water.

The salt water created problems. Not only did it corrode the great copper, but the source for the water was the very bay in which the ship was moored. They were thus using water that was polluted from the feces and debris from the old, rotting hulk and the bodies of her dead prisoners. This fact was not lost on young Hawkins, who observed that the careless guards collected the water for cooking from the same location "where all the filth and refuse [from the ship] were thrown." Plus, the derelict ship leaked so badly that, without constant efforts to pump the water from the bilge, it would sink. However, the bilge water was contaminated with the blood, vomit, and disease from the ship. Dring noted that the *Jersey*'s cook prepared his own food and the crew's with water from a different source. And he never used salt water for his own food. Accordingly, Dring refused to eat anything prepared in the great copper. He believed that act helped him survive.

The meat was often barely cooked. Therefore, some prisoners sought to boil their food beyond what the cook had done. They did this by fastening their own small pots and strings on hooks hanging from the kettle. Of course, not all the men had their own ladles or pots. They had to make do with what they had or hope someone in their mess was generous. There was also limited space around the kettle. Access was on a first-come, first-served basis, and prisoners were given little time for preparing and eating their food. As a result, there were frequent arguments around the kettle. At a certain point the cook simply rang the bell, thus ending mealtime. Men were then turned away from the kettle at bayonet point, whether or not they had cooked or eaten their food.

There was also a limited amount of fresh water to use for cooking. The officers in Dring's mess designed a system whereby the six of them took turns saving a bit of water from their daily ration. This was used for the entire mess to boil their food. In the face of extreme thirst and heat, Dring remembered that it required great discipline. But the mess worked together to enforce their system. It likely saved their lives.

Nor was there enough wood for cooking. The cook and guards were known to steal the supply of wood sent to the ship and then sell it to residents who lived by the bay or to those prisoners who boarded the *Jersey* with money. Those unable to procure wood either scavenged for splinters and chips of wood or dug at the rotting hull of the ship itself. Once when Dring went ashore on a burial detail, he found a small stump floating in the water and snuck it back aboard the ship. On another occasion, Dring had been assigned to load wood from a supply ship that had tied up next to the *Jersey*. Even though the guards watched the prisoners very carefully, with the help of his crewmates he managed to steal some of it. His mess hid the wood in the gunroom where they bunked, and they took turns guarding it day and night with "the most scrupulous and anxious care." These precious pieces of wood were cut with a knife into four-inch-long slices and carefully rationed to last many days. Dring enjoyed searching for, cutting, and rationing wood because it provided a welcome distraction from his day-to-day ordeal.

The cook was another problem. He considered the galley to be "his palace" and was notoriously "surly" and short-tempered. Ironically, the cook was himself a prisoner who had requested to be the cook when he realized there was no chance of escaping or being freed. All prisoners quickly came to despise the "inhuman monster" they sarcastically nicknamed "His Majesty the Cook." He rarely fulfilled anyone's requests and prisoners had to approach him very gingerly. Dring recalled that the officers in his mess took turns talking to His

Majesty to prevent one of them from always incurring his wrath and receiving reduced rations for the entire mess. Once, for instance, when angered, the "plump" cook splashed scalding hot water at the men in the queue, burning a few of them badly.

Dring was frequently on the receiving end of the cook's anger. He had once approached the window in the galley to light his pipe, but His Majesty threw a shovelful of burning cinders in Dring's face. It nearly blinded him, and it was several days before the pain dissipated and Dring could see again. The men were forced to simply put up with the "petty, unceasing insults" and "disgusting tyranny" of the cook. There was nothing they could do. They were also frustrated with him because His Majesty the Cook had plenty of flesh on his bones. It was obvious that he took more than a fair share of the rations while the prisoners wasted away from a lack of food.

Not only were the prisoners in a constant state of starvation, but they were always thirsty. Fresh water was a precious and limited resource on the *Jersey*—so much so that a few elderly marines were assigned to guard the water supply. One of them was always on duty, standing next to the barrels of water with "a drawn cutlass."

Fresh water was brought aboard the *Jersey* from a spring on General Johnson's family farm next to Wallabout Bay. Under guard, four prisoners were tasked with rowing to shore in a small launch and collecting the water in containers. It was then poured from the accommodation platform through a leather hose into the large barrels. The ship housed so many prisoners that crews were required to go ashore on a regular basis. Dring estimated that the daily consumption of water on the old hulk was seven hundred gallons, which was still well under a gallon per person per day for the tasks of drinking, cooking, bathing, and cleaning.

Whenever the work detail returned with water, the parched prisoners clamored to get a drink. But they had to assemble at designated times at the large cask. Three copper ladles were chained to the container and used by the prisoners to collect their water ration, which was limited to just one pint of water at a time. At night, according to Sherburne, each prisoner was only permitted one small tin cup of water. They had to make sure they were in line before the hatches were shut and then not spill it while climbing down the ladder. Not surprisingly, men constantly begged for additional water, especially at night. But their requests fell on deaf ears. Once, for instance, when he became too sick to get in line for his ration of water, Sherburne made a deal with another prisoner: if the man filled his cup of water, he could have Sherburne's ration of bread. The situation was so dire that it had come to such sad arrangements.

Even though the water was from a nearby spring, it was anything but safe. Swamps and estuaries ringed Wallabout Bay. Of the "fresh" water, one prisoner said simply that it was "disgusting and poisonous." Dring described it as "very brackish" and guessed that another problem was the hose and water casks, which "had never been cleaned since they were placed" on the ship. He suspected that the drinking water "caused the death of hundreds of the prisoners, when, to allay their tormenting thirst, they were driven by desperation to drink this liquid poison, and to abide the consequences."

Going ashore to pick up water was not the only work the prisoners were required to perform. Prisoners carried out a variety of other chores, including setting up the guards' awning on sunny and rainy days, hoisting wood and supplies on board the ship, and helping to serve meals. One of the regular jobs was manning the pumps to keep the rickety old ship afloat. The *Jersey* was constantly taking on water, and the prisoners complained about the exhausting task of having to pump out the bilge in the lower deck.

Prisoners were organized daily into a "working party" consisting of "able-bodied men." These working parties functioned in "daily rotation" and were overseen by the guards. According to Andros, the armed guards made the work a hellish experience for the prisoners by shoving and beating them. "Little else could be heard," he remembered, "but a roar of mutual execrations, reproaches and insults" from the cruel guards. Within each party, one of the prisoners who had been an officer was put in charge of the detail and given the naval title "boatswain." The men received no monetary compensation for working, but they sometimes received a half pint of rum as the only payment for their hard labor.

One of the most difficult jobs was cleaning the lower decks and gangways. To accomplish this, working parties were given old brushes and buckets and sent below to scrub the urine, blood, and vomit as well as the general dirt and grime that accumulated in the very old, very crowded prison ship. Andros remembered that the old buckets and brushes were so broken that they could hardly be used. Even with proper equipment, it would have been a difficult job because, he recalled, "the whole ship, from her keel to the tafferel," was a mess.*

Many of the prisoners did not mind washing the upper deck, however. It afforded them a chance to be outside in the morning and escape the disease, heat, and foul air of the holds. Moreover, if the conditions were right, the men could peer across the river and see the tops of buildings and masts of ships. If the wind was blowing in their direction, it was even possible for the ear to catch an occasional sound from the city. Dring said, "This privilege alone was a sufficient compensation for all the duty which was required of them."

Occasionally prisoners were temporarily transferred off the *Jersey* so that the whole ship could be cleaned. Dring recalled one such moment, saying that "for a few hours, our existence was in some degree tolerable" because the ship was empty and quiet. But the task of getting so many weak and sick prisoners off the *Jersey* was not easy. Once, when the men were transferred to a transport ship it was discovered that the new ship was far too small. "The condition," recalled Andrew Sherburne, "was absolutely distressing." The men could not move and were forced to urinate in their clothing. To make matters worse, soon after the transfer a violent storm struck. The prisoners

---

* The tafferel was a panel decorated with carvings, typically located on the upper part of the ship's stern.

were stuck on the transport and those on the upper deck were pummeled by driving rain and high winds. Soaking wet and chilled, many of them caught pneumonia. Ironically, the cleaning made things worse because many of the prisoners returned to the *Jersey* with colds. If the old hulk was not already functioning as a hospital ship, it now was.

The worst job was cleaning the large tubs used as latrines. The tubs frequently filled up and overflowed, and the task of emptying them was a precarious one because it was difficult to keep the waste from spilling over the sides and onto the men in the work detail. Dring was selected for this "highly offensive" job. As bad as it was, after they had emptied the tubs the men in the work detail had a few quiet moments on the upper deck. "It was during this brief interval, when we breathed the cool air of the approaching night, and felt the luxury of our evening pipe." But then the work party was ordered to carry the waste tubs back belowdecks and "descend to our gloomy and crowded dungeons." As was the routine every night, the hatches were hammered shut above them.

Another job for the working parties was helping the sick and dying who were unable to get in or out of their hammocks. The workers prepared the hammocks and bunks each evening and stored them before breakfast. Tragically, sunrise was usually met by the grim reality that some of their peers had perished during the night. After guards shouted down to the prisoners, "Rebels! Turn out your dead!" it was the work parties who had to gather the corpses and carry them to the upper deck. There the dead were stripped of their clothing, "sewed up in a blanket," and lowered by rope into the "dead boat." Typically, the dead boat would fetch the deceased from the handful of other ships nearby before pulling alongside the *Jersey* each morning for its final human cargo.

The first night belowdecks for Thomas Andros was filled with terror. But in the morning he was able to climb the ladder to the upper deck to breathe the fresh air and feel the rising sun upon his face. Yet he recalled the shock of watching men from a working party carrying the dead up through the hatches. The gruesome image of several bodies being dumped into the dead boat was "a most appalling spectacle." He stood transfixed as he watched "a boat loaded with dead bodies" taken to the shore. As a morning ritual, Andros took to counting the number of dead and even the number of times a shovelful of sand was thrown over the bodies during the rushed burial. He determined that the number of corpses was often more than the number of shovels of sand thrown over them. Numerous accounts claim that a half dozen to a dozen dead men were taken off the *Jersey* each day, a number that matches Andros's observations.

A few prisoners were sent ashore as the burial detail. After rowing to the nearby banks of Wallabout Bay, they loaded their deceased comrades in wheelbarrows and carted them to one of several shallow, sandy burial sites. The guards stood watch as the prisoners dug makeshift mass graves, but did not permit them to dig proper graves or even convene a brief service for the dead. Instead, as soon as the corpses were interred the guards barked orders and shoved the prisoners back into the dead boat.

When Thomas Dring's friend and former crewmate Robert Carver died, the former master's mate asked the guards if he could be a part of the burial detail. The guards agreed but proceeded to make a "mockery" of the burial. They were completely unaffected by the horror of so many dead prisoners, as "if we were burying the bodies of dead animals instead of men." However, on this one occasion after Dring buried his friend, he begged the guards to allow him and his fellow prisoners to wash themselves in the bay and remain a few minutes to breathe the fresh air. The request was denied at first, but the guards then changed their mind and allowed the small party to remain there for thirty minutes after the burial. It was not on account of compassion, Dring guessed, but rather that the guards did not want to return to the polluted, malodorous ship either. The only prisoner in the party with shoes that day, Dring quickly kicked them off in order to feel the earth below his feet. He remembered feeling "high gratification" at the chance to breathe clean air and stand on "our native soil." He even dug up a small patch of turf, which he took back with him to the boat so that the other prisoners could feel the dirt and smell the grass. The appreciative prisoners passed it "from hand to hand," eagerly inhaling its scent "as if it had been a fragrant rose."

The irony of knowing they too might soon be dumped into one of the graves must have weighed on the prisoners, especially Dring and others in the burial detail. But, despite the grisly assignment, the men often volunteered for the interment detail so that they could say a final good-bye to a friend. Mostly, Dring admitted, there were always volunteers "not so much from a feeling of humanity, or from a wish of paying respect to the remains of the dead (for to these feelings they had almost become strangers), as from the desire of once more placing their feet upon the land, if but for a few minutes." Dring returned from burying his friend filled with sadness. Although he was glad to be momentarily off the ship, he admitted the "visit to the land caused me to feel the extent of my wretchedness, and to view my condition with feelings of greater abhorrence, and even of despair."

One winter, a prisoner named Isaac Gibbs asked permission to go ashore to bury his father, who had died on the old hulk. The guards let him join two other prisoners on the burial detail that day, but would not provide them with coats. All three men returned to the ship shivering and with frostbite, and died soon afterward. Another time, a sailor named Gavot from Providence was sewn up in a blanket with other corpses and was about to be loaded on the dead boat for burial. Just then a royal captain on the upper deck saw that Gavot was still alive. Reluctantly unsheathing his knife and cutting Gavot free, the captain joked, "If he is not dead, he soon will be." Such inhuman incidents soon became commonplace on the *Jersey*.

As if all that was not enough, because the graves were so hastily dug and shallow the remains of the deceased were often carried away by the tide. Ironically, Andros believed that had they not been so easily "disinterred" by the waves and wind, there would soon have been an enormous pile of bones. Indeed, he had boarded the *Jersey* with thirteen members of his former crew. All but three died "in short time." Even the young and strong succumbed to the deadly conditions of the Hell Ship. Yet he, far less "muscular" and healthy than his shipmates, was spared by "mercey." The experience made Andros a devout Christian. He promised God that if he ever made it off the ship, he would devote the remainder of his life to the Almighty.

11

Tempest

Black as the clouds that shade St. Kilda's shore,
Wild as the winds that round her mountains roar,
At every post some surly vagrant stands,
Cull'd from the English or the Scottish bands.
Dispensing death, triumphantly they stand;
Their muskets ready to obey command,
Wounds are their sport, as ruin is their aim;
On their dark souls compassion has no claim;
And discord only can their spirits please:
Such were our tyrants; only such as these.

—Philip Freneau, "The British Prison-Ship" (1781)

The prison ship *Jersey* was crewed by Captain David Laird, two mates, a cook, a steward, a dozen sailors, and roughly one dozen "old invalid marines." Thomas Dring remembered that "the crew had no communication whatever with the prisoners," and he recalled seeing an officer only on rare occasions when they boarded or disembarked by boat. Approximately thirty soldiers from various units quartered throughout Long Island were stationed on the *Jersey* to provide extra security. They rotated their assignment on the ship and were replaced by a "fresh party" each week; these consisted of British regulars and "refugees," who were Americans loyal to the Crown who had fled to British-occupied New York when the fighting started. However, "the soldiers in charge of the Prison ships were mostly Hessians, and were universally hated as mercenaries." Some of these were the same Hessians who had earlier crushed General Washington's army at Brooklyn, murdering in cold blood many of those who attempted to surrender.

All of the different guards behaved with "great cruelty" toward the prisoners. The veteran Thomas Andros attributed the brutish behavior to their view that the Americans were "rebels and traitors" rather than prisoners of war. Accordingly, no punishment, no torment, and no deprivation was too extreme. "We had," Andros explained, "risen against the mother-country in an unjust and wanton war." So "they seemed to consider us as not entitled to that humanity which might be expected by prisoners taken in a war with a foreign nation."

Ironically, even though the Germanic mercenaries were feared by the Americans and had gained a reputation for their brutality in war, several prisoners commented that the Hessian guards were not as bad as the British, Scottish, or American loyalists. Dring was one of them, saying the prisoners "always preferred the Hessians, from whom we received better treatment." The mercenaries were simply following orders and did not care one way or another about the Americans, but the British and Scottish guards loathed the prisoners and enjoyed attacking them. One account even claimed the prisoners debated whether or not the British and Scottish guards vied in a sort of sick competition to see who could be the cruelest. An example of this was documented by Thomas Andros. When a bag of apples was once brought aboard the *Jersey*, the guards made it into a "cruel sport" whereby the apples "were hurled promiscuously into the midst of hundreds of prisoners crowded together as thick as they could stand, and life and limbs were endangered in the scramble." So desperate were the prisoners and so savage was the melee that, rather than attempt to get an apple, Andros "fled to the most distant part of the ship" to save himself.

The British guards had grown disillusioned with the long war and were repulsed at having to serve on the disease-infested prison ship. Any sense of humanity, Dring observed, had quickly "withered," and "self-preservation appeared to be their only wish." The good news for the prisoners was that the guards, like the crew of the ship, limited their interaction with the detainees. Therefore, they almost never ventured belowdecks, where the prisoners were housed. When prisoners asked questions, the guards would typically not answer them. Guards were even forbidden by Commissary David Sproat, under threat of punishment, "to relieve the wants of the distressed." Instead, the guards simply "pointed to their uniforms, as if to say, 'We are clothed by our Sovereign, while you are naked.'" Dring also remembered that when the guards did talk, they always referred to the prisoners as "rebels" or simply cursed them. Once, a prisoner named Thomas Philbrook was dragging a corpse to the upper deck to be placed in the dead boat. A guard recognized him and spat, "What! You alive yet? Well, you are a tough one."

The "refugees," however, were the worst. While the Hessians were "just following orders," the American loyalists viewed their brethren with "scorn and hatred" and routinely acted with great "severity" and "violence." So much so that when these loyalists were assigned to the ship, it created great "tumult" among the prisoners who "could not endure the sight of these men, and occasionally assailed them with abusive language." Indeed, the entire mood on the prison ship changed when the loyalists reported for their tour of duty. There were frequent, bloody clashes between prisoners and the loyalist guards.

A prisoner for fourteen months, William Burke of Newport, Delaware, documented many of these "cruelties" by the loyalists. He saw, for instance, "many American prisoners put to death by the bayonet." The problem was made worse because the loyalists were, at times, stationed along the gangways that the prisoners used to move about the ship. Dring remembered, "We dared not approach near them for fear of their bayonets." Instead, the prisoners resorted to crawling on their stomachs along the booms in order to move fore and aft on the ship.

Not surprisingly, when one of the loyalist guards completed his tour of duty, prisoners would gather by the ladder or crowd around the portholes and cheer!

Each daybreak was met by the sound of boots on the upper deck. Whether they were British, Scottish, Hessian, or American "refugees," it was always the same. The guards walked the old, creaking planks of the ship to the hatch. Keeping their bayonets and swords at the ready, they threw open the entrance to the holds and, with a handkerchief or sleeve shielding their noses and mouths from the onslaught of the stench, yelled, "Rebels! Turn out your dead!" And so the day began for the prisoners on the Hell Ship.

Throughout the long nights, as the prisoners tried to sleep in the dark, dank holds, they heard the sentries above call out every hour, "All's well!" Of course, all was not well belowdecks. Life was unbearable in the severely overcrowded, disease-riddled ship. Aside from the lack of food and water and the barbaric treatment by the guards, another source of constant torment was the lack of basic hygiene. The prisoners were permitted to wash only occasionally and then only with salt water. The result was that most prisoners saw their skin turn sallow and brittle from the salt. There simply was not enough fresh water to ration it for drinking, cooking, *and* washing. As a result, when it rained, men desperately stripped naked and tried to wash their clothing and themselves.

Dring was shocked every time he looked at his fellow prisoners. They had all become covered in filth, "their long hair and beards matted and foul; clothed in rags; and with scarcely a sufficient supply of these to cover their disgusting bodies." Many had no clothing at all, except bare remnants of what they had initially worn when first captured. Prisoners tried but were usually unable to get a razor or soap, much less needle, thread, or anything to repair or make clothing. Some had scissors or shears, so they clipped one another's beards or hair. Even then, recalled Dring, such effort, "though conducive to cleanliness, was not productive of much improvement in their personal appearance."

Others were simply too ill or had been confined so long that they became "indifferent" to their personal appearance. Soon "ordinary cleanliness was impossible" and the prisoner's skin began to hang from his emaciated body.

Several diseases tore through the *Jersey* during the years it was moored at Wallabout Bay, periodically decimating the population belowdecks. Thomas Andros, who had watched fellow soldiers die of disease during his years in uniform, called the *Jersey* "the King of Terrors" because every disease imaginable plagued the ship. Smallpox, dysentery, yellow fever, and other contagions ran rampant in the crowded holds and contributed to the shockingly high death toll. "The lower hold and the orlop deck were such a terror," described Andros, "that no man would venture down into them."* He poetically and powerfully concluded that "the whole ship, from her keel to the taffrail, was equally affected . . . that disease and death were wrought into her very timbers."† The Hell Ship, it seemed, "contained pestilence sufficient to desolate a world."

Thomas Dring recalled that contagion and disease were already widespread on the ship when he and his crewmates arrived. Many prisoners contracted one of the ship's "putrid fevers" as soon as they stepped foot on the old hulk. Moreover, Andros and Dring complained, many men became ill because the healthy and sick were "mingled" together in close, confined spaces, especially after sundown, when they were forced belowdecks and the hatches sealed. Everyone ended up contracting some ailment.

Young Christopher Hawkins shared the assessment of his fellow prisoners: "The small pox and scurvy, with diverse fevers, raged from

---

* The orlop was the lowest deck on large sailing ships.

† A taffrail is a carved panel, often with a painting or carving, on the flat upper part of a ship's stern. It is sometimes referred to as "tafferel."

stem to stern; and lice and other vermin were [my] constant companions and tormentors." Nor were the crew or guards safe. They also contracted the fevers and disease that infested the ship. In fact, according to Dring, disease was part of the reason the *Jersey* was "removed, and moored, with chains and cables," to the "solitary and unfrequented" bay. There remained concern throughout the war that the "destructive contagion" on board was so bad that it might spread to Brooklyn and Long Island. The British intended the notorious prison ship to be a visible reminder of what would happen to those who took up arms against them, but it was so wretched that it also threatened the nearby population still loyal to the Crown.

At any one time, there were usually a half dozen male nurses on board the *Jersey*. Their main role was to assist in accommodating the afflicted until they could be transferred by a small launch to one of the hospital ships. But several of the prisoners pointed out the misnomer of calling them nurses, as they were not trained. Many of the so-called nurses were themselves sick and were prisoners who volunteered their services solely in order to get extra rations.

There were also ten or so nurses selected from the prison population assigned to each of the nearby hospital ships, but most of them neither cared about nor helped their patients. Sherburne remembered them playing cards all day while the prisoners suffered. At night, the nurses never ventured belowdecks to tend to the sick and ignored the shrieks, moans, and requests from the dying men. When a prisoner died, the nurses confiscated any belongings and clothing to sell to other prisoners, prompting one prisoner to recall, "The nurses took more interest in their death, than they did in relieving their wants." Sherburne offered a similarly dreary assessment of the hospital ships, concluding, "The depravity of the human heart was probably as fully exhibited in those nurses, as in any other class of men."

Dring also suggested that it would have been more accurate to call the nurses "thieves," as they were good at commandeering a sick or dead man's belongings. He remembered one such incident aboard the *Jersey* clearly. Dring's friend and crewmate Robert Carver, a gunner on board the *Chance*, had become very sick but was given no pillow or bedding. Carver knew the nurses would steal his extra clothing from his chest, so he put on several layers including a coat and hat even though "the weather was excessively hot." When Carver became delirious, Dring took off his heavy coat and folded it like a pillow under his friend's head, then went to get him some tea. As he was returning, he caught one of the "thievish" nurses with Carver's coat. Dring demanded the nurse return it, but the man refused, saying it was the only perk the nurses had and that Carver would soon die anyway. Dring grabbed the nurse and forcibly took the coat. Carver, despite being a "strong and robust" man, died quickly. He was one of the last survivors of the privateer *Chance*. Dring would end up being the only member of his crew to survive the *Jersey* and after the war returned the coat to Carver's family.

A surgeon was assigned to the HMS *Hunter*, a hospital ship floating next to the *Jersey*. However, according to Dring, the doctor rarely visited the Hell Ship and only "when the weather was good." Andrew Sherburne said the physician visited the ship only once every several days while he was on board, and that his "stay was short." Nor did the doctor "administer much medicine." Philip Freneau, the famous "Poet of the Revolution," was sent to the *Hunter* and remembered that a Hessian physician arrived from Brooklyn only a few times but usually ignored the sick. Yet that was fine with Freneau, who said of the doctor, "He kill'd at least as many as he cur'd." The poet even stated that he preferred the "frequent blows" of the guard's "cane" to the doctor's treatments.

Even if a physician was brought aboard the ship, Andros admitted, the situation was such that "death was next to certain, and his success in saving others by medicine in our situation was small." The exception was in the case of vaccinations. Andros estimated that about four hundred of the prisoners on the *Jersey* had never had smallpox and could have been saved with an inoculation. But the guards and crew did not permit the precaution. Rather, they let fate run its course. In fact, it is probable that this omission was by design, as it greatly increased the death toll and instilled fear among those on the ship and those under arms opposing Britain. Once, Andros remembered, two prisoners who arrived on the ship were physicians, which occasioned some hope among the men. But after a few days the commissary issued an emergency pardon or exchange and they were taken off the *Jersey*. It would not serve the ulterior motives of the British command to have the prisoners healthy and receiving care.

Either way, there was little that could be done for most of the prisoners; the surgeon ended up doing little other than recording the names of the dead.

The problem underlying all the others was overcrowding. While earlier prison ships and the latter hospital ships moored near the *Jersey* would hold, on average, about two hundred prisoners, the Hell Ship typically carried at least a thousand in its rotting holds, and by the last year of the war the population was up to twelve hundred. Young Hawkins described the ship as "cramped up with hundreds of others" belowdecks and "for most of the time . . . [they] were deprived of the light of day." There were so many sick and dying prisoners on board that even the hospital ships floating nearby were overcrowded. The captain was frequently forced to establish temporary quarters on the upper deck for the sick and erect bunks at the starboard stern as a makeshift hospital. The overcrowding also added to the scarcity of food and water, exacerbated the spread of disease, and even caused injuries, as the men were prone to stepping on and tripping over one another at night.

As days turned into months and months into years for the prisoners, severe frustration and depression set in. Tempers flared belowdecks and there were fights among prisoners. Above deck, the violent treatment at the hands of the guards seemed to grow worse with time, and the death rate on board the old hulk also worsened. A half dozen prisoners a day were dying aboard the *Jersey* when she was first moored in Wallabout Bay, but that number increased to seven, eight, or nine a day by 1781, and was averaging a dozen a day by the end of the war. One prisoner estimated that eleven hundred men died on the *Jersey* and the hospital ships anchored near her in the winter of 1780–81 alone. A simple extrapolation of these surviving estimates and numbers over the time the ship served as a floating dungeon puts the total death count well above ten thousand. Overcrowding, concluded General William Heath of the Continental Army in a report, was the chief culprit. "Closely confined in great numbers," he wrote, "produce[d] almost certain death."

In a letter written on August 21, 1781, to Captain Edmund Affleck, an officer in the Royal Navy garrisoned in New York City, General George Washington complained about the overcrowded conditions on the *Jersey* and demanded relief for the prisoners. Captain Affleck replied later that month: "I take leave to assure you, that I feel for the distresses of mankind as much as any man, and, since my coming to the naval command in this department, one of my principal endeavors has been to regulate the prison and hospital ships. The government having made no other provision for naval prisoners than shipping, it is impossible that the greater inconvenience, which people confined on board ships experience beyond those confined on shore, can be avoided, and a sudden accumulation of people often aggravates the evil."

While prisoners suffered during the hot, humid days of summer, where temperatures belowdecks routinely passed the 100-degree mark and there was no fresh air, winters presented the opposite problem. Alexander Coffin, a prisoner on the *Jersey* during the winter of 1782, said that most of the men lacked warm clothing and were forced to huddle together to "keep from freezing." But it was often to no avail. One newspaper report summed up the hellish conditions, saying, "No fires warmed her occupants in winter, no screen sheltered them from the August sun; no physician visited the sick, no clergyman consoled the dying there." The shocking description continued, "Poor and scanty food, the want of clothing, cleanliness and exercise, and raging diseases that never ceased their ravages, made the *Jersey* a scene of human suffering to which the Black Hole of Calcutta might be favorably compared."*

There were, at various times, two or three hospital ships moored roughly two hundred to three hundred yards southeast of the *Jersey*. These included some combination of the *Falconer, Frederick, Good Hope, Scorpion, Strombolo, Weymouth*, and *Hunter*, which also held medical supplies and housed the physician and nurses. The sickest of the prisoners from the *Jersey* were transferred to one of the hospital ships but, as one prisoner cautioned, "the sick were seldome removed from them." Thomas Dring knew of only three men who ever returned from one of those ships. These floating hospitals were visible from the deck of the *Jersey* as ever-present reminders for the prisoners of what awaited them and may have had even higher death rates per capita than the Hell Ship. Accordingly, Dring said of these "terrible" hospitals that "their appearance was more shocking than that of our own miserable hulk."

Despite the horrors on board, the hospital ships contained awnings and openings for fresh air. Because the prisoners sent there were so sick, the guards did not worry about their escaping. Therefore, the hatches remained open at night, which allowed for some fresh air and moonlight into the holds. Depending on the nurses on the hospital ships, the patients were occasionally treated to a pint of wine. But as the prisoner population continued to grow and as conditions aboard the *Jersey* grew ever more wretched, the hospital ships soon became overcrowded. In fact, in both 1781 and 1782, they became so grossly overcrowded that the sick had to be transferred back to the *Jersey*, disease and all. Some were placed back into the general prison population; others were housed on the lower gun deck or simply piled up on the upper deck.

---

* The Black Hole of Calcutta was the infamous dungeon in India. In 1756, a Bengali army of 50,000 marched on Fort William, which was defended by only around 170 British soldiers. After the fort fell on June 20, the surviving soldiers as well as English women and children were forced into the small, dank, disease-ridden dungeon. By the time the doors were opened, most had died.

The real horror of the hospital ships was that they were filled with diseased and dying men. To be sent there was, in effect, a death sentence. Thomas Andros recalled that only three of his thirteen crewmates who went aboard the hospital ships survived their stay, while Andrew Sherburne lost eight of his thirteen mates, and nearly all of them died "exceedingly fast." Another prisoner said of the death toll on the hospital ships, "I verily believe that not one out of a hundred returned or recovered."

Sherburne became ill in January 1783 and was taken to the hospital ship *Frederick*. It was so crowded that two men had to share a "wretchedly unsanitary" bunk. Sherburne bunked with a young man from Massachusetts named Wills, whose health was declining "fast." He remembered that, a few nights later, Wills succumbed and, in his struggles, died "stretched across me." Sherburne was so weak he could not move the body and repeatedly begged the nurses to help him, but had to wait thirty minutes for the corpse to be removed. Andros had a similar experience on a hospital ship, remembering waking up to find that the man with whom he shared a cot had died during the night.

Even without the dead bunkmate, Sherburne was unable to stand to "relieve" himself and had the misfortune to bunk near a porthole. In the winter, cold wind froze the prisoners and "snow would blow through the seams onto my bed." Sherburne remembered one particularly bad storm when, "in the morning, the snow was three or four inches deep up on my bed." He awoke shivering and had to rub his hands and feet together to keep from freezing. Frostbite set in on one of his legs. It did not kill him, but for the remainder of his life Sherburne suffered numbness and pain and was forced to wear a laced stocking on the leg.

The young boy survived the frigid winter and time on the hospital ship because his uncle, who was also imprisoned on the *Jersey*, managed to save one dollar. He gave it to his nephew before the boy was transferred to the hospital ship. Sherburne used it to purchase a cup, a spoon, some sugar, and a "few" oranges from a nurse. The oranges, he believed, kept him alive. But when Sherburne recovered and was sent back to the *Jersey*, he could not find his uncle. He discovered that while he was gone his uncle had become ill and was sent to a different hospital ship, where he died. He also learned that his friend Daniel Davis, a gunner from their privateer, had frozen to death on the *Jersey* during the bad storm. Sherburne spent days looking for others from his privateer, but only one member of his crew and mess was still on the *Jersey*, a boy named Stephen Nichols.

The weather remained very cold and Sherburne never fully recovered, and soon afterward he was sent to another hospital ship, the *Weymouth*. There he found John and Abraham Fall, two brothers who had served on his privateer. They bunked together and Sherburne was on a cot next to them. One night Sherburne heard Abraham complaining to his brother to "get off of him." It turned out that John had died. Soon after, Abraham passed away. Sherburne was stricken with grief over the loss of two more friends. His own bunkmate on the hospital ship was one of the nurses who had recently contracted a disease from a patient and was himself now a patient. During the bitterly cold winter, severe frostbite afflicted the man's legs and feet. Sherburne remembered watching the flesh rot and the nurse's toes eventually fall off.

The idea that these ships served as floating hospitals was, in the words of one prisoner, a "mockery." Prisoners suffered aboard them without the "least sympathy or attention." It seemed, the prisoner concluded, that the hospital ships were moored next to the *Jersey* simply for "historical record," certainly not for "humanity."

Given the wretched conditions aboard both the hospital ships and the *Jersey*, the prevalence of sickness and disease, the brutality of the guards, and the exceedingly high likelihood that the prisoners would not live to see their families again, the men struggled with hopelessness and despair. Many prisoners became severely depressed, others simply went mad. Dring alluded to this affliction, the worst aboard the *Jersey*, as "sickness of the heart." It was followed by homesickness, especially among the many teenagers. Missing their families, the boys were in a near constant state of "dejection and anguish." Dring observed that these boys "died that most awful of all human deaths, the effect of a broken heart."

Such torment and sadness were most prevalent during the initial days in captivity. When they first boarded the old hulk, young sailors typically "became dismayed and terror stricken." Many gave up and died quickly. He was reminded of a poem he knew, which helped him to understand their suffering:

> *Denied the comforts of a dying bed,*
> *With not a pillow to support the head;*
> *How could they else, but pine and grieve and sigh,*
> *Detest that wretched life, and wish to die?*

Though a strong and stoic man, Dring admitted that he struggled to keep his will to live. The despondency struck him mostly at night. The distressing sounds of diseased and dying prisoners and the constant buzzing drone of mosquitos, rather than the somber serenade of the night breeze, made sleep difficult, even for men exhausted by illness and long hours of tedious work. Nighttime also brought out the "vermin." Rats infested the ship. "These loathsome creatures," he bemoaned, "would be my constant companions and unceasing tormentors" each night. Dring wore a black handkerchief around his neck but once took it off and placed it with his meager possessions. He discovered it was immediately covered in rat droppings.

As days turned into weeks, and weeks blurred into months of captivity, even the hardiest of men fell into despair. Some men found religion, and their only hope came from daily prayer. Thomas Andros was one of them, and he longed for the presence of a preacher. But no man of the cloth, representative of government, or comforter ever appeared on the ship. Others drew strength from their shipmates. Dring made friends during his two years of captivity. They had "been through the furnace" together, and formed an unbreakable bond that would help them survive. But other prisoners wished that death would "not long delay to release them from their torments." As time went by, the surviving prisoners found that even the prospects of release or escape failed to inspire them.

Perhaps the toughest challenge—even more so than the hellish nights trapped belowdecks—was seeing their futures in the ghostly stares of the walking dead around them and the corpses dragged daily off the ship. Dring recalled another poem whose words seemed written for the Hell Ship:

Night and day,
Brooding on what he had been,
what he was;
'Twas more than he could bear.
His longing fits
Thickened upon him.
His desire for Home
Became a madness.

Negotiations

Conveyed to York we found, at length, too late,
That Death was better than the prisoner's fate
There doomed to famine, shackles, and despair.
Condemned to breathe a foul, infected air,
In sickly hulks, devoted while we lay,—
Successive funerals gloomed each dismal day

—Philip Freneau, "The British Prison-Ship" (1781)

There was an ever-present answer to the suffering on board the *Jersey*, and it came in the form of a pardon. A regiment of refugees "with green uniforms" was stationed at Brooklyn. Healthy prisoners were invited to join them by swearing an oath of loyalty to His Majesty the King. Surprisingly, despite "their unbounded suffering" and "their dreadful privation," very few prisoners accepted the terms. In the words of one of the prisoners, most defiantly "preferred to linger and die, rather than desert their country's cause." Many prisoners were inspired by such patriotism, including Dring, who boasted, "During my whole period of my confinement, I never knew a single instance of enlistment from among the prisoners on the *Jersey*."

General Sir William Howe.
(LIBRARY OF CONGRESS)

General George Washington's forces retreating from Long Island in 1776.
(LIBRARY OF CONGRESS)

Sketch of the Old Sugar House and Middle Dutch Church used as temporary prisons in New York City until the prison ships were hulked.
(NEW YORK PUBLIC LIBRARY)

The prison ship *Jersey*. This illustration mistakenly contains a mast and it omits the ladder and landing platform beside the ship.
(LIBRARY OF CONGRESS)

The prison ship *Jersey*. (*NEW YORK PUBLIC LIBRARY*)

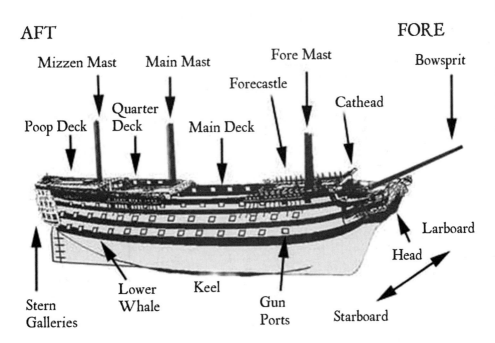

Diagram of a typical three-decker ship, based on the HMS *Rose*.

Interior of the prison ship *Jersey*. Note, however, that the guards were rarely belowdecks. *(LIBRARY OF CONGRESS)*

A sketch of the prisoners aboard the *Jersey*. (*The History Project, University of California, Davis; from the collection of Alan Taylor; Fordham University Library/Charles Allen Munn Collection*)

American hero Ethan Allen in the notorious Provost prison.
(LIBRARY OF CONGRESS)

Joshua Loring, selected by the British command to oversee American prisoners of war; painted by the noted artist John Singleton Copley.

David Sproat, the infamous prison commissary who oversaw the prison ship *Jersey*; painted by the famous artist John Trumbull. *(NEW YORK HISTORICAL SOCIETY)*

Ebenezer Fox, one of the few prisoners aboard the *Jersey* who lived to tell his story.

Philip Freneau, the "Poet of the American Revolution," who was held prisoner aboard a British prison ship.

Andros also said that "no one [was] seduced into the British service," despite the offers from the guards. The men had become hardened in their love of country. The British had hoped that the brutality aboard the *Jersey* would help end the war, but for countless patriots horrified by the gruesome accounts of the infamous prison ship and for a few prisoners, it produced the opposite effect.

But there was another way off the ship: prisoner exchanges.

One of the earliest factors to impact negotiations for prisoner exchanges was the detainment of an American hero—Ethan Allen, the legendary patriot and leader of the Green Mountain Boys. It was Allen who captured Fort Ticonderoga, near Lake Champlain, in May 1775. After his subsequent attempt to sack Montreal, however, Allen was captured on September 25. Allen was one of those prisoners sent back to England to be incarcerated. The voyage was brutal. He and thirty-three other Americans had their wrists and ankles put into irons and were confined in the dark, crowded bowels of a schooner named *Gaspee*. The irons were so tight that he could not even rest on his side, and when the British learned who he was, they spat in his face and confiscated his clothing, boasting as they gave him rags instead, "Those will be good enough for you to be hanged in!" For forty days Allen and his men suffered from poor ventilation, rats and lice, little food or water, and no provision for bathing or washing. The two tubs used for human waste overflowed and were not emptied, which made all the prisoners sick. Later on the journey, nearly all the prisoners contracted fever. Their only comfort was one pint of rum each day.

The *Gaspee* landed at Falmouth and the prisoners were paraded in public as a curiosity for local residents to see. Allen spent well over two years in Pendennis Castle in Cornwall and aboard prison ships. Fortunately, the conditions there were far better than on the prison ships in Wallabout Bay. The main challenge was the constant harassment by the guards and warden, who threatened, "You shall grace the halter at Tyburn, God damn ye!"* But Allen's long incarceration caught the attention of military and political leaders back home.

Even Benjamin Franklin weighed in on the plight of Allen and other American prisoners, complaining about the harsh conditions in the prisons and ships back in England and pressuring the British to conduct exchanges. Franklin also took matters into his own hands, sending funds and arranging for the release of prisoners and their passage back to America. Allen himself expressed concern for his fellow prisoners, writing, "I have seen several of the prisoners in the agonies of death, in consequence of very hunger, and others speechless and very near death, biting pieces of chips; others pleading for God's sake for something to eat, and at the same time shivering with the cold. Hollow groans saluted my ears, and despair seemed to be imprinted on every of their countenances. The filth . . . was almost beyond description." He concluded, "I have seen . . . seven dead at the same time, lying among the excrements of their bodies."

So high-profile was the imprisonment of Allen that General Washington inquired about it. Washington wrote to his British counterpart, General Howe, that the hero had "been treated without regard to decency, humanity, or the rules of war; that he has been thrown into irons, and suffers all the hardships inflicted upon common felons." This prompted General Howe to write back to London for instructions. In the meantime, the Continental Congress supported General Washington's advice to keep captured officers such as General Richard Prescott under close control in the event it would be necessary to use them as leverage.

Allen and General John Sullivan were finally exchanged in May 1778 for General Prescott, who had been captured during the fighting in Montreal.† A year later, Allen published a gripping account of

---

* A halter is a rope or noose, and Tyburn was the location of so many executions in London that it came to be known as "God's tribunal" and the hanging post was known as the "Tyburn tree."

† General Richard Prescott had the dubious distinction of being captured twice. After a small unit of Americans snuck at night into his headquarters in Rhode

his ordeal as a series in the *Pennsylvania Packet*. It was later released as a book, and the story was described in numerous newspapers on both sides of the Atlantic, including the touching account of Allen's son dying while his father was in prison. Allen's imprisonment was well known throughout the colonies and further raised awareness of the cruelties of the British prison ships.

There had long been a custom of prisoner exchanges in warfare, dating to the chivalrous ideals of combat during medieval times in Europe. While the Revolutionary War was being fought in America, prisoner exchanges were occurring on the other side of the Atlantic between the British and other European powers. However, a number of factors limited prisoner exchanges between the British and Americans, one of the foremost being the fact that the British did not recognize their former colonies as a legitimate nation and therefore did not consider colonials under arms to be soldiers. Rather, they viewed the Continental Army and especially the militias and privateers as rebels and criminals.

Furthermore, as one scholar has noted, "captured Americans created exceptionally awkward problems, since neither wholesale release nor wholesale trial for treason or piracy was practicable, and *habeas corpus* made indefinite imprisonment illegal." The British somewhat resolved the dilemma on March 3, 1777, when the North Act temporarily suspended *habeas corpus* when it came to those charged with "high treason" in the American colonies and on the "high seas." Although most captured American soldiers and sailors were never formally charged with a crime, they ended up being detained indefinitely on accusations of treason and piracy.

Another practical problem facing the Americans and British was that neither could afford to keep prisoners. After defeating the

---

Island, Prescott was caught in bed and further humiliated by not being allowed to dress. He was later exchanged for the American general Charles Lee, despite the fact that Lee had conspired against George Washington and was also caught in his bedtime clothing after a night of illicit partying in New Jersey.

Americans in New York in the summer and fall of 1776, General Howe faced a far worse enemy—starvation and a winter without adequate clothing and provisions. These factors claimed more lives than colonial muskets. A historical account of the British headquarters in New York reveals the severity of the problem fully three years later: "Flour exhausted. Hessians at Brooklyn received damaged oatmeal. If the British could not feed their own soldiers, how could they accommodate thousands of American prisoners?" Indeed, this created yet another problem. Another record of the war stated, "The known shortage of provisions in New York during November and December, 1776, and January and February, 1777, from which the British Army suffered, had a good deal to do with the famine and mortality of the prisoners of war at that period. Washington himself attributes them to this cause."

But the challenges presented an opportunity. Funds and food were in such short supply that in some cases the British decided to allow prisoners to purchase their freedom. At the same time, such an arrangement was an incentive to capture even more American prisoners. Prisoners would, perversely, help pay for the war.

There continued, however, a general unwillingness by the British to come to the negotiating table. But that changed when the Americans began winning battles and took prisoners of their own. Even though informal prisoner exchanges began, there never was an official policy on the matter. For the Americans, the individual states (through their governors or committees of prominent citizens), rather than the Continental Army, oversaw exchanges. During such negotiations, an officer was more valuable than an enlisted man, and Britain insisted on a level of deference for their captured officers. Indeed, when generals such as the American Charles Lee and British "Gentleman Johnny" Burgoyne were captured, both sides managed to secure their quick release.

In Europe, soldiers were typically exchanged rank for rank. For instance, when French privateers were captured by the British, they exchanged them in France for English sailors. Oftentimes the British would parole prisoners incarcerated in England—in Mill Prison near Plymouth, Fortran Prison near Portsmouth, smaller prisons in Liverpool and Weymouth, and Kinsale in Ireland. Such prisoners were even free to live in the town, but under certain restrictions. One condition used in Cape Breton in Newfoundland was that they work in coal pits. But when privateers were caught in American waters, a different fate awaited them.

The political situation among the upstart Americans was such that, even if Washington wanted to negotiate for the release of all prisoners, he was not in a legal position to do so. Privateers, for instance, were not a part of the Continental Army, volunteers were not regulars, and the militia units fought for the colonies where they were organized. The general also had trouble ordering American privateers to either imprison or hand over British sailors. Privateers often did what made them money. At the same time, the privateer captains did not have the resources to detain prisoners and often purposely kept poor records. Nor did American prisoners taken from privateers have the same claims as those taken from the Continental Army or even the makeshift navy, because they were not regular soldiers. As one old account of the prison ship dilemma stated, "The men on the *Jersey*, if unable to purchase their liberty, could only wait for peace or death; they were the victims of circumstance." Both sides were limited in their ability to release or exchange privateers.

But there were some efforts to improve the conditions in the prisons and on the prison ships, and to secure the release or exchange of the prisoners. In August 1775, only months after the first shots of the war, General Washington wrote to General Thomas Gage, the British commander at the beginning of the war, complaining about the inhumane treatment of the prisoners taken at Bunker Hill earlier that summer. Washington claimed Americans were being treated like common criminals and deserved the "Rights of Humanity." Washington also expressed frustration that the British failed to distinguish between officers and enlisted men in their prisons. Gage was defiant, responding that because the king had not bestowed the officer's rank or provided any rights to the prisoners, they were rebels and could be hanged.

Before leaving his post as commander of British forces in America, Gage wrote to Washington: "The Britons, ever pre-eminent in mercy, have outgone common examples, and overlooked the criminal in the captive. Upon these principles, your prisoners, whose lives by the laws of the land are destined to the cord, have hitherto been treated with care and kindness, and more comfortably lodged than the King's troops." The statements were anything but accurate.

Gage then accused Washington of mistreatment: "I understand there are some of the King's faithful subjects . . . laboring like Negro slaves to gain their daily subsistence, or reduced to the wretched alternative to perish by famine, or take arms against their King and country."

Washington was outraged by the lie and insolence. Not only did Gage fail to comply with any requests, but most of the colonials taken at the Battle of Bunker Hill in May either died in custody or were killed by their British captors. One group of surviving prisoners was murdered on September 14, 1775, prompting General Washington to report the incident to the Continental Congress and request a response. Washington was right to fume about Gage, for the British general helped craft the brutal policy on prisoners at the outset of the war.

Gage was replaced by William Howe in September 1775, and Washington continued the discussion about the treatment of prisoners. However, angered by Gage's reluctance to improve conditions, Washington tried a new approach with Howe. It contained threats: "My duty now makes it necessary to apprise you that, for the future, I shall regulate my conduct towards those gentlemen who are or may be in our possession, exactly by the rule you shall observe towards those of ours now in your custody." It had become an eye for an eye, Washington warned. "If severity and hardship mark the line of your conduct, painful as it may be to me, your prisoners will feel its effects. But if kindness and humanity are shown to ours, I shall with pleasure consider those in our hands only as unfortunate, and they shall receive from me that treatment to which the unfortunate are ever entitled."

But Howe, like Gage before him, refused to consider the conditions of the prisoners.

Another architect of the cruel prisoner policies was Lord George Germain, the minister in charge of the colonies in 1775. Unlike Gage, however, the scandalous and inept Germain worried about Washington's threat to treat captured British officers as his own men were treated. This prompted him to write to General William Howe in 1776 about the American prisoners: "It is hoped that the possession of these prisoners will enable you to procure the release of such of His Majesty's officers and loyal subjects as are in the disgraceful situation of being prisoners to the Rebels for, although it cannot be that you should enter into any treaty or agreement with Rebels for a regular cartel for exchange of prisoners, yet I doubt not your own discretion will suggest to you the means of effecting such exchange, without the King's dignity and honour being committed, or His Majesty's name used in any negotiations for the purpose."

General Howe also initially favored punishing American prisoners. When his massive army seized New York City in 1776, the war appeared to be in its final throes. Accordingly, Howe did not worry about the ramifications of his brutal treatment of prisoners or about any retaliation by the Americans on British prisoners of war. Howe had no qualms about imprisoning thousands of soldiers and sailors, or about the shockingly high death toll in the prisons, sugar houses, churches, and ships.

General Washington repeatedly made requests to the British command to improve the situation. In another letter to Howe, he informed his foe that "those who have lately been sent out, give the most shocking account of their barbarous usage, which their miserable, emaciated countenances confirm." Writing to General Howe again in March 1777, Washington stated his "wish that every reasonable indulgence and act of Humanity should be done to those whom the fortune of War has or may put into our hands."

Washington sent yet another letter to Howe later in 1777, writing diplomatically, "I am sorry that I am under the disagreeable necessity to trouble your Lordship with a letter, almost wholly on the subject of the cruel treatment which our officers and men, in the naval department, who are unhappy enough to fall into your hands, receive on board the prison-ships in the harbor of New York." Washington continued, "I call upon your Lordship to say, whether any treatment of your officers and seamen has merited so severe a retaliation. I am bold to say, it has not. And I hope upon making the proper inquiry, you will have the matter so regulated, that the unhappy persons, in captivity, may not in the future have the miseries of cold, disease, and famine, added to their other misfortunes."

Washington ended his letter less diplomatically, issuing another threat: "You may call us rebels, and say that we deserve no better treatment. But, remember, my Lord, that supposing us rebels, we still have feelings as keen and sensible as loyalists, and will, if forced to it, most assuredly retaliate upon those upon whom we look as the unjust invaders of our rights, liberties and properties."

After the British again failed to comply with the requests, Washington repeated the warning in another letter to Howe: "I would beg, that some certain rule of conduct towards prisoners may be settled; and, if you are determined to make captivity as distressing as possible, let me know it, what we may be upon equal terms, for your conduct must and shall regulate mine."

By the end of 1777, an exasperated Washington appears to have lost his patience with Howe and other British commanders who pretended to be interested in exchanges and claimed incorrectly to have provided adequate care for prisoners. The general fired off an angry letter to Admiral Robert Digby, one of the British commanders in America, saying, "It is preposterously cruel . . . to confine 800 men in one ship at this sultry season." He also reminded his foe that he too held prisoners. "We have the means of retaliation in our hands, which we should not hesitate to use, by confining the land prisoners with as much severity as our seamen are held."

Like other American leaders, Washington believed British cruelty aboard the prison ships was in part designed to deter colonials from joining the war and also to get Americans to enlist in the Royal Navy. In another letter to General Howe after the British took Philadelphia, Washington protested that the treatment there was intended "to Oblige them to inlist in the Corps you are raising." Similarly, writing to his fellow commander and French ally, the Comte de Grasse, Washington expressed his continued frustration, noting, "This unhappy class of men are now languishing under every species of inhumanity in the Prison Ships of the British, who pursue this conduct with a view to forcing the men to enter their service."

Even in his personal letters, the general revealed his disgust with British impressment. Such was the case when he complained to his aide Colonel John Laurens, "Admiral Digby is capturing all our Vessels, and suffocating all our Seamen who will not enlist into the Service of His Britannic Majesty as fast as possible in Prison Ships." Yet Washington did not give up hope of improving the conditions aboard the British prison ships, as is evident in a letter written to Admiral Digby later in the war: "If the fortune of war, sir, has thrown a number of these miserable people into your hands, I am certain your Excellency's feelings for the men must induce you to proportion the ships, (if they must be confined on board ships,) to their accommodation and comfort, and not, by crowding them together in a few ships, bring on diseases which consign them by the half-dozen in a day to the grave."

Washington was joined in his efforts to end the suffering aboard the prison ships and bring about prisoner exchanges by other American leaders, including Robert Morris, the superintendent of finance and one of the financiers of the war effort, who wrote to the Board of War urging it to make provisions for exchanges. Thomas Jefferson wrote to General Howe about the American prisoners taken at the Battle of Germantown in 1777, expressing concern that they were "so long without any food furnished them, that many perished with hunger." Jefferson added, in vivid terms, "Where the bodies laid, it was seen that they had eaten all the grass around them, within their reach after they had lost the power of rising, or moving from their place."

The presence of increasing numbers of British officers being captured and Washington's numerous threats to do unto them as was being done to his own troops finally brought slight changes to British policies. While conditions in prisons and on the prison ships remained deplorable through 1776, the British demonstrated more interest in exchanges. One of the first exchanges occurred in the summer of 1776 when General Howe proposed to General Washington that a total of 43 officers and 848 men be released. He wrote, "I shall redeem them by a like number of those in my possession; for which purpose I shall send Mr. Joshua Loring, my commissary, to Elizabethtown, as proper place for the exchange of prisoners, on any day you may appoint, wishing it may be an early one, wherein I presume you will concur, as it is purposed for the more speedy relief of the distressed."

One of the other early efforts to exchange prisoners occurred around the same time, on July 20, 1776, when Washington met with Colonel James Patterson, an aide to General Howe. Colonel Patterson was sent to negotiate because the British command worried about the safety of captured officers such as General Richard Prescott. Patterson and Washington discussed Prescott's treatment but were not able to agree. Washington pressed the point that General Prescott was being treated far better than the American prisoners and that several of the paroled British prisoners had violated the terms of their release by returning to military service.

The first instance where British treatment of prisoners improved was after Washington's surprise victory over the Hessians at Trenton after Christmas of 1776. General Howe understood that Washington's victory meant the war would continue beyond 1776. It would not be the short, year-long affair many British commanders had predicted.

Washington also now had hundreds of Hessian prisoners. In January 1777, the exchange occurred—some of the Americans taken at the Battle of Brooklyn the year before were freed. Minor improvements occurred again in October 1777, when almost six thousand British and Hessian soldiers and officers under General "Gentleman Johnny" Burgoyne were forced to surrender at Saratoga, giving the Americans more leverage in prison negotiations.

The decision facing General Washington as to whether or not to exchange prisoners, however, was impossibly complicated. It was not advantageous from a military perspective to exchange healthy British regulars for emaciated, ill, and poorly trained colonial volunteers, just as it was strategically problematic to redeem seasoned British sailors for young boys who had only recently joined the crews of privateers. Any man or boy could serve as a privateer, and the Americans had more than enough motley crews shipping out on any available schooner or merchant craft. The British had the upper hand in the matter and both sides knew it. Accordingly, on the rare occasion when British commanders proposed exchanging prisoners, Washington was forced more than once to decline the offer, especially when it was one-for-one—which effectively meant a professional, veteran soldier for a farmer-turned-volunteer. Plus, American militiamen and privateers generally enlisted for very short periods of time, meaning they would not be back in uniform if exchanged. The general also realized that prisoner exchanges often only prolonged the war by providing the British with more soldiers and sailors, noting, "It would be contrary to the practice of other nations and the soundest policy, by giving the enemy a great and permanent strength." These realities frustrated the general, who genuinely felt "urged by humanity" to try to secure the release of his men.

Making matters worse was the fact that General Howe and Admiral Howe also understood their advantage and Washington's predicament. Moreover, the Howes had a few tricks up their sleeve. They occasionally exchanged sailors, but only those who served on merchant ships, not seasoned naval seamen. At other times, they exchanged only those prisoners who were closest to death and thus unable to fight after their release. Washington complained about British deceit, writing, "Exchanging seamen for soldiers was contrary to the original agreement. Officers should be exchanged for officers, soldiers for soldiers, seamen for seamen, and citizens for citizens."

The British, according to another account, were exchanging prisoners "unfit for exchange because of the severity of their treatment." In 1777, Joshua Loring, the British commissary of prisoners, confessed that he only released those in "deplorable condition." David Sproat, the naval commissary, did the same thing aboard prison ships. This was observed by Thomas Andros: "It was evidently the policy of the English to return for sound and healthy men, sent from our American prisons, such Americans as had but just the breath of life in them, and were sure to die before they reached home." Andros recalled hearing the British admit as much.

The British continued to only release the sickest among the prisoners and those of little military value to Washington. For instance, in December 1778, a cartel in New London managed to secure the release of five hundred men from Connecticut. But the local newspaper's account of the exchange described the prisoners as "sick with various diseases—they had frozen limbs—and many were infected with small-pox. They died all along the way through the Sound, and every day after their arrival for three weeks."

Sadly, such troubling reports were common. One of the earliest exchanges was also one of the most unconscionable. On July 16, 1776, 150 prisoners were released by William Cunningham, the savage warden in New York City. Before their trek home, the men were given bread, which they ate "ravenously." Unbeknownst to them, the bread had purposely been poisoned so that the prisoners would die before arriving home. Another tragic exchange occurred a few months later, on December 2, 1776, when another group of prisoners from New York City was released. Some of them were so weak and ill that they died while walking home. One of the few to make it home was

Lieutenant Oliver Babcock. But he brought along smallpox, which soon killed him and the members of his family.

As the war dragged on, the British took more and more sailors and privateers as prisoners. In December 1781, General Washington faced the predicament that the British were seizing prisoners simply to advantage themselves in exchanges. He grumbled, "The suffering of seamen for some time past arises mostly from the want of a general regulation . . . so that the balance of prisoners is against the Americans." And with the number of privateers entering the fight increasing every year, the situation would only worsen.

On January 5, 1781, the Continental Congress had formally decreed that Washington and other American commanders could retaliate against British prisoners. Yet, even though Washington had long ago lost his patience with British commanders, he did not resort to the intentional abuse and neglect of his prisoners, as the British had done on the prison ships, nor did he give orders for or condone such behavior among his subordinates.

July 4

In slumbers deep I hear the farewell sigh,
Pale, plaintive ghosts with feeble accent cry;
At distance far with sickly aspect move,
And beg vengeance at the throne of Jove.

—Philip Freneau, "The British Prison-Ship" (1781)

Given the shockingly high death toll aboard the *Jersey*, the daily abuses suffered at the hands of the guards, and a war that dragged on for years, the prisoners had little to bolster their spirits. But there were a handful of developments and individuals that helped keep the men alive. One of them, in the words of Thomas Dring, was a "very corpulent old woman."

One of the few indulgences permitted by Commissary Sproat and the guards on the *Jersey* were routine visits by a woman known to the prisoners as "Dame Grant." Every other day, two local boys would row Dame Grant, whose considerable bulk filled the entire back of the skiff, to the accommodation platform beside the *Jersey*. She came to sell wares and food from a box placed at the front of the small boat. It contained bread, fruit, sugar, tea, and a few assorted items that the guards would purchase for their own consumption or resell to prisoners who had money. On rare and special occasions, depending on the guards on duty, the prisoners were allowed to organize near the accommodation ladder to purchase items directly from Dame Grant. This, however, never happened when the angry loyalists were on duty. Either way, in anticipation of Dame Grant's arrival prisoners would eagerly line up along the side of the ship.

Dame Grant's boat typically contained roughly the same items each visit and it was the only chance for prisoners to obtain fresh, edible food, a pinch of tobacco, or much-needed items such as needle and thread. The enterprising old woman's arrival was also one of the connections prisoners had with the outside world. However much the men looked forward to the dame's visit, the event always elicited mixed emotions, as the old woman reminded them of their own mothers or grandmothers—and of their captivity.

On the other hand, Dame Grant's visits were tough on prisoners without the means to purchase her items. Thomas Dring, for instance, described the "distress" of seeing the faces of "famished wretches" without money peering hopelessly at the exchange taking place on the upper deck. Outstretched hands jutted from the iron bars of the holds, begging for food. Remembered Dring, "Whenever I bought any articles from the boat, I never enjoyed them; for it was impossible to do so in the presence of so many needy wretches, eagerly gazing at my purchase, and almost dying for want of it."

If the prisoners were lucky, a friendly guard would pass along a request to Dame Grant for an item of clothing, comb, pipe, or apple. The old woman would "always faithfully procure" that rare luxury for the prisoners. However, one day Dame Grant failed to arrive at the boat. The prisoners "awaited with extreme anxiety" for her next scheduled visit. But that day too came and went without an arrival. News finally reached the *Jersey* that the kind old woman had died of a fever she had contracted from the prisoners she served. Her absence, remembered Dring, created "a void which was never afterwards filled up."

In the months following the dame's passing, a sutler—an entrepreneur who followed armies in hopes of selling them food and supplies—occasionally came to the prison ships to sell products. As was the case with Dame Grant, the items were usually purchased by the guards and then distributed to the prisoners through an opening in the bulkhead. Unfortunately, these sutlers, unlike Grant, gouged the prisoners, charging exorbitant fees and providing little in return. The most popular item was spirits. Andrew Sherburne was one of the prisoners who had managed to bring money on board, although he never purchased alcohol. The teenager had just over five dollars and rationed it in order to occasionally purchase sheep liver, pepper and salt, and meat pudding from the sutlers.

Another source of comfort for some of the prisoners was religion. However, Thomas Andros recorded that he never saw a Bible on the *Jersey* and the ship received no visits by clergy, even during the daily burials. Such comforts that would render hope for the prisoners were likely prohibited by decree from the commissary David Sproat. Andros was greatly disturbed by the absence of clergy and religious services on the ship and the general lack of prayer among many prisoners, who, he noted, seemed to have lost their faith on account of the ordeal. "I know not that God's name was ever mentioned, unless it was in profaneness or blasphemy," Andros complained. Rather, it seemed to him that "when they most needed religion, there [then] they treated it with the greatest contempt."

Some prisoners such as Andros, who had become increasingly devout during his ordeal, attributed their survival to faith. During his captivity, Andros tried to remember sermons and scripture. He also found comfort in a poem in Latin he had heard as a child and recited often during the most trying hours on the *Jersey*:

Which things,
most worthy of pity,
I myself saw.
And of them was a part.

Additionally, the officers among the prisoners had organized codes of conduct for those aboard the Hell Ship, one of which was to observe the Sabbath. The Rhode Islander Thomas Dring recorded that one of the prisoners finally agreed to serve as a proxy preacher. The man, whose name was Cooper, was not a man of the cloth, but rather a "common sailor." Dring and other prisoners described Cooper as well educated and possessing good manners. The Virginian was also quite charismatic and articulate, allowing him to capture the prisoners' attention with his stories, the most popular of which was about his running away from home to become a sailor. Each Sunday, when the prisoners were permitted on the upper deck, Cooper would climb atop the spar. From there, his thundering voice would call upon his fellow prisoners. The Virginian would recite the bylaws developed by the sailors, share personal stories, and offer them heartfelt words of faith and hope.

While reading the bylaws, Cooper made reference to the prisoners before him who had developed the "Rules of Conduct" as "the framers." Poetically he evoked their memory, suggesting that they were "in all probability sleeping in death, beneath the sand of the shore before our eyes." The man the prisoners called "the Orator" and "the Elder" also encouraged the prisoners to adhere to these codes, noting that in them was a token of civility and the hope of survival.

Cooper peppered his "sermons" with warnings he had received before his capture that, should he become a sailor, he would end up aboard the dreaded *Jersey*. The notorious Hell Ship, he had been told, would send him to meet his maker. "The first of these predictions has been verified," warned Cooper, "and I care not how soon the second proves equally true, for I am prepared for the event. Death, for me, has lost its terrors, for with them I have been too long familiar." This particular sermon resonated with the other prisoners because, like Cooper, many of them had known about the old hulk before they were captured; it had become synonymous with British oppression. While it had inspired some to fight, others had whispered the name in hope that they would never be captured and put aboard Hell.

But one Sunday, Cooper, from his perch atop the spar, went too far. He roared that Satan had sent his demons to torment the prisoners and chief among these tormentors was David Sproat, the commissary of prisoners, whom he called the "most active of these infernal agents." The prisoners listening worried that the guards would beat or kill "Parson Cooper," and they begged the Orator to cease making statements that could get him in trouble. However, Cooper refused, stating firmly that their "keepers could do nothing more, unless they should put him to the torture." But even that, the parson declared, did not scare him. Rather, he hoped his words would convince Sproat and the guards to permit members of the clergy to come aboard the ship.

No preachers arrived. But aides to Commissary Sproat did arrive and ordered that Cooper be brought to them. The guards dragged Cooper to the upper deck, and Sproat's agents then took him away in a boat. The parson waved while sailing away. Cooper's removal greatly disturbed the prisoners, who revered the gifted orator and had come to rely on his weekly sermons for hope. Most of the prisoners believed Cooper had been killed by Sproat. Dring held out hope that he was from a powerful family who had purchased his freedom. They never found out what became of him.

The prospects of escaping the *Jersey* or being released from the imprisonment were slim. As was mentioned earlier, one option was to purchase freedom, but few prisoners carried enough money with them at the time of incarceration or had family members with the means to secure their release. Another option was impressment. The British were in need of sailors and often resorted to "pressing" sailors from the American colonies and elsewhere into service, not infrequently at the tip of a bayonet. The Royal Navy secured new "recruits" by taking patients from hospitals, swooping in on drunks in pubs, and having press gangs seize mariners from merchant vessels. But they also used prisoners.

The British came to be so reliant on impressment that a bizarre plan was formulated in the last full year of the war by the son of the legendary British general Lord Jeffrey Amherst. The young officer imagined an entire military unit consisting of naval prisoners that would be sent to fight for the Crown in the West Indies and elsewhere. Although the proposal never came to fruition, the British did press countless numbers of Americans into service. Press gangs operated at the discretion of the captains of warships but were also a part of Royal Navy policy. Admiral Mariot Arbuthnot was responsible for pressing many hundreds—and possibly thousands—of Americans into service on his warships. The admiral's press gangs targeted imprisoned sailors and privateers in New York by either offering them the chance to get off the prison ships or simply forcing them into service. The British were so desperate that they even visited the disease-plagued *Jersey*.

Ebenezer Fox remembered that after his warship, *Protector*, was captured by two larger Royal Navy vessels, about one-third of his crew were forced into the service of His Majesty's navy. Many did not go willingly. He recalled that most of these unfortunate souls were never heard of again. But even that fate seemed preferable to being taken to the *Jersey*. Fox had heard frightening tales from older sailors about the notorious prison ship. Yet, as he stated, "The idea we had formed of its horrors fell far short of the realities which we afterwards experienced."

Fox was on the Hell Ship when Admiral Arbuthnot's press gangs boarded in April 1780 hoping to find a few experienced sailors among the sick and malnourished prisoners. Fox remembered that "a British officer with a number of soldiers came on board. The prisoners were all ordered on deck, placed on the larboard gangway, and marched in single file round to the quarter-deck, where the officers stood to inspect them, and select such ones as suited their fancies without any reference to the rights of the prisoners." Confused and afraid, Fox did as he was told. "We continued to march round in solemn and melancholy procession, till they had selected from among our number about three hundred of the ablest, nearly all of whom were Americans, and they were directed to go below under a guard, to collect together whatever things they wished to take belonging to them. They were then driven into the boats, waiting alongside, and left the prison ship."

Even though Fox loathed the British, he and the others left behind were so sick and hungry that they "almost envied" their peers who were pressed into service.

The conditions were so hellish that Fox and a few others planned to escape. It would happen the next time British sloops anchored near the *Jersey* in order to press prisoners into service. As Fox described it, "[We] conceived the design of rising upon the guard, and seizing upon the sloop, and running her aground upon the Jersey shore." However, the British guards were "watchful" and "well armed; while a guard of soldiers stood at the head of the companion way, to prevent any communication with the prisoners upon the deck." There would be no escape for Fox.

Both Thomas Dring and Thomas Andros noted that they and their crewmates refused offers from the guards and officers aboard the *Jersey* to join the Royal Navy. These two prisoners proudly boasted of the patriotism of their comrades in choosing the wretched conditions of the Hell Ship over joining their enemies. However, for other prisoners the choice was not so easy or obvious.

Ebenezer Fox's strength eventually wore out. After suffering for too long on the *Jersey*, he and a dozen other prisoners enlisted with a British regiment shipping off to Jamaica. He expressed guilt and tried to rationalize the difficult decision by saying, "Again we heard the tempting offers, and again the assurance that we should not be called upon to fight against our government or country, and with the hope that we should find an opportunity to desert, of which it was our firm intention to avail ourselves when offered, with such hopes, expectations, and motives, we signed the papers, and became soldiers in his Majesty's service."

The Royal Navy did not want to risk the chance that these new recruits would try to escape when near an American port or sabotage combat operations against an American warship or privateer. As such, pressed sailors were often shipped to distant waters, where they had little incentive to escape and virtually no chance of ever making it back home. Thus was the fate of Ebenezer Fox. One of the few to live to tell the tale was a young seaman named John Blatchford, who, along with more than eighty other sailors, was sent to the East Indies. He alone made it back home, in the year 1783.

There was one other way of coping with imprisonment on the nightmarish ship—resistance. And that is precisely what the prisoners on the *Jersey* did on July 4, 1782.

As is true for prisoners of war throughout history, several of the men confined belowdecks on the *Jersey* dealt with their bleak situation by fighting back against the oppressive guards. The prisoners used every trick and tool at their disposal to resist. Ebenezer Fox described one such tactic that took advantage of the swarms of rats, lice, mites, and other pests that filled the ship. The prisoners would put "vermin" inside an empty "snuff box." When a British officer boarded the *Jersey*, they purposely opened the box and poured the creatures on his coat in order to infect him.

Perhaps the largest organized resistance occurred on July 4, 1782. With the war all but over, the prisoners planned to celebrate Independence Day with a demonstration of resistance and camaraderie. Planning began several days before July 4 when the prisoners started saving and hiding rations of food and water, gathered supplies and materials, and spread the word among fellow inmates. Hoping "to make ourselves merry," the men made small American flags and thought of patriotic songs to sing. The celebration would occur when the prisoners were permitted on the upper deck, but in such a way as not to invite "trouble" or "insult" the guards. Yet that is precisely what happened.

While the guards on duty that day were not the feared Hessians or the vindictive loyalists, they included a group of aggressive and foul-tempered Scots, whom the prisoners deemed second only to the loyalists in terms of their aggressive and violent dispositions. On the morning of the fourth, the prisoners symbolically placed thirteen small flags on and around the booms of the ship. However, the guards ordered the prisoners to remove the flags. The prisoners refused, citing their right to mark the occasion with song and camaraderie. They stood in defiance and silent solidarity, tensions building. Then one of the prisoners began singing patriotic songs; soon all of them were singing. They were ordered by the guards to stop singing, but only sang louder.

The guards reluctantly gave in and permitted the men to sing, but did manage to block access to the upper deck so that no additional prisoners from the holds could join their comrades. Those stuck belowdecks ended up spending the entire day trapped in the dingy and stiflingly hot holds. Yet, from below, they joined in the chorus. Prisoners on deck and below celebrated all day, singing and sharing stories and sparse rations with one another.

By late afternoon the guards had had enough of the celebration. Around four o'clock they ordered the prisoners to cease the merriment. The prisoners only sang louder and began cheering. Their order ignored and their patience wearing thin, the Scottish guards tore down the flags and "triumphantly demolished and trampled them under foot." A few prisoners attempted to stop the act, but the guards responded with violence. Fighting soon broke out across the upper deck. Prisoners rushed the guards, but their advantage was short-lived. The guards eventually gained the upper hand, driving the prisoners belowdecks with bayonets and whips, shouting, "Down, Rebels, down!"

The guards finally succeeded in beating the prisoners down the stairway. That done, they locked the hatches. One account described the chaos and bloodshed: "The helpless prisoners, retreating from the hatchways as far as their crowded condition would permit, were followed by the guards, who mercilessly hacked, cut, and wounded everyone within their reach; and then ascending again to the upper deck, fastened down the hatches upon the poor victims of their cruel rage, leaving them to languish through the long, sultry, summer night, without water to cool their parched throats."

At suppertime, the prisoners were denied food and water. This lasted through the night, but in defiance the prisoners started singing again. As the chorus grew louder, the guards shouted threats down to their charges, but their warnings were drowned out by the singing. Ultimately, the guards could stand the singing no longer. Around nine that evening, they opened the hatch and charged down the stairway "with lanterns in one hand and cutlasses in the other." Steel flashed in the dim twilight and flickering wicks of lanterns, as swords were thrust into anyone unable to get away in time.

Men had nowhere to hide and little room even to move in order to avoid the attack. Soon the guards retreated up the ladders, and cries of wounded and dying prisoners echoed throughout the holds. Several men were killed, with accounts varying from ten to twenty-five, while many other prisoners were injured in the melee. A few of them later died from their wounds. The bodies of those killed on the upper deck during the uprising were simply thrown overboard.

Thomas Dring survived the Independence Day massacre by re-treating to the gunroom. He described the ordeal that followed: "It had been the usual custom for each person to carry below, when he descended at sunset, a pint of water, to quench his thirst during the night. But, on this occasion, we had thus been driven to our dungeon three hours before the setting of the sun, and without our usual supply of water." The situation was made worse because "the day had been sultry, and the heat was extreme throughout the ship." Dring continued, "The usual number of hours during which we had been crowded together between decks; the foul atmosphere and sickening heat; the additional excitement and restlessness caused by the unwanted wanton attack which had been made; above all, the want of water, not a drop of which could be obtained during the whole night, to cool our parched lips; the struggles and groans of the dying; together formed a combination of horrors which no pen can describe." Dring concluded, "Of this night I cannot describe the horror."

Hatches were again fastened shut. Any request for a drop of water to quench a parched throat was met only by taunts from the guards above deck. Likewise, no medical attention—no dressing for the wounds, no gauze for the blood—was offered for the wounded who had survived the attack by the Scottish guards. Dring recalled that few prisoners slept that night, not only on account of their thirst but because of the groans and cries from wounded and dying prisoners. In the pitch blackness of the holds, Dring sat near a small grate and stared out into the dark sky all night. Sleep eluded him.

The next morning, the men awoke to a ghastly scene. Several of their fellow prisoners had died in the night or were barely clinging to life. Denied water all night, they were parched and eagerly awaited the morning meal with its ration of water. But it did not come. Mealtime usually occurred like clockwork on the *Jersey*, but the morning of July 5 came and went with no food, water, or access to the upper deck. Nor did the guards open the hatches for the usual morning ritual of collecting the dead. Desperation set in as a few delirious prisoners began to panic. Others worried they would be left to starve as a punishment for the celebration.

Finally, after several hours, the hatches opened and a mob of "thirsty wretches thronged to the water cask," but the guards dispersed them at bayonet point and made them wait even longer. Cruelly, the prisoners could see the water but not drink it. The guards' taunting was "more spiteful than violent." Thomas Andros remembered trying to reach for the water cask and being attacked by a sentry. He barely escaped with his life.

Food rations also arrived very late that day, and the prisoners were not allowed access to fire to cook their food. The time allotted on the upper deck was limited for the next few days, as were the rations of food and water. It was a particularly difficult period for many of the prisoners. But finally the guards rotated off duty and a group of Hessians arrived, causing "great joy" among the prisoners.

The massacre on July 4 was not the only effort by prisoners to resist the guards; nor was it the only instance when the guards attacked their unarmed charges. For instance, after continual beatings and savage treatment aboard the ship *Strombolo*, the prisoners revolted. Several prisoners were wounded or killed in that uprising. Their bodies were piled on top of one another on the upper deck and left as a cruel reminder for the living. It had the desired effect, especially when a few wounded men too weak to stand were included in the pile. The prisoners watched in horror as one mortally wounded comrade piled among the dead gasped for breath and begged, "For god's sake . . . a little water." An officer kicked the prisoner in the face with his boot and screamed, "Damn you! Take that, you damn'd rebel rascal!"

Back on the *Jersey*, the tragedy of July 4 had another effect.

—— 14 ——

Escape

These all in freedom's sacred cause ally'd,
For freedom ventur'd and for freedom died;
To base subjection they were never broke,
They could not bend beneath a tyrant's yoke.

—Philip Freneau, "The British Prison-Ship" (1781)

Many prisoners owed their lives to Elizabeth Burgin. Unfortunately, very little is known about her except that she must have been a remarkable and courageous woman. Burgin, a mother of three and most probably a war widow living near the prison ships of Wallabout Bay, risked disease by delivering food to the prisoners aboard the floating dungeons. As she was returning home from the prison ships one evening in early July 1779, an American officer secretly approached her with a plan to help prisoners escape. The details of the operation remain obscure, but it appears a group of officers had infiltrated British-occupied New York, followed Burgin's moves, and decided to recruit her to help them.

The British sometimes permitted women to board prison ships in order to sell or distribute food and provisions, or at least conduct the exchanges at the accommodation platform or ramp. Burgin had been one of those women and had gained the trust of both the prisoners and guards aboard the ships. Despite the grave risks, Burgin agreed to help.

While providing food and wares to the prisoners, Burgin slipped the prisoners a note apparently drafted by the officer who recruited her. The note contained the details of the plan, which appears to have involved the prisoners hiding on the small boat she used to travel to and from the prison ships. Over the next few weeks, she repeatedly risked her life by going back to the prison ship to help more prisoners escape. In total, Burgin smuggled perhaps two hundred men to freedom, a handful at a time, and may even have sheltered some of them at her home.

The ruse continued until the officer who had recruited Burgin was captured by the British, which not only jeopardized further escapes but put her life in danger. Whether by coercion or in an effort to secure her husband's freedom, the officer's wife informed the British that Burgin was an accomplice. On July 17, 1779, the British ordered Burgin arrested on grounds that she was "suspected for helping the American prisoners to make their escape." A £200 reward was offered for her capture, a considerable sum of money at the time.

The details are unclear, but what is known is that Burgin was nearly caught. Knowing she was being hunted and that her home was being watched, the fugitive hid for two weeks before getting friends to help her escape to Long Island. She hid there for five weeks and then boarded a whaling boat that took her to Connecticut. A letter written by Burgin while she was still on the run in November survives. In it, she asked a minister named James Calville for help, writing, "I am now sire, very desolate, without money, without Cloaths or friends to go to. I aim to go to Philadelphia, where God knows how I shall live, a cold winter coming on." She went on to explain her ordeal, saying, "Helping our poor prisoners brought me to want, which I don't repent."

It appears the reverend helped, possibly by contacting General George Washington. What is known is that Burgin wrote to the general asking for his help and informing him that the British had confiscated all her possessions. She also offered the names of American officers and former prisoners who could vouch for her good character and deeds. Men whose lives had been saved by Burgin came forward with their stories. Moved by her heroic sacrifice, Washington wrote to the Continental Congress requesting assistance. "Regarding Elizabeth Burgin, recently an inhabitant of New York," said Washington, "from the testimony of our own Officers who have returned from captivity, it would appear that she has been indefatigable for the relief of the prisoners, and for facilitating their escape. For this conduct she incurred the suspicion of the British, and was forced to make her escape under disturbing circumstances."

Burgin later traveled to Philadelphia and then resettled in Elizabeth, New Jersey. Although history did not record how, she managed to be reunited with her three children. One of the grateful former prisoners she had aided offered her a home, others came forward with money, and Washington's intervention resulted in a pension for Burgin that began in 1781. The full story will likely never be known, but Burgin wrote back to Washington, the man she called "Kind General," thanking him for championing her cause. Elizabeth Burgin remains one of the little-known heroines of the war.

The conditions aboard the *Jersey* were so abysmal that many prisoners attempted to escape even if the chances were slim. Prisoners on other ships, as was mentioned earlier, were at times so desperate that they set the ships on fire. One such account was reported in the newspaper *Rivington's Gazette* in 1780. "Last Saturday afternoon the *Good Hope* prison ship lying in the Wallebocht Bay," read the story, "was entirely consumed after having been wilfully set on fire by a Connecticut man named Woodbury, who confessed the fact. He with others of the incendiaries are removed to the Provost." Not all the prisoners were sent to the notorious prison. Presumably many died in the fire, while others were sent to the *Jersey*. But a few escaped during the inferno. As reported in the paper, "The prisoners let each other down from the port holes and decks into the water."

One weakness in the *Jersey*'s security was the size of the crew and guards. Ebenezer Fox, the former prisoner who, late in life, recorded an account of his ordeal for his children and grandchildren, described the old warship as having a crew that was at minimal strength. The British needed every available soldier—including mercenaries—for the war. Therefore, Fox remembered, guards on board the old warship numbered only about thirty and were uninspired to be stuck aboard a noxious, diseased hulk. While such a force could mount some defense of the ship, there was upward of a thousand prisoners on board, which presented for the prisoners the possibility of mutiny.

Other factors, however, deterred mutiny. Most of the prisoners aboard the *Jersey* were so weak and sick that they lacked the ability to revolt. Furthermore, as Fox observed, "the physical force of the prisoners was sufficient at any time to take possession of the ship, but the difficulty was to dispose of themselves after a successful attempt." Because the *Jersey* had been completely hulked, it could not sail and stayed afloat only if water was continually pumped from its bilge. The putrid marshlands and mudflats surrounding the ship made swimming and walking exceedingly difficult.

Those lucky enough to escape then had to navigate their way through what was at the time the main British stronghold in America and a countryside filled with loyalists who would report escapees to the military. Reduced to skeletons and wearing rags, the prisoners stood out no matter where they went. As Fox noted, prisoners were "occasionally . . . brought back who had been found in the woods upon Long Island and taken up by the Tories."* Moreover, unsuccessful attempts at escape were met with severe punishment. Fox and a few other prisoners tried to escape in 1780 but were caught and punished "by having our miserable allowance reduced one third in quantity for a month." He and his crewmates were starving before

---

* Tories were colonists who supported the British during the war.

the punishment, but the reduction in rations was now "hardly sufficient to sustain life."

Whenever such attempts were successful, the prisoners still on the
ship would cheer loudly, which further angered the guards. The result was that the prisoners suffered when their escape attempts failed,
but also after their crewmates succeeded. Nevertheless, even though
escape was difficult and those caught attempting to do so were severely punished, efforts to escape continued. This was especially true
as the war dragged on and on. After the failure of so many attempts
to negotiate prisoner exchanges and after brutal incidents such as the
July 4 massacre, they had no choice but to try and escape.

Some prisoners did escape. The simple fact of knowing they were
about to be taken to the notorious *Jersey* was an incentive for many
prisoners to make an attempt. So vile and widespread was the Hell
Ship's reputation that a group of prisoners including Thomas Hitch-
cock, Lieutenant Eliakim Palmer, and John Searles from Connecticut, when they discovered they were headed to the *Jersey*, pulled off a
simple but daring escape.

There are accounts of the escape in newspapers from May 1780.
They reported that a few prisoners were being transferred from the
Scorpion and the *Falmouth*. As the prisoners lined up to disembark
for the *Jersey*, "one having, as by accident, thrown his hat overboard,
begged leave to go after it in a small boat, which lay alongside." Surprisingly, the guards agreed that he could fetch the hat before being
transferred to the *Jersey*. The hatless prisoner and two others were
put in the rowboat along with a guard to supervise them. The prisoners rowed the vessel to retrieve the hat and purposely acted as if
they did not know how to steer the boat. Watching from the prison
ship, the other prisoners and guards roared in delight at the hapless
landlubbers. All the while, the three men from Stonington took the
launch further and further from both their ship and the *Jersey*. Finally, the officers and guards back on the prison ships realized the

boat was too far away and hollered for them to return. It was too late. At that moment, the prisoners overpowered the unsuspecting guard. Experienced sailors, the three men rowed quickly away. "Though several armed boats pursued, and shot was fired from the shipping," according to the newspapers, it was in vain. The prisoners were gone, headed to New Jersey and to freedom.

Another dramatic escape occurred in December of that year when four officers from Connecticut seized an opportunity. A small launch was fastened to the gangway on a cold, stormy afternoon. Earlier the men had gotten hold of a crowbar, which they used to pry open a hatch. With no guards in sight and the wind howling, the four prisoners raced across the deck, down the accommodation ladder, and to the launch. The guards were too slow, sounding the alarm only after the prisoners had put some distance between their launch and the prison ship. A second boat was sent out in pursuit of the escapees, but the prisoners made it back to Connecticut.

Ebenezer Fox recorded in his memoir that there were successful escapes from the *Jersey* during his incarceration, although they were few and far between. One of them occurred amid the stifling June heat in 1780 when thirty sailors and five officers jumped overboard and swam for shore. The guards scrambled to action and began firing their muskets into the water, but according to both Fox and the *New Jersey Gazette*, most if not all of the prisoners made it to land.

Another escape occurred around the same time when the guard stationed by the accommodation ladder leading to the water was talking to a visitor to the ship. A prisoner seized the opportunity and, with the guard distracted, came upon the sentry, knocked him hard to the ground, and jumped overboard. Hearing the commotion on deck, other prisoners attempted to rush to the upper deck and revolt, but the guards "overpowered" them and violently beat them back belowdecks. Nothing is known about the fate of the escapee.

American newspapers were filled with stories of successful escapes, which gave families hope. But such escapes accomplished much more. With the revolutionary cause desperate for victories, the stories of escaped prisoners were welcome news. At the same time, the accounts in newspapers exposed the public to the wretched and violent conditions on the ships, which helped rally support for the war. The same was true when stories emerged of prisoners' dying while trying to escape. One such instance occurred in January 1780 when fifteen prisoners escaped from a prison ship in the East River. The men crossed the frozen river, but one man died on the ice. Several others, "frost bitten and unable to endure the cold," returned to the ship rather than freeze to death. One man, however, managed to reach New London to tell the story.

Each successive attempt to escape became more difficult, as the officers and guards on the *Jersey* increased security every time a prisoner tried to escape. But some prisoners still tried, including the brave boys profiled in this book.

—— 15 ——

Run!

Hunger and thirst, to work our woe, combine,
And mouldy bread, and flesh of rotten swine,
The mangled carcass, and the battered brain,
The doctor's poison, and the captain's cane,
The soldier's musket, and the steward's debt,
The evening shackle, and the noon-day threat.

—Philip Freneau, "The British Prison-Ship" (1781)

In late September 1781, Christopher Hawkins, the cabin boy from Rhode Island imprisoned on the *Jersey*, met a friend who likely ended up saving his life. William Waterman was roughly the same age as Hawkins, and in early October the two began the "hazardous project of making their escape from the prison ship." The plan, according to Hawkins, was a simple one: jumping overboard and "swimming to Long Island, a distance . . . of two and a-half to three miles." There were hazards, Hawkins admitted, including "the sentinels posted along the shore."

The main challenge, the boys reasoned, was not the long swim but getting off the ship. It was, they knew, almost "impossible to leave the upper deck, without being discovered." They ruled out a nighttime escape because all prisoners were confined to the lower deck after dark and the gun ports were "secured by iron bars, strongly fastened to the timbers of the ship."

Their break came when the boys managed to "secure an old axe and crow-bar" apparently left behind by a work crew. At night they "went to work during a heavy thunder storm," and successfully "removed the bars from one of the port-holes of the lower deck." They worked night after night but each day before sunrise "replac[ed] them temporarily to prevent detection." The two boys managed to cut a small opening in the side of the rotting ship through which their emaciated bodies could squeeze.

The night of the escape, Hawkins and Waterman "stowed the little money they had, with some other articles, into their knapsacks, which they fastened to their backs by passing the lashings under their arms and across the breast." They then enlisted a few trusted prisoners to help lower them down into the water by an "old service-rope which they had obtained." Once in the cold, dark waters of Wallabout Bay, the two boys swam along the side of the old hulk and back to the stern. There they used the "beacon light on the shore" of Long Island as a compass and began swimming for freedom.

Three problems faced the boys. The first was arriving at a spot not swarming with British soldiers. The second was something they had not anticipated: the waterlogged rucksacks on their backs became very heavy and "greatly impeded" their swimming. Third, in the dark night Hawkins and Waterman became separated but could not call out to each other for fear of alerting the guards on the ship. The two would never see each other again, and Hawkins never found out what happened to his friend.

After looking frantically but to no avail for Waterman, Hawkins spotted a light some ways off, roughly a "gun-shot distance" from the coast, and swam toward it. However, the weight of his rucksack became too much. Exhausted, Hawkins tried to adjust it, but the lashings became "unraveled" and the pack started to sink below the surface. "Unwilling to part with it," the boy quickly dove down and managed to grab it. Treading water and gasping for breath, Hawkins tried to hold the heavy sack above the waves. It was hopeless, but he tried again and again "to retain it by taking it first under one arm and then under the other." Eventually the sack, like his tired arms, became too heavy and he let it sink below the waves with all his earthly belongings.

Later that night Hawkins neared the shore of Long Island. He was so close that he heard British sentries calling out "all's well." After three hours in the cold water Hawkins was freezing and his body began shutting down. Despite the guards, he could stay in the water no longer. Miraculously, he managed to make it ashore undetected and, wearing only "an old hat," hid in the bushes. He hoped the spot was free from soldiers because he was too "cold, stiffened, and nearly exhausted" to run. But at least he was alive and free from the ship.

After resting a few moments, Hawkins struggled to walk along the shore, creeping quietly through the dark looking for his friend, but Waterman was nowhere to be found. Eventually he abandoned the search and snuck through the countryside looking for a barn. He needed a place where he could rest undetected. But while searching for a barn in the dark night, Hawkins tripped over a stone and fell hard to the ground. He was cold, afraid, tired, and alone, with no barn in sight, and now he was injured. But he willed himself forward. Twigs and thistles cut at his naked body as he stumbled blindly onward in the dark.

Early in the morning, the teenager finally came upon a barn. There was no food to be found, but after climbing a ladder to a loft Hawkins spotted an old, torn blanket. He longed to sleep and a pile of hay tempted him, but he continued on, taking the blanket to warm his naked body and knowing he needed to move under cover of darkness. Before sunrise "a hard storm of rain" poured down from the dark clouds. "Naked and hungry," wet and cold, Hawkins sought shelter as the sun was beginning to peek above the horizon. When he found another barn, he curled up in the corner in an inviting pile of hay and slept.

Hawkins awoke around noon. Peeking out from a window in the barn, he realized he was in trouble. The entire area was "infested with Tories, and straggling bands of Hessians were prowling about the country." The young boy decided to head east and put some distance between himself and the British stronghold, but he had to be very careful.

While sneaking through the farm fields he felt the sharp pangs of hunger. It had been a full day since he last ate. Finally, in one field he found a few potatoes still in the ground. Hawkins quickly gathered them but resisted the urge to eat them. Instead, he thought it wise to get out of the open field and ran toward the cover of some nearby trees. Dashing through the field, he almost ran straight into a young woman holding a basket with fruit and vegetables.

The two surprised each other. The sight of Hawkins wearing nothing more than a hat and a tattered old blanket startled the young woman, who screamed, dropped her basket, and ran to the nearby house. Hawkins turned and ran for his life in the other direction, still carrying a few potatoes cradled in one arm. He darted into a wooded area, surprised at how "nimble" he still was despite his weakened condition. Along the way, he scooped up a branch to use to defend himself if he was caught. A small river offered him the chance to avoid detection in the event the British or Tories used hounds to track his scent. Hawkins crossed the water and came ashore some distance away.

He could run no farther. Hawkins found another barn filled with fresh flax, which he used to make a bed.* Hawkins then ate the raw potatoes and slept soundly. A long sleep and the potatoes left him feeling a bit rejuvenated and able to continue his journey. Hawkins avoided roads and kept to the woods.

However, partway up Long Island, near Oyster Bay, he was caught by a group of loyalists who accused him of being a prisoner on the run. The angry "refugees" from the war treated him poorly

---

* Flax is a flowering plant cultivated for its seed. The fiber from the stalk is used as a textile.

and placed him under arrest for "some time." To his horror, Hawkins learned that they planned to take him back to Brooklyn to be put aboard the *Jersey*. The gesture, they informed him, would ingratiate them with the British military.

Fortunately for Hawkins, a local patriot helped him escape at night. The man even provided Hawkins with food and money, and showed him how to travel farther up Long Island and then across the sound to Rhode Island.

With the exception of the potatoes, it had been days since the boy had a meal. Satisfying his hunger and quenching his thirst were his new priorities, so Hawkins approached another farmhouse. He crept low and quietly to avoid the people in the fields and came upon a young boy working in a garden. Hawkins decided to take a chance. He approached the boy and asked him for food and clothing. The boy did not run or scream. Instead, he simply went inside to ask his mother. Hawkins was prepared for the worst, but the "old" and "kind" woman invited him in to eat.

As Hawkins devoured the food, the young boy brought him a pair of pants and the woman asked him questions. He informed her that he was going home to see his mother in Providence. The woman was remarkably calm and caring, saying to him, "Oh, how I wish you were at home!" Hawkins had the sense that his host knew from where he had come. As they spoke, he discovered he was right. It turned out that the woman's husband had enlisted, been captured, and was imprisoned on the *Jersey*, where he died. This explained, he reasoned, why the woman was so "timid and cautious in her manner," yet so "kind hearted."

Hawkins told her his story and they both agreed that the "pestilent old hulk" was a living hell. After he had eaten his fill and dressed, the woman packed Hawkins food for his trip and sent him on his way with "her blessing" and an extra shirt and pair of pants that had been hanging on a line to dry. Showing him the best way to travel undetected, the kind widow informed Hawkins of the location of a canoe and told him to row across the small bay to Sag Harbor; from there he could try to cross the wide sound to Rhode Island. She made only one request: that he tell no one she had helped him. Fear of the *Jersey* had spread throughout the colonies and she still had a son at home.

Hawkins found the canoe, crossed the bay and sound, and eventually arrived in Rhode Island. The young boy's incredible ordeal came to an end a few days later when he made it home. His father was not home, as he had volunteered for the war, but Hawkins was welcomed by his tearful mother, to whom he admitted that he was finally "pretty well cured this time of his sea-faring propensities."

For quite some time, Thomas Dring and an officer from Philadelphia named Lawrence had been planning to escape from the *Jersey*. Despite the concerns of all but one of their fellow officers, Dring decided to join Lawrence in cutting a hole in the side of the old, rotted ship, as young Hawkins had. It was essential, they agreed, to keep the plan a secret. No one could know outside of the small group of officers. Desperate prisoners were prone to snitching on their fellow inmates in an effort to curry favor with the guards and perhaps gain an extra ration of food or water. Someone always seemed to be awake and unable to sleep, and everyone had too much idle time on their hands, so the challenge would be to bore the hole quietly and at times when other prisoners bunking in the small, crowded gunroom would not discover it. It was a risky plan, but Dring believed it was their only chance to beat death.

The men, led by Lawrence, worked in shifts, concealing their labor by hanging a blanket over the hole. The side of the ship was four inches thick and, even though much of it was rotting, cutting through oak was difficult. They had only a single small jackknife and a gimlet.* All the officers in the mess assisted Dring and Lawrence in cutting the hole, working in rotation. It was a slow process, but

---

* A gimlet is a T-shaped tool with a screw tip used to bore holes.

eventually they neared completion. It was time to plan the moment of their escape.

The officers agreed that after squeezing through the hole and dropping down into the bay, they would wait until the last one was off the ship. Only then would they begin swimming. During their time on the upper deck, they planned the location where they would come ashore and agreed on a spot about a quarter mile away.

A few nights later, a heavy squall swept through the bay. It was time! The rain and wind would help cover their escape. At midnight, the final section of wood was cut out. The officers undressed and tied their clothing together. They crawled through the hole one at a time and passed down their clothes. Four men were out and Dring was next. But after the fourth man dropped down into the water it happened.

The guards had known about the plan all along. One of the prisoners must have tipped them off. Yet the guards did not stop the prisoners from trying to escape. Rather, in what Dring described as a "perverse" idea, they remained "vigilant" and waited in a rowboat near where the prisoners dropped into the water in order to catch them in the act and ambush the unsuspecting sailors. Musket shots rang out, freezing Dring and the other prisoners waiting quietly in the gunroom. They heard shrieks coming from the water below as the guards used bayonets and swords to finish off the escapees. Dring peered out through the hole to see what was happening, but in the darkness of the storm, he could see nothing. The prisoners began panicking, not knowing what to do, as news of the escape "ran like wildfire through the gloomy and crowded dungeons of the hulk." Dring realized how fortunate he was that he was still in the gunroom.

A few minutes later, the hatch above opened and the guards came down the ladder, dragging a wet, naked, and bloodied prisoner. It was Lawrence, and he was hurt badly. One arm had been nearly "severed" by a "cutlass," and he had also been shot. While Lawrence cried in pain, the guards informed the prisoners that they had shot him while he was holding on to the gunwale at the back of the ship and that the other three escapees were dead.

Even though candles were not permitted belowdecks after dark, the guards lit a small flame next to Lawrence. It was psychological warfare—the guards wanted the other prisoners to see Lawrence's bloodied body and his suffering. After the guards went up the ladder, prisoners crowded around Lawrence's bunk. The scene unnerved them. Dring and the other officers dressed Lawrence and, after washing his wounds, wrapped a rag around the exposed bone and flesh of his arm to try to stop the bleeding. It did not work. They also tied a wet handkerchief around his head. Dring had seen many men die on the ship, but Lawrence's painful ordeal struck terror into him, and everyone else. Amid Lawrence's shrieks of agony, few men slept that night.

In the morning, the gratings were not removed at the usual hour; the hatches remained shut. As punishment, the prisoners were given no food or water until ten o'clock, even though it was an especially hot and humid morning. The guards eventually allowed the men to eat and go to the upper deck, but never provided a surgeon and made no inquiry about Lawrence. Dring's friend lived through the night, though he was delirious in the morning. He died later that day, and his body was left on deck as an "example" to the other prisoners.

The guards made Dring and his fellow officers cover the hole they had cut in the ship with a plank and punished them by reducing their rations of food and water. Dring began working on a new plan—to attack the guards and throw them overboard.

Thomas Andros, another one of the prisoners suffering on the *Jersey* in 1781, admitted, "While on board almost every thought was occupied to invent some plan of escape; but day after day passed and none presented that I dared to put into execution." He and other prisoners knew the ship was contaminated by smallpox, yellow fever, and other diseases. He had contracted both and, although he was a man of faith, believed it was only a matter of time before he came down with another disease. Sure enough, Andros became ill again and was taken off the *Jersey* to a nearby hospital ship. Luck remained with him—he eventually recovered. However, before he was transferred back to the *Jersey*, Andros assisted the nurses with the sick prisoners and contracted yet another disease. He knew it was time—if he recovered from the present malady, he had to get off the ship.

Hope came this time in the form of an announcement by the guards of a prisoner exchange. With the men gathered on the upper deck, the names of prisoners to be exchanged were read aloud. The list included the crew from the ship on which he had served! Andros "immediately stepped forward" and announced his name, but he was informed that he was not a part of the exchange. Andros attributed the rejection to the preference by the British for prisoners "whose flesh was ready to fall from their bones" rather than "sound and healthy men." Even though Andros was weak from a bout with yellow fever and sick with another ailment, one guard growled at him, "You have not been here long enough, you are too well to be exchanged."

Andros became desperate, writing, "But the time had now come when I must be delivered from the ship, or die. I could not be delayed even a few days longer; but no plan could I think of that offered a gleam of hope. If I did escape with my life, I could see no way for it but by miracle." In "utter despair," Andros and a few other prisoners developed a desperate plan: "The next night, to steal down through a gun-port which we had managed to open . . . unbeknown to the guard, and swim ashore."

Barely able to walk, Andros worried that he might not be able to swim. Moreover, he knew that there were always informants who ratted out their fellow prisoners and that those caught trying to escape were severely punished. Such an incident had just occurred on the *Jersey*. A captain named Young from Boston had tried to escape during a prisoner exchange, hiding in a large chest belonging to one of the prisoners being exchanged. However, as the chest was being carried off the *Jersey*, another prisoner named Spicer from Providence told the guards that Young was inside the chest. Young suffered mightily at the hands of the violent guards, who were eager to make an example of him. However, the angry prisoners attacked Spicer, one of them pulling out a confiscated knife and holding it to the rat's throat. As the prisoner was about to dispatch Spicer, the guards intervened and drove the prisoners belowdecks.

The prisoners remained in an agitated state and it appears that Spicer got what was coming to him later that night. In the throes of disease and depression, Andros drew comfort from reciting a verse: "When helpers fail and foes invade, God is our all-sufficient aid." Sure enough, the aid materialized the next day in the form of a new opportunity to escape: the guards were selecting prisoners to join a work party charged with getting water and carrying it back to the *Jersey.*

Andros believed it was the work of God, "who had something more for me to do than to perish in that ship." The sailing master, a man named Emery, was taking the launch ashore. "Without really considering what I said and without the least expectation of success," Andros stood and yelled, "Mr. Emery may I go on shore with you after water?" Emery agreed, and Andros clambered into the small boat. As they were about to shove off, however, a prisoner on the upper deck hollered, "What is that sick man going on shore for?" To his horror, Andros was ordered back aboard the *Jersey* by the guards. But he had been called back because he had forgotten his "great coat," without which he would freeze in the chilly October wind.

Once more in the rowboat, Andros grabbed an oar and tried to be useful. He did not want to be kicked off the boat. He was nearly taken off the work detail again when one of the guards ordered, "Give me the oar, you are not able to use it, you are too unwell." The oar was yanked out of his hands but, surprisingly, the guard allowed Andros to remain on the launch.

On land, some men in the small work party were given baskets and told to collect apples. Others were sent to fetch water. Because he was so weak, Andros was initially instructed to remain in the launch, but Emery said loudly, "This fresh air will be of service to you." The guards then told Andros to go get apples.

Andros had to climb a slope roughly thirty feet high to get to the apple orchard. "My state of health was such," he admitted, that he almost "did not make it." They walked past a "dense swamp of young maples and other bushes" a half mile away. While the other prisoners went ahead of him, Andros hid in the swamp. He was not sure what to do next. He had not thought that far ahead. In every direction there were villages full of loyalists, and a British sentry patrolled the edge of the orchard. Fortunately for Andros, it appeared that the sentry's job was to protect the apples rather than look for runaway prisoners. There in the swamp, Andros found a "huge log, twenty feet in length, having lain there for many years." He believed the log was a godsend, "spread over on both sides with such a dense covering of green running briars as to be impervious to the eye." He hid under it.

The work party returned to the launch and, after a short wait, sailed back to the *Jersey* without Andros. Years later he learned that when the guards had questioned why one of the prisoners was not present to return to the *Jersey*, another guard dismissed the concern, saying Andros was so sick and weak that "he will never live to go a mile."

Andros remained hidden for several hours. A storm blew in and it began to rain, but the old log offered him some protection. As he waited, he felt guilty for abandoning his fellow prisoners and worried that his escape might result in punishment for Emery and the others in the work party. He vowed then and there that if he lived, he would write a letter to Emery apologizing and explaining that the sailing master had been "God's chosen instrument to save me." Presumably, a correspondence with Emery after the war explains how Andros learned of the guards' conversation about him. After the rain subsided, he headed away from the bay and to freedom, looking back one last time at the old, black ship with "greatest horror." What he saw motivated him to keep moving.

That first night on the run was difficult. Andros recalled that it "rained in torrents," which made walking difficult. But under cover of darkness he headed to the east end of Long Island. It was a difficult trek in the moonless night. He tripped often, became entangled in bushes, and was shivering from the cold, wet night. He was thankful he was wearing his greatcoat; it most likely kept him alive. Again, Andros interpreted it as divine intervention.

Andros found a road and followed it through the night, ready if need be to duck into the woods that lined the path. In the predawn hours he saw another person on the road and barely had time to seek cover until the person passed. Andros vowed to be more careful. One precaution he adopted was to cover his head with a handkerchief (he had lost his hat in the swamp) in order to hide his sickly appearance.

In the morning, Andros arrived at a village. He heard the fife and drums of soldiers but was fortunate that the poor weather kept most people inside. It also gave him an excuse to hide his gaunt body and his face under the coat. Near collapse, suffering from the lingering effects of yellow fever and hunger, he stumbled through town, close to giving up. But he saw a barn. As he was about to go inside, Andros heard voices in the barn. He mustered the strength to turn and run away. Good fortune remained, and Andros found another barn outside of the village that was empty. Hay was stacked high in the surrounding fields and he found enough of it inside to make himself a bed in the upper loft. Exhausted, Andros sank into the comfortable, warm hay and quickly fell asleep.

The next morning he awoke stiff, hungry, and still wet. He also awoke with a cold to go along with the yellow fever. It had stopped raining, but cold northern winds blew into the barn and across the fields. Andros knew he had to be on his way, but opted to rest a bit longer in the barn. As he was about to shut his eyes, a young woman entered the barn to milk a cow. Fortunately, she did not go up into the loft. When the woman finished, Andros came down from the loft and snuck out of the barn. Only a half mile away, he saw a sight that nearly brought him to his knees in fear and repulsion: a group of escaped prisoners from the floating dungeons had been caught and were being marched back to Wallabout Bay.

Andros melted into the thick woods, reminding himself once again to be more careful. There he stripped off his coat and clothing and laid them out in the sun to dry. He rested an entire day. Happily, it had stopped raining and his cold did not worsen. Before sunset, Andros dressed and headed back out to the road. As he did, two British units marched around the corner. Rather than run, which would have aroused suspicion, he simply pulled the collar of his coat up around his face and walked casually past them.

The routine of traveling by night, hiding by day, and resting in barns or woods continued for days. An unexpected incident nearly ended his escape when he was chased by a pack of dogs. There were more close calls, but he kept walking. Every few days he managed to find apples and vegetables in barns, and once he came upon an orchard of pear trees. His gleanings kept him alive, but they were never enough to quell his hunger, and the pangs eventually prompted Andros to risk capture.

Driven by hunger and frustration, one night he approached a house lit by candles, and he knocked at the door. A woman appeared. She seemed to know immediately that he had been a prisoner, but revealed to him that she was a patriot and not a loyalist. Andros asked the woman for milk, but she replied that British soldiers in the area had consumed all of it. However, she gave him food and told him how to avoid British soldiers stationed in the area. Andros saw the gesture as another act of providence.

Not long afterward, Andros was again nearly captured. To get out of the cold rain, he had snuck into another barn, but was caught by the farmer. Andros apologized and asked for food. The farmer and his wife took him into their home and fed him. They recognized from his ghostly appearance that he had been on the prison ships and told him they opposed the British. Two other escaped prisoners had arrived at their farm days earlier, presumably also from the prison ships. It seemed that everyone was aware of the *Jersey*, which worried the farmer. Citing his concern that a loyalist neighbor or soldier might see the escaped prisoner in his home, the farmer asked Andros to be on his way. Before leaving, Andros gave the farmer the three coins he had in his pocket to thank them for feeding him and not turning him in.

Andros was racked with guilt about having stolen food over the previous several days. He originally had justified it as an act of desperation, but came to believe that his behavior would "not stand the test of the Day of Judgment." God had taken care of his needs, even though he was unworthy. But then another sign of providence appeared. While seeking shelter in another barn, Andros found it held several horses and realized too late that it was a military stable. Before he could escape, a soldier appeared holding a sword and asked, "Who goes there?" Andros responded, "A friend," and then asked in as calm a voice as he could muster, "Where is the well? I want to get some water." Amazingly, the soldier did not arrest him but showed him to the well.

Lying and quick thinking would again save his life when four soldiers found him picking apples in a field. "Have you any cider?" they asked, mistaking him for the farmer. "No," replied Andros, "but we expect to make some next week; call then and we shall be glad to treat you." But the ordeal of his escape had become almost too much to bear. Andros's nerves were worn from the many brushes with recapture. He began to "sink under such trials," his soul pained by his constant thievery, the lies he needed to tell, and his inability to repay the poor farmers who fed him. And his fever returned, draining the little strength he still had. Andros could go no longer. He collapsed and everything went black.

Upon awakening, Andros discovered that a family had found and sheltered him. In his state of delirium, he told them the truth about his escape. Luckily for him, they turned out to be patriots, like the other families he had encountered on his escape. After burning his ragged clothing, they gave him new garments, allowed him to bathe, and showed him to a spare bedroom. It was the first real bed Andros enjoyed since initially leaving Connecticut. In the morning, the couple sent him on his way, rested and with a full stomach. Their charity was too much for Andros to bear. Finally, after many days on the run and this act of mercy, he broke down and sobbed uncontrollably. Andros would later say he learned a lesson in compassion and humility.

Arriving in Sag Harbor on the end of Long Island, Andros encountered two of his crewmates who had also escaped the *Jersey*. The three of them found passage on a fishing boat whose captain agreed to drop them off in New London. He was nearly home, he thought. But the boat was stopped by an American privateer who suspected the fishermen of trading with the British. The privateer threatened to fire on them unless their captain allowed the ship to be inspected in New London. The privateer's suspicions proved correct: the fishermen had in fact been trading illegally and even carried the confiscated wares on board!

Andros could not believe the turn of events. He had survived the *Jersey*, the long trek to freedom, and countless close encounters, only to wind up facing the wrath of fellow American privateers. However, on the way to New London the fishermen managed to elude the privateer and escape. Andros was horrified to discover that both privateers and fishermen preyed on their fellow Americans, looting any ship they could. The captain did, though, make good on his promise to put the three former prisoners ashore in Connecticut. In port, Andros observed the crew members accost a woman and steal her necklace. Andros was disgusted by the entire situation.

He had traveled 150 miles and made it to Norwich by the end of October. At that point his fever returned and Andros found himself too sick to go any farther. To come this far only to die so close to home would be a sign that he had fallen from God's favor. But Andros's eldest brother had heard news that prisoners had arrived in Norwich and had traveled to see if his little brother was among them. Andros was finally taken home and reunited with his mother, but his fever "raged" for another three weeks, reducing him to a state of "derangement." A preacher and physician were summoned to the house. Both announced that Andros would soon meet his maker. The family began preparations for the funeral.

Somehow Andros recovered. He attributed his relapse to God's wrath because he had stopped praying. Filled with "guilt, remorse, terror, and despair," Andros asked God for forgiveness and promised that if he lived, he would devote his life to serving Him. As spring was about to arrive, Andros's health finally recovered enough for him to make good on his promise. He became a preacher.

—— 16 ——

Turning Point

American, on thy own plains expire,
A glorious victim to the hostile fire;
In thy own ship expect the deadly blow,
But be no captive to this tyrant foe;
Yield not alive to glut their greedy jaws,
First faint, first perish in thy country's cause;
Prefer to meet the winged, wasteful ball,
And cut to atoms for lov'd freedom fall.

—Philip Freneau, "The British Prison-Ship" (1781)

In the words of the historian John Ferling, "Perhaps more than any defining moment in American history, the War of Independence is swathed in beliefs not borne out by the facts." Indeed, even though the Revolution is often "a child's first encounter with history," there are many misconceptions about the founding of the nation.

Not all Britons supported the war, just as not all colonists in America favored independence. Yet mobilization across the colonies to fight was quite impressive, especially considering that most people lived in sparsely populated farming villages and that there were few newspapers and roads. For example, when word spread on April 19, 1775, that the British army was marching from Boston to Lexington, hundreds of militiamen scrambled to arms within a matter of hours. The number soon turned into thousands, as the farmers, blacksmiths, and clerks who constituted the ragtag force repelled the British army and saved the arsenal in Concord. Days later, roughly sixteen thousand men from four colonies in New England answered the call of duty and assembled outside Boston. Massachusetts alone organized twelve regiments, each numbering from roughly 450 to 800, while 6,000 volunteers from Connecticut went to war that spring, a number that amounted to fully one-quarter of the colony's males of military age.

Perhaps over 100,000 men served in colonial forces. In 1781, George Washington commented on his countrymen, "A large majority are still firmly attached to the independence States, [and] abhor a reunion with Great Britain." These numbers ebbed and flowed throughout the war. Farmers, for instance, were hesitant to fight because it meant abandoning their fields for an entire growing season or longer, and most battles were fought in the spring through the fall. Consequently, many of those who came forward to fight were those who had the least to lose: recent immigrants who were young and poor, without a profession or land. A shocking one in four militiamen from Pennsylvania were young immigrants living in abject poverty.

As the war dragged on, losses mounted, and funding all but disappeared, American commanders often struggled with shortages of manpower. The colonies resorted to offers of money, clothing, land, and short enlistments in order to field armies, just as the Continental Congress was forced to address the revolving door of troop strength in 1777 by increasing the length of enlistments from three months to three years or until the conclusion of hostilities, whichever came first. There was even talk of a draft throughout the country, and in 1778 several states began conscripting men to supplement their volunteer units. At the same time, New England's political leaders began enlisting black soldiers.

Not only were there fluctuations in troop strength during the war, but we will likely never know the exact number of colonists who supported the Revolution. What is certain is that some did while others remained loyal subjects to the Crown. Still others were likely conflicted about the issue or perhaps wanted only to continue selling their crops to England or importing goods from the mother country. One well-known theory on the topic is known as "the Adams Third," which postulated that about one-third of colonists supported the war, one-third opposed it, and another third were uncertain or tried to remain neutral. The "rule" comes courtesy of John Adams's postwar writings. Said Adams in a letter to a Massachusetts senator in 1815, "I should say that a full one third were averse to the revolution. . . . An opposite third . . . gave themselves up to an enthusiastic gratitude. . . . The middle third, composed principally of the yeomanry, the soundest part of the nation, and always averse to war, were rather lukewarm."

Letters written in 1813 between Adams and Thomas McKean, a former member of the Continental Congress, also discussed the degree of support for independence. While Adams is a very reliable source, his oft-repeated estimates may be about public support for the French Revolution, not the American Revolution. The great Founder was not clear in his "meandering" letter, which touched on many issues. Yet over time the number has often been repeated by scholars.* But Adams and McKean did discuss matters closer to home, with McKean recalling that "the great mass of the people were zealous in the cause of America" and Adams countering by reminding his friend of the strong loyalist sentiment of the time.

Various estimates have been offered by historians such as Paul H. Smith, who suggested that roughly 16 percent of the population were loyalists. This matches the estimate by historian Robert Calhoon, who believed loyalists numbered about 15 to 20 percent of adult white

---

* "The Adams Third" was popularized in the famous book *The Struggle for American Independence*, written by Sydney George Fisher at the dawn of the twentieth century.

men, while just over 40 percent of the population supported the cause of independence.

It is difficult to determine the views of the average citizen, as paper was exceedingly rare and prohibitively expensive at the time, many people were illiterate, and newspapers seldom recorded the views of regular people. Nevertheless, at the time the Declaration of Independence was written, it appears that patriots held a slight edge over loyalists, at least among the colonies' political and economic elite. As Adams summed up the debate in a letter to McKean, "Divided we ever have been, and ever must be." The consensus among historians that the public was divided in its support of the Revolution echoes Adams's clever quip.

While there appears to have been more support for the war than opposition to it, "at most not more than a bare majority" backed the Revolution. Many recent immigrants from Europe may have had little loyalty to either side and probably tried to avoid involvement in the war altogether. In terms of raw numbers, the historian Thomas Fleming suggested that there were perhaps 75,000 to 100,000 loyalists in America during the war. The vast majority of them moved away at the end of the war. But not all loyalists fled, fought, or switched their allegiances. The loyalist Anglican minister Jonathan Boucher, for instance, did abandon his parish in Maryland as the Revolution was beginning but maintained his loyalty to both Britain and God. The reverend continued to preach in America, though he did so with loaded pistols in the pulpit!

Without a majority of the population and local political establishment behind them, Britain was in an impossible position: despite their victories over the Continental Army, they could only control those parts of America where they had a military presence. British forces seized Philadelphia in 1777, Savannah the next year, and Charleston in 1780. But their rule was unenforceable outside of those communities. Foremost among the British strongholds was New York City, including the surrounding areas such as Brooklyn and the rest of Long Island. The loyalist population there grew as pro-British refugees from around the country fled to New York seeking protection from harassment, public humiliation, and the confiscation of property at the hands of zealous patriots and rowdy Tea Party mischief-makers.

Loyalists were found throughout the colonies, including farmers in New York, German immigrants in Pennsylvania, Scots in North Carolina, Anglican clergy in Connecticut, and Iroquois Indians. Many of these loyalists, considering themselves to be war "refugees," even fought alongside the British army.* Scholars have put the number of loyalists serving in the British army at nineteen thousand, along with another ten thousand fighting in loyalist militia units known as "associations." Such numbers are high when one considers the limited population living in the colonies at the time.

The exact number of Americans who were loyalists versus patriots will never be fully known; nor will the extent to which certain events contributed to the fluctuations in public support for the war effort. However, it is undeniable that one of the primary factors in rallying patriots to the cause was the *Jersey*.

As young Christopher Hawkins said of the *Jersey*, "Of those confined within her walls, but few, comparatively, ever returned to their homes." Hawkins went on to note that "occasionally a poor sufferer would escape to tell his dismal story to his countrymen, but such instances were rare." Yet when this did occur, the harrowing tales of life aboard the Hell Ship alarmed the public. Likewise, the sight of emaciated, diseased prisoners arriving home ghost-like after a negotiated prisoner exchange was hard to forget. Moreover, because the British purposely sought to exchange only the sickest among the prison population, for every prisoner who survived the exchange there were often several who died en route or soon after making it home, which only increased the public's shock and anger.

---

* Loyalist units fought at such battles as Camden, Cowpens, Guilford Court House, King's Mountain, and elsewhere.

Newspapers throughout the colonies, but most especially in Pennsylvania, New York, and Connecticut, began printing disquieting stories of the survivors. As early as January 1777, the *Freeman's Journal* reported, "General Howe has discharged all the privates who were prisoners in New York. Half he sent to the world of spirits for want of food: the others he hath sent to warn their countrymen of the danger of falling into his hands, and to convince them by ocular demonstration, that it is infinitely better to be slain in battle, than to be taken prisoner by British brutes, whose tender mercies are cruelties." The prison ships continued to serve as psychological weapons of terror, none more so than the *Jersey*, even though the British commanders' plans ended up producing the opposite result: for every colonial worried about the threat of imprisonment on the ghostly ship, several others were inspired by British cruelty to take up arms.

Survivors also told stories about how the British shipped prisoners to faraway lands. Holt's *New York Journal*, for example, published the warning, "As every rebel, who is taken prisoner, has incurred the pain of death by the law martial, it is said that Government will charter several transports, after their arrival at Boston to carry the culprits to the East Indies for the Company's service." The article went on to say that patriots would be "forced into slavery with the East India Company" and that it was "the intention" of the king to put to death any "ring-leaders" of independence.

The public clamored for news about the prison ships, and papers responded. On March 22, 1781, the *Connecticut Journal* proudly proclaimed, "Captain Calhoon with four others escaped from a prison ship to Long Island in a boat, March 8, notwithstanding they were fired on from the prison and hospital ships, and pursued by guard boats from three in the afternoon to seven in the evening." Another newspaper in the state, the *Connecticut Gazette*, announced the details of a prisoner exchange on January 8, 1777: "A flag of truce vessel arrived at Milford . . . from New York, having about 200 prisoners." The article described their "rueful countenances" and the "ill treatment they received in New York" before noting that "twenty died on the passage, and twenty since they landed."

A few years later in nearby New London, the local newspaper reported in the winter of 1782 that "130 prisoners landed here from New York, December third, in most deplorable condition. A great part are since dead, and the survivors so debilitated that they will drag out a miserable existence." The paper declared that it would "melt the most obdurate heart to see these miserable objects landed at our wharves sick and dying, and the few rags they have on covered with vermin and their own excrements." The papers painted shocking visuals for their readers.

One prisoner managed to get a letter off the ship, but was too afraid to reveal his name. The letter was reprinted in 1780 in the *Connecticut Gazette*. The touching story began, "I am now a prisoner on board the *Falmouth*, a place the most dreadful; we are confined so that we have not room even to lie down all at once to sleep. It is the most horrible, cursed, hole that can be thought of." Another prisoner gave his name, Christopher Vail. He was on the *Jersey* in 1781, and recounted for the paper's readers what happened when someone died on the ship: "When a man died he was carried up on the forecastle and laid there until the next morning at 8 o'clock when they were all lowered down the ship sides by a rope round them in the same manner as tho' they were beasts. There was 8 died of a day while I was there. They were carried on shore in heaps and hove out the boat on the wharf, then taken across a hand barrow, carried to the edge of the bank, where a hole was dug 1 or 2 feet deep and all hove in together."

Robert Sheffield of Stonington, Connecticut, who escaped from a different prison ship in 1778, told a similar story in July 1778. In the article, he claimed that "the air was so foul that at times a lamp could not be kept burning." The result was that prisoners who had succumbed to disease and starvation in the dark holds "were not missed until they had been dead ten days."

Yet another letter from a prisoner appeared in the *Pennsylvania Packet* in 1781. In it, the man, who was on board the *Jersey*, concluded, "There is nothing but death or entering into the British service before me." The letter stated that most of the men in his crew had died aboard the ship and that they buried between six and eleven men a day, with "200 more sick and falling sick every day; the sickness is the yellow fever, small-pox, and in short every thing else that can be mentioned." The prisoner ended his poignant tale with these words: "I had almost forgot to tell you, that our morning's salutation is, 'Rebels! Turn out your dead!'"

Several newspapers alleged that the British were purposely "starving our people" in order to entice the prisoners to join His Majesty's army and instill terror into the American public. It worked, but in a way not foreseen by the British. Public opinion across the land was changing. Anti-British sentiment was being fueled by, among other incidents, the alarming stories about the *Jersey*.

British leaders had underestimated the support for the war among colonists, as they underestimated the blowback from their brutal prison ship policies. The same phenomenon had occurred in response to the Stamp Act, Intolerable Acts, and Boston Massacre years before. Their violent policies undermined the legitimacy of British rule, especially when force had been a measure of last resort for the colonists. Conducting "a war of ravage and destruction" only created "an irrecoverable hatred" among colonists. More than the heroics of John Paul Jones or George Washington, British mistakes and the change in public opinion helped the Revolutionary cause by making it a "just war" in response to injustices.

A number of events helped rally colonials to the cause of war, including Paul Revere's depiction of the Boston Massacre, the Committees of Correspondence established by colonial leaders to organize resistance, and Thomas Paine's *Common Sense.** Indeed, a revolution

---

* General Washington ordered his officers to read *Common Sense* to the army in order to build support for the war.

rooted in concepts such as "the will of the people" and "representative government" required both broad public support and an ongoing commitment to the effort by the people. Ironically, the *Jersey* would play a role in both matters.

To counter such damning stories, which appeared with increasing regularity in American newspapers, the British resorted to propaganda. Like the leaders of the Revolution, they too needed to sway the hearts and minds of both colonials and taxpayers back in England who footed the bill for the war. And so they did. Newspapers whipped up anti-American feelings in England, labeling the "disloyal" colonists "outlaws," "rebels," and "traitors."

One effort involved denying that the prisons and notorious hulks were that bad. William Cunningham, the monstrous prison warden, appears to have forced prisoners to write complimentary accounts of their incarceration. Such was the case when the pro-British newspaper *Gaine's Mercury* published an article on November 25, 1776, saying of the prisoners, "Their situation must have been doubly deplorable, but for the humanity of the king's officers. Every possible attention has been given, considering their great numbers and necessary confinement, to alleviate their distress arising from guilt, sickness, and poverty." The New York–based newspaper repeatedly made the case for the British, inventing fictitious accounts of the prisons.

Another approach was to try to use the suffering in prisons and aboard the *Jersey* against the Americans. On November 25, 1776, the loyalist newspaper *Gaine's Mercury* published a propaganda piece that claimed, "There are now 5,000 prisoners in town, many of them half naked. Congress deserts the poor wretches,—have sent them neither provisions nor clothing, not paid attention to their distress nor that of their families." Likewise, British officers and guards on the prison ships regularly told the prisoners that their government and countrymen had given up on them. Prisoners were informed that General Washington refused to agree to prisoner exchanges because he did not care about the men on board the old hulks. Another loyalist newspaper claimed to have letters from American sailors who said they felt "deserted by our own countrymen." It went on to claim that the British wanted to negotiate more prisoner exchanges but Washington did not.

The reality of the matter was that the British admiralty and commissaries regularly refused Washington's requests to inspect the prison ships. Instead, they conducted their own "investigation" into the allegations of neglect, abuse, and murder on the ships. It was headed by Captain George Dawson. On February 2, 1781, Dawson informed a three-member naval board of inquiry that he found no evidence of poor treatment aboard the prison ships. Incredibly, he even claimed the prisoners were well fed and received "full allowances" of bread, beef, pork, and butter. Captain Dawson also denied that the ships were overcrowded and blamed the prisoners for the high death toll, saying the "sickness at present among the prisoners arises from a want of cloathing and a proper attention in themselves in their own cleanliness." The report, titled "The Extensive and Impartial Enquiry on Board His Majesty's Prison Ship *Jersey*," was sent to Washington and also contained coerced confessionals from the prisoners. The wicked commissary David Sproat conducted fake investigations as well, claiming that conditions on the prison ships were good, except that the prisoners needed more clothing.

Furious with the outright lies and propaganda, Washington sent a letter a few days later saying that the British seamen in American possession would, from then on, receive the exact same substandard rations. Worried about the reprisal, Admiral Mariot Arbuthnot responded to Washington's letter in April, writing, "I give you my honor, that the transaction was conducted with such strict care and impartiality that you may rely on its validity." The preponderance of evidence suggested otherwise, and Washington knew it. The British concocted such reports, coerced prisoners into giving false testimony, and refused independent verification and access to the ships. As one American commissary complained in 1782, "I was refused permission to visit the prison-ships, for which I can conceive no other reason than your being ashamed to have these graves of our seamen seen by one who dared to represent the horrors of them to his countrymen."

On the other hand, there were several reports on the conditions of British prisons and prison ships organized by colonial politicians and military leaders. One of the earliest efforts was led by Major Levi Wells, who collected affidavits from escaped and paroled prisoners, and issued his findings to the Connecticut Legislature in early December 1776. The colony's governor, Jonathan Trumbull, was so disturbed by the report that he notified General Washington of the plight of the prisoners. "Their confinement is so close and crowded that they have scarce room to move or lie down, the air stagnant and corrupt; numbers dying daily," he wrote. Trumbull also received a letter from a Connecticut sailor named Oliver Babcock, who was imprisoned aboard the *Whitby* in Wallabout Bay. The letter, written in January 1777, was filled with such painful descriptions of suffering that it prompted Trumbull to urge Washington to conduct prisoner exchanges.

Numerous other reports were based on affidavits and depositions, such as those by the Committee for Detecting Conspiracies in New York and the Maryland Council of Safety, who found evidence that prisoners were "most cruelly and Inhumanely treated, confined in churches without fire, and Dying in great numbers." Another study in 1777 by the Pennsylvania Council of Safety claimed in a letter of "Utmost Importance" to General Washington that, astonishingly, more than eleven thousand American prisoners had already died from a lack of food, water, and medical attention, and that the numbers continued to grow.

Across the Atlantic, more accurate reports about the war and prison ships began finding their way to the public and political leaders. One result was that even the noted British statesman William Pitt, the Earl of Chatham, questioned the war. Pitt, a former prime minister and influential leader during the French and Indian War in America, proclaimed in 1777, "If I were an American, as I am an Englishman, while a foreign troop was landed in my country, I never would lay down my arms—never—never—never!" And the colonists did not.

Even at the beginning of the war, General Thomas Gage admitted that his troops were experiencing increasing opposition, to the extent that they were virtually "surrounded" in New England by an army of angry farmers. One British soldier observed, "The Americans lose 600 men in a day, and eight days later 1,200 others rejoin the army; whereas to replace ten men in the English army is quite an undertaking." Likewise, as the historian John Shy described, "From the British viewpoint, the militia was the virtually inexhaustible reservoir of rebel military manpower." And so it was. By the end of the war, the British found themselves under constant harassment by guerrilla-style attacks. It was a "constant skirmish" wherever the British went in the colonies. In the words of General Nathanael Greene, one of George Washington's best commanders, the Americans' motto was "Fight, get beat, rise, and fight again!"

The longer the war dragged on, the more the British economy and trade suffered and support for the war back home plummeted. The British were not able to restore order by armed force alone and they never really seriously considered another approach. More important, they lost the battle for the hearts and minds of the colonists. It is safe to say that toward the end of the war most Americans no longer were interested in negotiating an end to hostilities or a return to British rule.

As one historical account described, "Associations of intense horror are linked with the memory and the records of the cruelties practiced and sufferings endured in the prisons and prison ships at New York." Foremost among them was the Hell Ship, which, according to a survivor, was so woeful that "for years, the very name of 'the old *Jersey*,' seemed to strike a terror to the hearts of those whose necessities required them to venture upon the ocean." Story after gruesome story filled the pages of newspapers and were whispered with chilling effect in pubs, shops, and homes throughout the colonies, thus making the ship notorious. Another historical account stated in stark terms that "the mortality which prevailed on board her was well known throughout the country. . . . To be confined within her dungeons, was considered equal to a sentence of death, from which but little hope of escape remained." The mere mention of the *Jersey* struck fear into patriots everywhere.

Christopher Hawkins, Thomas Andros, and other escapees found this to be the case while they were on the run. Colonists they encountered, even if assistance was rendered, recoiled at the realization that they were meeting a survivor of the infamous ghost ship. The woman who gave Hawkins clothing during his escape was so afraid of getting caught that she told him he must not acknowledge her help; if asked, she said, he should lie and tell anyone he encountered that he stole the items. She did not want to be seen as aiding a prisoner from the *Jersey*, lest she be labeled a patriot or risk her son being sent to its wretched holds. The prisoner Thomas Dring even noted that a popular nickname for yellow fever became "the Old Jersey fever" and that both the term and awareness of the ship as a floating Hell were "well known throughout the whole country."

These grim stories had a devastating effect on the British war effort. They sparked outrage in the colonies and built support for the Revolution. As the morbid truth behind Britain's prison policies became known, and as people learned the barbaric details about life on the *Jersey* and the ship's shockingly high death toll, a public outcry for retribution and justice erupted. It might be said to have been the *Jersey* effect.

---- 17 ----

Freedom

Remembrance shudders at this scene of fears,
Still in my view some tyrant chief appears,
Some base-born Hessian slave walks threatening by,
Some servile Scot, with murder in his eye,
Still haunts my sight, as vainly they bemoan
Rebellions manag'd so unlike their own.

—Philip Freneau, "The British Prison-Ship" (1781)

Many prisoners died on the *Jersey*, and a few managed to escape, but others were released through prisoner exchanges. The Continental Congress had favored exchanges since the beginning of the war, passing a measure for prisoner swaps on December 2, 1775. As was mentioned earlier, a protocol was established whereby equivalent numbers of prisoners would be exchanged of similar rank—an officer for an officer, a soldier for a soldier.

One of the first exchanges involved ships and was described in the *Virginia Gazette*: "The prisoners taken at Lexington were exchanged. The wounded privates were soon sent on board the *Levity*. At about three a signal was made by the *Levity* that they were ready to deliver up our prisoners, upon which General Putnam and Major Moncrief went to the ferry, where they received nine prisoners." The newspaper wrote that a few prisoners cried with joy. Nevertheless, General Washington wrote to General Gage, his British counterpart, angry that the men had been jailed "with no consideration of their rank" and were not "treated with care and kindness."

Most of the exchanges were organized by cartels, who collected food and clothing for the prisoners, negotiated the time and date of the exchange, and took delivery of the prisoners under a flag of truce. The *Connecticut Gazette* chronicled one such effort by a local cartel that was supported by the Connecticut Assembly, who assisted them in gathering "a sufficient supply" of shirts and pants for the prisoners.

Several colonial governors, such as Jonathan Trumbull of Connecticut, organized their own cartels and exchanges, as did towns such as New London. Governor Trumbull wrote to General Washington asking for help in supporting the cartels, pleading, "In New York between three and four thousand prisoners, the privates all close confined, upon about half allowance; great number of them almost naked; their confinement is so close and crowded that they have scarce room to move or lie down, the air stagnate and corrupt; numbers dying daily." Governor George Clinton of New York was also an ardent advocate for exchanges, providing food, clothing, and funds to them from 1777 all the way until the final months of the British occupation of New York. As late as September 1783, during the final days of the war, he was still funding relief missions to the prison ships.

A number of other cartels were established, including a few that operated from the beginning of the war. In one such instance, a cartel from New London negotiated with General Howe in November 1776 to exchange sailors. Another cartel from the town was able to obtain the release of 136 prisoners from Connecticut in February 1779. Sadly, sixteen of the prisoners died on the way home and another sixty were so weak and ill that they could not even stand. The exchanges were covered by newspapers, which reported the gruesome details of the treatment of prisoners and conditions aboard the prison ships. The account rallied the people of New London and elsewhere to demand more exchanges. And it happened.

According to a New London newspaper, that August the town's cartel secured the release of "five or six hundred American prisoners . . . chiefly from New England," followed by another 117 in September 1780 and 130 in December 1781. As the New London paper reported, these men were in the "most deplorable condition; great part since dead, and the survivors so debilitated that they will drag out a miserable existence." The British did not even try to clean or assist the prisoners during such exchanges, reflecting their attitude toward their former colonists. As another report stated, one of the cartels returned in September 1779 with 180 prisoners whose "countenances indicate that they have undergone every conceivable inhumanity." The men had been on the *Jersey*.

Some of the earliest descriptions of the suffering and brutality aboard the prison ships came from newspaper reports of prisoner exchanges. Such reports only further incited revolution and emboldened the cartels, of which those in New London were among the most active and effective. They also prompted the Continental Congress to initiate an official inquiry into the prison ships in April 1777. The findings were disturbing. "The prisoners, instead of that humane treatment which those taken by the United States experienced," the report found, "were in general treated with the greatest barbarity. Many of them were kept near four days without food altogether. . . . Multitudes died in prison." The report concluded in flourishing terms that such brutality was "never known to happen in any similar case in a Christian country."

Anger and impatience with British policies were growing throughout the colonies. The public demanded more exchanges. One of the frustrated leaders was General Samuel Holden Parsons, who had been born in Connecticut and raised in Massachusetts. Parsons even went so far as to develop a plan in May 1777 to conduct a military raid in New York to rescue the prisoners. Although Washington cared deeply for the prisoners and was emotionally torn by the situation, he disapproved of the lawyer-turned-general's plan and rejected it. Despite the growing support for the war and exchanges, Washington had little choice save to back the difficult but strategic decision that exchanging dying farmers and blacksmiths who had volunteered for service for relatively healthy, professional soldiers benefited the British. As he stated in a letter to the Continental Congress, "It may be thought contrary to our interest to go into an exchange, as the enemy would derive more immediate advantage from it than we should. I cannot doubt that Congress will authorize me through commissioners to settle a cartel, any resolutions heretofore to the contrary notwithstanding." Intense pressure was building on both sides for additional, massive exchanges.

Then entered an unexpected development in the form of Admiral Sir George Rodney, the man believed to have ordered the *Jersey* converted from hospital ship to floating prison because it was "unfit" and "totally useless." In 1780, Rodney seized fourteen hundred American sailors and, reflecting the earlier policy of using the hellish prison ships as a psychological weapon of terror, announced that capturing additional prisoners and refusing to release them would weaken the American navy and deter privateers from joining the war. He also maintained that the Americans were not worthy of exchanges, as he indicated in a letter to the Admiralty: "The Wretches with which their Privateers are Mann'd have no principal whatever, they live by Piracy." Rodney complained that, when exchanged "out of humanity to return to their families and live by honest Industry, they forget the Mercy that had been shown them, and instantly return to renew their Acts of Piracy."

Rodney's views were shared by Admiral Mariot Arbuthnot and Commissary David Sproat, who had long advocated harsh treatment of prisoners and forcibly pressing them into the service of the Royal Navy. Accordingly, during Admiral Rodney's tenure with the Royal Navy, more prisoners were captured and fewer were exchanged. The prisoner population on the ships exploded and conditions worsened.

At the same time, British wardens and commissaries such as Joshua Loring, William Cunningham, and David Sproat viewed the cartels and exchanges as a way of making money. As one historical account of the negotiations noted, "It is a known fact, also, that whenever an exchange was to take place, the preference was always given to those who had, or could procure, the most money to present to the commissaries who conducted the exchange." But the Americans responded by demanding payment as well. The British proved willing to pay when it came to senior officers even though, ironically, it contributed to the high costs of the war and helped provide funding for the Americans.

With the war in its final, fitful throes, one would expect both sides to have embraced prisoner exchanges. But even after 1781 there were still political, military, and personal impediments to prisoner exchanges. Thousands of Americans continued to suffer aboard the floating dungeons. Hope came in the form of Admiral Arbuthnot resigning his post after becoming ill in 1781 and returning to England, and the appointment of Admiral Robert Digby that September as commander of the North American station. It would be Digby who would end up presiding over the British evacuation of New York in late 1783.

Not only was Digby more inclined toward exchanges, but after General Lord Charles Cornwallis surrendered at Yorktown in 1781, the British were desperate to secure the release of their soldiers and officers. As General Washington remarked in a letter, "There is scarce any price which they would not give for their veteran Troops now prisoners." Admiral Digby worried about the "distressed Situation" of British prisoners who would be treated as the American prisoners had been treated, and so he signaled a shift in policy governing releases and exchanges. Still, the British continued to raid American ships seeking additional prisoners and possible recruits. Washington, aware that the Royal Navy was targeting "every thing that floats on the face of the Waters" during the summer of 1782, understood that the British were still playing games with prisoners.

On March 25, 1782, Parliament finally declared Americans to be "prisoners of war," a designation of much importance. A month later, Benjamin Franklin eagerly submitted a report from France on the benefits of the law. "The Parliament of Britain have just passed an act for exchanging American prisoners. They have near eleven hundred in the jails of England and Ireland, all committed as charged with high treason. The act is to empower the King, notwithstanding such commitments, to consider them as prisoners of war, according to the law of nations, and exchange them as such." Franklin gushed with the good news that "this seems to be giving up their pretensions of considering us as rebellious subjects, and is a kind of acknowledgement of our independence. Transports are now taking up to carry back to their country the poor, brave fellows who have borne for years their cruel captivity, rather than serve our enemies and an equal number of English are to be delivered in return."

One of the many prisoners exchanged at the end of the war was Andrew Sherburne, who was clinging to life after bouts with various diseases. A schooner dispatched from a cartel in Rhode Island arrived at the *Jersey* in February 1782. Prisoners were ordered on deck, and they waited anxiously as names were read aloud. However, when Sherburne's name was read, he was not on the *Jersey*. Suffering from yet another illness, he had been taken off the ship and put aboard a nearby hospital ship. Sherburne nearly missed being exchanged, but at the last minute one of the prisoners announced that his fellow prisoner was still alive and was on the hospital ship. Surprisingly, the guards brought Sherburne to the schooner at anchor next to the old floating prison.

Filled with prisoners, the schooner sailed for Newport, Rhode Island. There they disembarked, but many, like Sherburne, were barely able to walk. The weather was cold, and Sherburne and a few of his crewmates went to a bakery to warm themselves. Fortunately for them, the baker was a kind man who invited the men to his home to eat. Sherburne remembered worrying about infesting the home because of the "lice and vermin" on his clothing and in his hair. But he was ravenously hungry and was treated to his first meal in months—ham, eggs, and chocolate! The former prisoners were so malnourished that they had to be careful not to eat too much. While they were eating, both the baker and his wife interrupted the feast to ask the men if they were from the *Jersey*—tales of the notorious Hell Ship were well known in New England coastal villages.

With a full stomach, Sherburne thanked the kind couple and went on his way. He had no money, was wearing torn clothing, and had as his only possession a hammock he had taken from the *Jersey*. Without a coat, he was worried he would freeze to death before making it home. But, as Sherburne recalled, "We had not walked twenty rods from the wharf" when a man called out to him and the other former prisoners, asking if they were from the *Jersey*. Sherburne responded in the affirmative, and a small crowd of people gathered to meet the men and welcome them home. Everyone, it seemed, knew about the wretched prison ship. The man who addressed them was the captain of a small ship, and he invited Sherburne and his mates to sail with him to Providence.

Sherburne arrived in the city in late March and experienced a similarly warm welcome. A young girl noticed the men and invited them to her home, introducing them to her mother by saying, "I really believe these men came from the same place." It turned out that a family friend had been imprisoned on the *Jersey*. When the girl's mother said the prisoner's name was Jack Robinson, a hatter from Providence, Sherburne was in shock. He knew Robinson and was overjoyed to announce that the hatter had also been released to a cartel. At the surprising news, the young girl raced out the door to the Robinsons' hat store to inform the family that their son was alive and on his way home.

Sherburne was taken to the Robinson home, where he was greeted with sobs of "God bless you!" He was fed, clothed, and invited to sleep at their house, which he did, curling up with blankets near the warm fireplace.

On the road to the family home in Rye, New York, Sherburne was met by his brother Samuel, who had heard from neighbors that a prisoner had arrived. The family that had sent him away for years as a boy now welcomed him home. Sherburne's mother, likely filled with guilt for neglecting her son as a child, nearly fainted at the sight of her long-lost boy. Sherburne remembered that his first order of business was to wash.

His physical recovery was long and tedious—he had, after all, survived several illnesses during his incarceration. Once he recovered, Sherburne's next priority was to visit the families of crewmates throughout New York who had perished on the *Jersey*.

Thomas Dring survived the deadly nighttime attack at the stern of the *Jersey*. His friends who had attempted to escape, however, were not so fortunate. It was a trying few weeks for the Rhode Island officer after the failed escape attempt. He and other prisoners were unnerved by the savagery of the Hessian guards and the painful death of their friend Lawrence. Not long afterward, a disease tore through the ship, and the mortality rate among the prisoners, which was already alarmingly high, increased. The result was that the prisoners on the Hell Ship were filled with despair and the sense that they all were going to die.

Too weak to attempt another escape, Dring and his fellow officers determined that the only way to survive was to appeal directly to General Washington for a prisoner exchange. In 1782, they wrote to General Sir Henry Clinton, the British commander who had replaced General Howe in New York, with a request that one of the officers aboard the *Jersey* be permitted to take a message to General Washington. Surprisingly, the request was granted—and not for just one, but for three officers from the ship to travel to meet with the American commander. Permission came from Admiral Digby, who agreed that the envoys could inform Washington of the "sufferings" on the prison ships. Worried about the threat of American retaliation on the large number of British soldiers and officers in American custody near the end of the war, Digby was now forced to recommend mass prisoner exchanges. Therefore, his decision to parole the three prisoners was likely meant to facilitate those exchanges. However, the condition was that they had to carry a letter, drafted by Digby's staff, that presented a watered-down version of the grim realities aboard the *Jersey*. The envoys also had to pledge to return to the ship or their fellow prisoners still aboard the Hell Ship would be made to suffer.

A large prisoner exchange had been in the works for several months. On June 1, 1782, Commissary Sproat wrote to his American counterpart, Abraham Skinner, with news that Admiral Digby was requesting the exchange. He also warned that the situation was dire, saying, "The very great increase of Prisoners and the heat of the weather baffles all our care and attention to keep them healthy." But Sproat tried to reassure Skinner that the Americans were well cared for, claiming falsely that "five ships have been taken up for their reception to prevent their being crowded, and a great number permitted to go on parole."

Skinner replied on June 9: "From the present situation of the American Naval Prisoners on board your Prison ship, I am induced to propose to you the exchange of as many of them as I can give you British Naval Prisoners for, leaving the balance already due you to be paid when in our power." The letters resulted in the release of more than thirteen hundred British prisoners. However, Sproat failed to uphold his end of the deal. He blamed the delay on the Americans not having released enough sailors from His Majesty's navy; Skinner had released soldiers because the Americans held few sailors in their custody.

Soon after, Skinner fired off a terse response. "We are unable at present to give you seamen for seamen, and thereby relieve the Prison ships of their dreadful burden," he explained, and he added a warning: "It ought to be remembered that there is a large balance of British soldiers due the U.S. since February last, and we may be disposed to place the British soldiers in our possession in as disagreeable a situation as the men are on board the Prison ships." The war was all but over, momentum for the exchange was growing, and the Americans held all the cards.

Accordingly, Washington managed to negotiate with Digby for slight improvements on the *Jersey*, including the construction of an awning to shield prisoners from the sun when on the upper deck, a wind sail for fresh air belowdecks, an allotment of bread and butter provided by the Continental Army, the ability to send correspondence, and an agreement that a surgeon from the hospital ship *Hunter* would visit the *Jersey*. The improvements were minor, but gave hope to the prisoners; several of them, however, recorded that they never saw the surgeon.

Washington agreed to meet with the three prisoners, but sent a letter to Digby expressing his frustration with the deplorable conditions on the "infectious prison ships" and the ongoing refusal by Commissary Sproat and the British command to allow his commissaries and officers to inspect the old hulk. Washington was still reluctant to engage in large-scale exchanges unless all his demands were met. He did not trust the British and hesitated to exchange British prisoners for anyone but members of the Continental Army under his direct command, of which there were few on the *Jersey*. Privateers were not a part of the army.

For the mission to meet Washington in the summer of 1782, the officers on the *Jersey* selected three men who had been officers on the *Chance*, the ill-fated privateer captured by the British. The envoys— the ship's captain, Daniel Aborn, the ship's surgeon, Joseph Bowen, and Dring—affixed their names to the document to be presented to Washington and departed for his headquarters, where they were given an audience with the commander. During the meeting, they told the general the full extent of the horrors of the Hell Ship and shared stories of prisoners accepting death as preferable to the torment of their captivity. The three prisoners also stated that if Washington agreed to the exchange, they would swear to join the Continental Army after their release.

The general heard their case but explained that it was difficult to exchange privateers for regulars in His Majesty's army. The Continental Army, they discovered, had far fewer British prisoners than the British had American prisoners. The general also shared with his three guests his successful efforts to get British generals and Commissary Sproat to improve the conditions aboard the ships and his goal of having Britain abandon all the floating prisons. He also told them of his threat to treat the prisoners he held in the same way. In the end, Washington agreed to intervene.

Dring returned to the *Jersey* carrying a letter from Washington. He ordered all the prisoners to assemble on the upper deck and read it. He also announced to his comrades, "[Washington] had perused our communication, and had received with due consideration the account which our messengers had laid before him; that he viewed our situation with a high degree of interest; and that although our application was made in relation to a subject over which he had no direct control, yet that it was his intention to lay our Memorial before Congress." To shouts of joy, Dring continued, "In the mean time we might be assured that no exertion on [Washington's] part should be spared which could tend to a mitigation of our sufferings."

It appears Dr. Bowen chose to flee rather than return to the Hell Ship. Captain Aborn, as the senior officer of the mission, was set free by the British, but asked his former first lieutenant, John Tillinghast, to make a list of all the men from their old privateer, *Chance*, who had died on board the *Jersey*. He also encouraged the prisoners to write letters to friends and family, and promised that he would deliver the letters of the survivors and pay respects at the homes of the deceased. Dring assisted Tillinghast in helping the men to draft letters. However, the guards on the *Jersey* required that the letters first be submitted to them for inspection. The men worried that the malicious guards would destroy all the letters, as usually happened, but this time the guards permitted them to be organized for Captain Aborn. The only one of the three emissaries to return to the holds of the *Jersey* was Dring.

Captain Aborn arrived the next day at the accommodation ladder to collect the lists and letters, but was careful not to board the ship because of contagion. Lieutenant Tillinghast delivered the materials to Aborn, who sent the lieutenant back with a promise that he would send clothing and supplies back to the ship, and work to arrange an exchange. And then he was off.

Even though the British seemed eager to release prisoners and had started sending many of the diseased and sick ashore to nearby Blackwell's Island, Commissary Sproat announced to the prisoners still aboard the *Jersey* that the mission by Captain Aborn, Dr. Bowen, and Dring was a failure.* The bad news was met with stiflingly hot weather and another outbreak of disease that tore through the ship. Dring worried that he could not hold out for the awaited exchange. Month after agonizing month, the men fought for their lives, taking solace from the hope that Sproat might be wrong and that Washington was arranging an exchange or that Captain Aborn was passing along letters to their loved ones back home and working on an exchange. Dring occupied the long days by helping the sick and trying to stay alive. However, he began to doubt that Captain Aborn had succeeded or that General Washington had pursued the exchange. To survive this long, only to perish at the end of the war . . .

Finally one October afternoon a sloop pulled up alongside the *Jersey*. The craft flew a white flag at her masthead, indicating that the sloop had been sent by a cartel to take the prisoners home. Excitedly the prisoners clamored to get to the upper deck, but the guards beat them back below the hatches. Men rushed to the grated openings on the side of the *Jersey* hoping to get a glimpse of their salvation, but a terrible sight awaited them. The sloop's deck contained roughly forty emaciated prisoners. There looked to be no room for additional passengers, and the officer standing on the deck was none other than David Sproat, the notorious prison commissary.

Small launches were lowered from the sloop and the prisoners began gathering in them. A few at a time, the prisoners were shuttled

---

* The narrow island is in the East River between Manhattan and Queens. In the nineteenth century it held a prison and asylum for the mentally ill. The island is now known as Roosevelt Island.

to the shore. As Dring and the men aboard the *Jersey* watched through the narrow grates with much agitation, they wondered what could be the reason for the transfer.

Finally an American captain named William Corey came aboard the *Jersey* with an announcement. He had been sent by a private cartel from Providence, Rhode Island, arranged by Captain Aborn with the blessing of General Washington, and the prisoners on the sloop who had been ferried ashore were British sailors and soldiers being exchanged for prisoners from the *Jersey*. Captain Corey informed the anxious prisoners that he was there to take the surviving members of the privateer *Chance* to freedom! The others' hearts sank as he went on to say that he was authorized to accept only forty prisoners. He then asked the *Chance*'s crew to line up and prepare to board the sloop.

Dring and the surviving members of the *Chance* ran belowdecks to gather their belongings. The bylaws on the *Jersey* stipulated that freed prisoners must leave their chests behind, which Dring did. He gave away his remaining possessions, which included a few items of clothing, a small bag, a tin cup, and some pieces of firewood. He then raced to the upper deck to be released.

The prisoners were ordered to attention while Lieutenant Tillinghast read the names of the parolees aloud. Commissary Sproat stood menacingly beside him on the quarterdeck. Dring felt his stomach tighten as he listened with anxiety, "well knowing that I should hear no second call, and that no delay would be allowed." When a prisoner heard his name he stepped forward and hollered "Here!" Others were called on to verify that the person was indeed the man whose name was called. One by one, the prisoners descended the accommodation ladder to the sloop. Finally Dring heard his name called. He remembered, "I never moved with a lighter step, for that moment was the happiest of my life." As he passed Sproat, the commissary simply pointed to the sloop. "In the excess and overflowing of my joy," Dring admitted, "I forgot, for a while, the detestable character of the Commissary himself; and even, Heaven forgive me, bestowed a bow upon him as I passed."

As he boarded the cartel ship, Dring was overcome with emotion. He had remained stoic during his entire incarceration, and his resourcefulness had saved the lives of many of his fellow prisoners, but now Dring finally burst into tears. All around him no one spoke. The prisoners simply sat in silence. Dring recalled, "It seemed impossible that we were in reality without the limits of the old *Jersey*." He glanced at his fellow crewmates, all of whom seemed to be worrying that something would go wrong. Dring "shuddered with the apprehension that we might yet be returned to our dungeons."

And then it hit him: there were only thirty-five survivors from the crew of the *Chance*, but forty British prisoners. Fortunately, Lieutenant Tillinghast had devised a plan. The lieutenant read five names of the former mates aboard the *Chance* who had died, but looked calmly at five friends who shared the gunroom with Tillinghast and Dring. The officers immediately picked up on the opportunity and came forward pretending to be the five deceased sailors. The ruse worked. No one said a word.

As sunset loomed, the exchange was completed. The sloop hoisted off and slowly sailed out of Wallabout Bay. Dring stared at the rotting hulk, watching prisoners shuffle slowly about on the deck as he had done each day for so long. As the sloop made sail in the twilight of the dying day, Dring caught his last glimpse of the *Jersey*. He was filled with "indescribable feelings of disgust." His five-month-long ordeal was over.

Death and Demise

By feeble hands their shallow graves were made;
No stone, memorial, o'er their corpses laid.
In barren sands, and far from home, they lie,
No friend to shed a tear when passing by;
O'er the mean tombs, insulting foemen tread,
Spurn at the sand, and curse the rebel dead.

—Philip Freneau, "The British Prison-Ship" (1781)

With the surrender by General Charles Cornwallis on October 18, 1781, at the decisive Battle of Yorktown, the die was cast for an American victory. There would not be another major engagement, but the war dragged on with smaller battles and skirmishes for another two years. In April 1782, the Continental Congress dispatched John Adams, Benjamin Franklin, John Jay, and Henry Laurens to Paris to open negotiations. However, Laurens was captured by the British and imprisoned in the Tower of London until the end of the war. A preliminary peace accord was worked out on November 30, 1782, yet numerous impediments remained, including what to do about the prison ships.

During the final two years of the war, a change in posture by the British was apparent. It began with the resignation in 1782 of Sir Henry Clinton, the commander of British forces in North America since 1778. That May, General Sir Guy Carleton arrived in New York to assume command. General Carleton did something his predecessors had never done—he visited the prison ships. The general also indicated his interest in relocating many of the prisoners from the ships to Blackwell's Island, in the East River. While some men were in fact taken to the island and the British began a gradual de-escalation of hostilities, they continued to seize prisoners and hold them aboard the *Jersey*.

Large groups of prisoners from the *Jersey* and other prison ships were released and exchanged throughout the early months of 1783, the final year of the war. Rather than "freeing" the prisoners, however, the prideful British claimed to only be "paroling" them. One by one, all the prison and hospital ships were abandoned. By August, the last ones were towed away, leaving only the unoccupied *Jersey* as the sole reminder of the horrors committed off the coast of Brooklyn. Throughout the drawdown, ads were taken out by the British in the loyalist newspaper *Rivington's Gazette* offering to sell the ships or parts for salvage. One ad featured "the hulks of His Majesty's sloops *Scorpion* and *Hunter*," the former fire ship *Strombolo*, and others. Earlier ships were scrapped, then sold; these final ships were never sold. The British did not even try to sell the *Jersey*.

On Sunday, April 6, 1783, British officers boarded the *Jersey* and ordered the remaining prisoners be assembled on the upper deck. The dreaded Commissary David Sproat stepped forward and read a royal proclamation stating that the war was ending. There were no congratulatory remarks, no medical assistance provided, and no apologies offered. Three days later, smaller ships anchored nearby in Wallabout Bay to take the prisoners to various ports in New England, where large and curious crowds gathered to see the living ghosts of the most notorious ship of the time. The long-awaited homecomings in late 1782 and early 1783 were not what people had hoped. As described in a New London newspaper, "The prisoners at N.Y. are sickly. Twenty were buried on Christmas day from the *Jersey*." According to the paper, the horrors on board the *Jersey* remained until the bitter end, becoming even worse after the other ships were abandoned and as supplies were completely exhausted. The British seemed to have given up completely on the ship. "We are creditably informed that 50 are buried weekly," the paper claimed.

After the last prisoners disembarked from the *Jersey* on April 9, the next day Commissary Sproat certified that the last prison ship was empty. The weakest and sickest among them, who had been transferred to Blackwell's Island, were shipped home on May 3.

But the ordeal was not over for the prisoners, many of whom died on the way home or soon after being freed. Others never regained their health. One of them was William Drowne, a Rhode Islander who was a friend of Thomas Dring's and had been captured by the HMS *Belisarius* in 1781. After being released in 1783, Drowne made it home, but the ghosts of the ship remained with him. Suffering from various maladies, Drowne eventually succumbed to them three years later. His story was all too common.

The old ship's fate had been sealed long ago. Unfit for further service, and with her prisoners having been released, "the old hulk, in whose putrefactive bowels so many had suffered and died, was abandoned where she lay," as one survivor remembered. Another commented, "The dread of contagion prevented everyone from venturing on board and even from approaching her polluted frame." The *Jersey* sat as a haunted spectacle in the polluted waters of Wallabout Bay for only a short time before sinking. Severely rotted and with no prisoners to operate her bilge pumps, the old warship soon filled with water and sank in the exact spot where she had been moored. In the words of one nineteenth-century account, the memories of "the thousands who had written their names upon her planks" joined the old ship in her watery grave.

The slowly decaying remains of the old dungeon were visible in the shallow waters off Brooklyn for years to come, an eerie reminder of the bloodiest battle of the Revolutionary War. Andrew Sherburne returned to Brooklyn in 1788 to visit the site of his incarceration, writing, "I took an opportunity to visit the navy yard, directly opposite to which, formerly lay that dismal ship, the old *Jersey*. I passed over her remains, some of which I could see laying in the bottom of the East River." Reminiscing as an old man in 1823, Sherburne counted his blessings and described the experience: "It caused my very soul to thrill when I passed over the remains of that wretched ship, and was approaching the shore to review the awful scenes I had witnessed, and the distressing suffering I had there endured through a long and tedious winter, more than forty years ago, and where more than two thirds of my shipmates had laid their bones."

Reports survive from 1795 and 1803 of other individuals claiming to have seen the rotted oak skeleton of the ship below the water. Another eyewitness description is found in a letter written by the son of Captain Roswell Palmer, one of the survivors. Palmer's son had been taken to the spot as a child and, "forty years after," wrote to the son of another survivor that "at low tide the huge remains of her unburied skeleton" were still visible.

Slumbering on the muddy bottom, the *Jersey* soon became a ghost ship, all but forgotten by history.

In mid-August 1783, Sir Guy Carleton, the last British commander in her former colonies, received orders from London to evacuate New York City. It stood as the final British toehold in what had once been the Crown's vast, lucrative colonies. Carleton planned a quick and unceremonious departure for the remaining British soldiers and sailors as well as for any loyalists and liberated slaves who wished to leave America. As Carleton was preparing for the awkward departure, word arrived that, after a long and difficult negotiation, the peace treaty had finally been signed in Paris on September 3, 1783.

Evacuation Day finally arrived. At noon on November 25 the British abandoned the city. A large flotilla of warships and transports set sail from the harbor on Manhattan Island with roughly 29,000 loyalists in tow. Crowds of Americans whooped and hollered from the shoreline as the British slunk out of the city. A single cannon from one of the warships fired at the hecklers. Fittingly, and to the delight of the Americans, the shot fell far short of its intended target. The scene was a far cry from the majestic arrival of the Howe brothers seven years prior.

Soon thereafter, General Washington entered the city with the Continental Army behind him. Across the Harlem River, through Manhattan, and down to the Battery at the foot of Broadway they rode triumphant in a grand parade, passing not far from Wallabout Bay and the scene of so much suffering. It was Washington's first time back in New York since retreating across the East River after the defeat at the Battle of Brooklyn on August 27, 1776. The humiliation of the defeat had long simmered in Washington, and he had always hoped to be able to retake the key city, though he never did. Now, though, after more than seven long years, the city was finally secured and back in American hands. After the festivities Washington put his trusted friend and artillery commander, General Henry Knox, in charge of the city.

Nine days later, on December 4, Washington gathered his officers at Fraunces Tavern, at the intersection of Pearl and Broad in the city. At an emotional banquet, the general bid them farewell. "With a heart full of love and gratitude, I now take leave of you," said Washington with his voice cracking. "I must devoutly wish that your latter days may be as prosperous and happy as your former ones have been glorious and honorable." Standing nearest to his commander, General Knox embraced his friend. And then, with tears on his cheeks, Washington invited every officer to come and shake his hand. One by one, the officers who had accomplished the impossible said good-bye.

After that, Washington rode to Annapolis to meet with the Continental Congress and resign his commission. There is no evidence he visited the old rotting hulk of the *Jersey* while in the city.

Although we will never know the final death toll aboard the *Jersey*, some partial records remain. Likewise, several newspaper articles from the Revolution, eyewitness descriptions from the time of the Revolution, and diaries of those who survived imprisonment on the ship exist; along with the work of a few historians, these allow for a reasonable estimate. All of the accounts are shocking, and most point to roughly 11,500 deaths on the *Jersey*.

One of the first tallies comes from General William Heath of the Continental Army, who arrived in New York five days after the last prisoners were released from the *Jersey*. Heath recorded that "11,644 American prisoners had died during the war in the prisons, and on board the prison-ships at New York." Calling it a "surprising number," he concluded that so many deaths occurred because the prisons and ships "were much too crowded, or not properly attended to in other respects." Though Heath never stated how he arrived at the number, his total is very specific, suggesting it is not an estimate. However, Heath states that his total is for *all* prisoners in New York City, not just those who perished aboard the *Jersey*.

David Sproat was known to keep meticulous records, including dates that prisoners died. A few other wardens and officers on the ships did as well, and it is possible Heath had access to their war records. Yet none of those reports has survived. It is likely they were destroyed by the British at the end of the war, and for good reason, as the evidence would have been damning.

Although Heath's death toll is for all American prisoners, other sources claim that roughly 11,500 men died on the *Jersey* alone. One of them was Charles West, a scholar from New York working in the nineteenth century. West was alarmed that history had largely forgotten the prison ship martyrs, and he sought to document their stories. As part of his research on the atrocities in Wallabout Bay, he concluded that over 11,000 American prisoners perished on the *Jersey* alone. Another nineteenth-century historian, George Taylor, put the number at 11,000 as well.

A third historian writing in the nineteenth century was Henry Onderdonk of Long Island. In discussing the revolutionary events of New York in his book, Onderdonk included the *Jersey* and quoted a story in a newspaper from nearby Fishkill written in May 1783, just days after the *Jersey* was finally abandoned. The article reads, "Tell it to the world, and let it be published in every Newspaper throughout America, Europe, Asia and Africa, to the everlasting disgrace and infamy of the British King's commanders at New-York: That during the late war, it is said 11,644 American prisoners have suffered death by their inhuman, cruel, savage and barbarous usage on board the filthy and malignant British prison-ship, called the *Jersey*, lying at N.Y." The author of the newspaper article was so appalled by the tragedy that he concluded, "Britons tremble, lest the vengeance of Heaven fall on your isle, for the blood of these unfortunate victims!"

Once again the number 11,644 is given, although this time it is for just the deaths aboard the *Jersey*. Still, questions remain about the reliability of these sources and reports. Two clues exist as to how the newspaper got the scoop on the fatality count. First, Fishkill is by the bank of the Hudson River, not far from General Washington's wartime headquarters at Newburgh.* Second, the noted publisher of the *New York Packet*, Samuel Loudon, had fled there in order to continue covering the war after the British took New York. Either incident could explain how the local newspaper had numbers relating to the notorious prison ship. Other newspaper stories written in 1783—including for the *Connecticut Gazette* and *Pennsylvania Packet*—used the same death count for the old prison ship. Onderdonk, however, points out that none of the newspapers name a source, leading him to ponder whether the figure is "baseless conjecture." Nonetheless, he concludes, "The number that perished was doubtless fearfully great, and needed no exaggeration."

---

* Washington headquartered at Newburgh from April 1782 to August 1783, the longest period of time spent at any headquarters during the war.

Another account from the time of the Revolution comes courtesy of Thomas Jefferson, who wrote about the *Jersey*. The author of the Declaration of Independence knew individuals who were imprisoned on the ships, including Philip Freneau. The noted author and poet was incarcerated on the *Scorpion*, and Jefferson took great interest in his good friend's experience. As the American minister to France, Jefferson felt compelled to inform the French about the horrors of the British prison ships of Wallabout Bay. While living in France, Jefferson also met a Pennsylvanian named Richard Riddy who had been on the *Jersey* and was presently doing business in Paris. The future president took an interest in Riddy's story and on August 17, 1786, recorded his deposition. The Pennsylvanian said that he had been captured in January 1783 and put aboard the *Jersey*. "While he was there," wrote Jefferson of the interview, "David Sproate Commissary general of prisoners to the British army informed him that upwards of eleven thousand American prisoners had died on board the prison ship the *Jersey*, and shewed him the registers whereby it appeared to be so."

While Jefferson was serving in Paris, a New Yorker named Henry Remsen Jr. was appointed as a clerk in the State Department. Remsen also took an interest in the legacy of the *Jersey*. The 11,000 number cited by Jefferson in the deposition was shocking to Remsen, who trusted Jefferson and rationalized that Sproat would have no reason to exaggerate the number. If anything, he had reason to understate it. Remsen therefore obtained Jefferson's deposition of Riddy, which had been sent to Washington, and conducted his own inquiry about the death toll. In his notes, Remsen wrote that "there is a person living now on Long Island, who informed me that the number of American prisoners who were buried from on board the *Jersey* prison ship, along the shore on his land, could not be less in number than 10,000." The individual in question was Remsen's relative, who lived on a farm by the burial ground at Wallabout Bay.

Another reliable source from the period is Elias Boudinot, one of the American prison commissaries. In a letter, Boudinot told the

poet Joel Barlow that 1,100 prisoners died in an eighteen-month period on the *Jersey*, "almost the whole of them from the barbarous
treatment of being stifled in a crowded hold with infected air, and
poisoned with unwholesome food." If one were to extrapolate Boudinot's death toll over the total period of time in which the *Jersey* served
as a prison ship, the number would be about 3,666. This is far smaller
than 11,644, but a staggering number nonetheless.

A handful of contemporary historians have tried to calculate
the number of fatalities on the Hell Ship using available accounts.
Larry Lowenthal puts it at roughly 10,950 and "perhaps many more."
The historian Eugene Armbruster suggests that between 10,000 and
11,000 perished on the *Jersey*, comprising 7,000 Americans and 3,550
foreign sailors. Perhaps the most conservative estimate comes from
the historian Howard Peckham, who in the 1970s estimated the total
death count on all prison ships in Wallabout Bay at "a conservative
8,500." On the other end of the spectrum, the author Edwin Burrows, who penned one of the very few reliable and scholarly accounts
of prisoners during the Revolution, concluded that the number of
Americans imprisoned and who died "was a lot larger than ever imagined." While many historians believed that roughly 18,000 Americans were captured by the British during the war and just under half
(roughly 8,500) of them perished, Burrows puts the number of captives at over 30,000, with over half of them (roughly 18,000) dying
during captivity.

One survivor of the Hell Ship recalled that three to eight prisoners died each day, while the American envoy to the peace accords,
Henry Laurens, wrote that in 1778 the ship was claiming five or six
lives a day. In a letter to Admiral Digby, General Washington also
wrote that the losses on the *Jersey* were devastatingly high and often
amounted to several prisoners a day. Thomas Dring, while admitting the total loss on the dreaded ship "has never been, and never
can be known," estimates that over 10,000 men died on the *Jersey*
and her three companion ships (*Scorpion, Strombolo,* and *Hunter*).

He also lamented that their "names have never been known by their countrymen."

There is little reason to doubt the veracity of the firsthand accounts of the prisoners, including Dring, who went ashore to bury the dead, and Andros, who stood on the upper deck and each day counted the bodies thrown into the "dead boat" for burial ashore. Most of the men who survived imprisonment on the *Jersey* wrote that somewhere from six to twelve men died on the dreadful ship every day. As such, one way to calculate the total fatality count on the *Jersey* is to multiply six deaths per day by the number of days (approximately 1,560) it served as a prison ship.* To do so would produce a conservative estimate of roughly 9,360 deaths. A high mark would come from calculating twelve deaths per day for the period the ship functioned as a floating dungeon, which amounts to approximately 18,720 total deaths. The prisoners' accounts suggested that the number of prisoners who died each day was closer to six when the *Jersey* was first used as a prison ship, but that the number gradually increased to a dozen a day by 1783 and the end of its service in the war. The total number of men and boys who died on the ship was therefore likely in the middle of the low and high estimates, which would produce a number larger than the 11,500 figure used by historical sources.

Another way to estimate the death toll is to determine how many prisoners were on the *Jersey*. Reliable accounts suggest that the ship initially held roughly 400 prisoners at a time but was crowded with up to 1,200 by the end of the war. In the 1960s the American historian Jesse Lemisch accessed what remained of the British Admiralty's records in London. After qualifying his estimate by saying that many of the records were missing and it was impossible to know for sure how many prisoners in total were either on the ship or perished aboard it, Lemisch confirmed that there were at least 7,773 total

---

* The *Jersey* was first used as a prison ship in December 1778. It was moved to Wallabout Bay in April 1780 and the final prisoners were removed from the ship in April 1783.

names on the *Jersey*'s prisoner logs.* The guards and officers on the *Jersey*, he concluded, "were far from faithful record keepers."

Similarly, in 1888, in an effort to raise money to build a memorial to the prison ship martyrs, the Society of Old Brooklynites published a report called *A Christmas Reminder*. It listed 8,000 names of prisoners who were on *Jersey*, beginning alphabetically with Garret Aarons and ending with Pierre Zuran. However, they too found that the records of the British War Department were incomplete, "carelessly kept," and that registers were missing for the other "floating Golgothas," as they called the prison ships. The society's report also said that "there is nothing to indicate what became of any of these prisoners, whether they died, escaped, or were exchanged." So the number was likely far higher, but the society did not list their sources.

The U.S. Department of Veterans Affairs in its report "America's Wars" officially lists the total number of American soldiers and sailors who died in combat during the Revolutionary War at 4,435. Some historians have argued that the number is low. One of them, Howard Peckham, attempted to list the estimated casualty count for all Revolutionary battles and conflicts, and guessed that there were perhaps 6,090 Americans lost in combat, with another 1,084 naval deaths at sea. At least another 10,000 American soldiers succumbed to disease, malnutrition, and the weather.

While these numbers are not overwhelming when compared to losses during the Civil War or Second World War, they are, proportionally, larger than most American wars in terms of the percentage of the overall American population that died. Therefore, because the American population during the Revolutionary War was only 1 percent of what it is today, the death toll aboard the *Jersey*, if extrapolated to today's population, would be akin to losing one million prisoners in a war. Taken yet another way, at the time of the Revolutionary

---

* No records have ever been found for the period November 21, 1777–August 2, 1778, and for December 25, 1780–February 14, 1781. And no records exist for the ships moored or anchored next to the *Jersey*, including the *Falmouth*, *Hunter*, *John*, *Prince of Wales*, *Scorpion*, and *Strombolo*.

War only a handful of cities in America had populations of at least 11,000—Boston, New York, and Philadelphia. The loss of 11,000 men on the *Jersey* would be comparable to losing the entire population of a major city today—New York, Los Angeles, or Chicago. Likewise, we can make an analogy with the Second World War, where 291,557 Americans died in combat and another 113,842 died in non-combat-related service; the loss on the *Jersey* would have been equivalent to the deaths of 850,000 men in a single prisoner-of-war camp!

Most of the historical accounts suggest that roughly 11,500 men perished on the *Jersey*. This number is used by the U.S. Merchant Marines, the History Channel, and the esteemed nineteenth-century war historian Benson Lossing, who nevertheless admitted, "The number of American prisoners buried at the Wallabout is not known." It is the figure given by Thomas Andros, one of the survivors, who added, "Doubtless no other ship in the British navy ever proved the means of the destruction of so many human beings."

There are discrepancies in the death toll from the *Jersey* and there is no reliable independent verification for the numbers. However, if 11,500 boys and men died on the *Jersey*, then over twice as many Americans were lost on that single, cursed ship than died in combat during the entirety of the long war!

Whichever estimate is most accurate, the *Jersey* was clearly a death ship. Add in the other prison and hospital ships, and Wallabout Bay was one of the deadliest places and events in American history.

Rediscovery

Hail, dark abode! What can with thee compare—
Heat, sickness, famine, death, and stagnant air.

—Philip Freneau, "The British Prison-Ship" (1781)

For several years after the war ended, bleached bones washed ashore in Brooklyn with the tides. As they piled up on the shoreline, residents collected them and buried them in a temporary vault on Hudson Street. Through the early 1800s, human bones and rotted timbers were still visible in the shallows of Wallabout Bay. For local residents, the ghosts of the *Jersey* were ever-present.

In 1791, a prominent citizen of New York named John Jackson acquired the land by Remsen's Mill along Wallabout Bay. The following year, Jackson began collecting bones on his property and placing them in caskets. A few years later, Jackson sought to make improvements to the long-abandoned property and sell it to the military for a naval yard. While digging in 1803, he unearthed a large pile of bones that turned out to be a mass grave for the victims of the *Jersey*. During the construction of the new Brooklyn Navy Yard more bones were discovered nearly every time they put a shovel into the ground. Eventually, thousands of bones were placed in the temporary vault on the property.

Jackson's discovery rekindled interest in the forgotten tragedy, but it also touched off a political debate about what to do with them. Many Brooklynites wanted the remains buried in a permanent resting place, preferably a nearby churchyard, but Jackson wanted the Tammany Society of New York, a politically influential organization, to take custody of the bones and gravesites. Politics intervened. Bad feelings from the bitter fight between the Federalists and Anti-Federalists during the 1800 election had not dissipated, and with elections looming in 1804 and 1808, both factions were posturing to appear more patriotic. The Federalists were planning to erect a statue of their beloved George Washington, so the Democratic-Republicans (or Republicans) of the Tammany Society, led by one of their congressmen, Samuel L. Mitchell, planned a monument for the prisoners of the Wallabout hulks in order to counter the proposed statue of Washington.*

The leaders of the Tammany Society presented a proposal for a memorial and tomb to Congress on February 10, 1803. But they were unsuccessful. Sadly, the issue faded from the headlines, and the bones continued to be placed in a temporary vault on Hudson Street as they were discovered. With the election of 1808 looming, the prison ship memorial was again thrust to the fore of the city's politics. The country was not happy with the trade embargo of 1807 or the sagging economy, both of which occurred under Jefferson's presidency. So the Republicans were eager to capitalize on the growing anti-British sentiment occasioned by the brutal policy of forcing U.S. sailors to serve on British ships.† The vault, they reasoned, would stoke anti-British and pro-Jefferson passions. It did.

However, the Republicans, favoring a Jeffersonian approach to government and seeking to make inroads with the "common man," replaced the idea of a grand marble monument with a humble and

---

* The Anti-Federalists were eventually known as the Democratic-Republicans.

† The policy, known as "impressment," was implemented because Britain needed more sailors in its war against Napoleon.

practical vault. Therefore, in the winter of 1807, leaders of the Tammany Society revisited the issue and appointed a committee headed by Benjamin Romaine to promote the construction of a new vault.* On April 13, 1808, the tomb was finally completed. It sat beside the Navy Yard on land donated by John Jackson near Hudson and Front Streets in Brooklyn. In a ceremony presided over by Jackson, a cornerstone was dedicated. It read, "In the name of the spirits of the departed free—Sacred to the memory of that portion of American Seamen, Soldiers and Citizens, who perished on board the Prison ships of the British at the Wallabout during the Revolution." Touching words were offered by Joseph D. Fay, a noted attorney who had once worked for Alexander Hamilton.

The simple vault, however, caught the attention of political leaders and the public. On May 26, a "grand" funeral procession marched through New York, passing through Main, Sands, Bridge, York, and Jackson Streets. The grand marshals—Major Aycrigg, whose father was imprisoned in a sugar house, and Captain Alexander Coffin, who survived two sentences aboard the floating dungeons—led the parade to the Brooklyn Navy Yard. There they reinterred the bones of the prison ship martyrs. The memorial was carried in a large wagon draped in black ribbons and crape and pulled by four horses. The obelisk was made of black marble and measured eight feet in length, six feet in height, and two feet in width. Four panels surrounded the pedestal, inscribed with the following words:

> Front panel: "Americans! Remember the British."
> Right side panel: "Youth of my country! Martyrdom prefer to slavery."
> Left side panel: "Sires of Columbia: Transmit to posterity the cruelties practiced on board the British prison ships."
> Rear panel: "Tyrants dread the gathering storm, while freemen's obsequies perform."

---

* In some sources, the name is also spelled Romeyn.

Standing next to the wooden frame that covered the vault, Dr. Benjamin Dewitt delivered a moving funeral oration that brought the crowd to tears. Artillery posted on the nearby hill fired a three-volley salute in honor of the event and a military band played solemn music. Standing at attention in a perimeter around the vault were nine soldiers carrying nine different flags, each one symbolizing a different American virtue—patriotism, honor, virtue, patience, fortitude, merit, courage, perseverance, and science. Thirteen bluestone coffins containing the bones of the martyrs were reinterred in the new memorial, which came to be known as the Tomb of the Patriots. An enormous blue flag waved from an eighteen-foot-high pole, with a globe and eagle perched majestically atop it, while thirteen posts—one for each colony—stood guard in front of the memorial. The patriotic occasion, which was attended by 104 veterans of the war as well as clergy, politicians, and "a vast concourse of citizens" believed to number around two thousand, had the desired political effect.

A few years later when the lot was sold, Romaine, who had been a prisoner on one of the wretched ships for seven weeks, purchased it and began restoring the vault. On it, he inscribed the following words: "The portal to the tomb of the 11,500 patriot Prisoners of War, who died in dungeons and pestilential Prison ships in and about the City of New York during the war of our Revolution." When Romaine died on January 31, 1844, at the age of eighty-two, he was buried alongside the remains of his former crewmates.

Efforts by Romaine before his death to raise funds for the upkeep of the memorial failed. A year later, the U.S. House of Representatives took up a bill to provide $20,000 for upkeep of the site, but it too failed. The $900 donation from Romaine's will soon ran out and the vault fell into disrepair. Additional efforts to memorialize the martyrs and find a permanent resting place would come and go with little effect, and the tragedy aboard the HMS *Jersey* would be largely forgotten.

One of those efforts was undertaken by Walt Whitman. The year after Congress rejected funding for the vault, Whitman published a poem and newspaper column about the tragedy at Wallabout Bay.

His efforts led to Congress's purchasing land around the site the following year. The grounds, known as Washington Park, prevented development from encroaching on the site and offered a proper setting for such a sacred memorial.

With the park now established, on May 2, 1855, a group of New Yorkers calling themselves the Martyr Monument Association met "for the purpose of devising and adopting the means necessary to secure the erection of a suitable Monument to the memory of the prisoners who died during the Revolutionary War, on board the Prison-Ships in the Wallabout Bay." They chose a small hill in Washington Park for the new, permanent site of a memorial. But the effort to build a new monument and reinter the bones would have to wait.

During an impromptu Sunday religious service one day on the upper deck of the *Jersey* by the spar, a man named Cooper, affectionately nicknamed "the Orator" by the other prisoners, had predicted a day would come when "their bones will be collected . . . and their rites of sepulture will be performed." The Orator comforted his fellow prisoners by saying they would be remembered by "a monument erected over the remains of those who have here suffered, the victims of barbarity, and died in vindication of the rights of Man."

That promise came a step closer to reality in 1867 when the famed landscape architect Calvert Vaux and his protégé Frederick Law Olmsted, the designers of Central Park in New York City, developed a new design for Washington Park and the crypt holding the bones of the prison ship martyrs. Finally, on June 18, 1873, a new vault was opened and the old tomb, which had long before collapsed and was overgrown with vegetation, was emptied. The remains were transported in twenty-two large boxes to be reinterred in the new mausoleum, which cost $6,500. Hundreds of bones were moved to the resting place, but they constituted only a fraction of the total lost on the ships and even just a fraction of those buried in the first vault in

1808—in the intervening years the tomb had been repeatedly vandalized and many of the bones stolen.

The new mausoleum, twenty-five feet by eleven feet, was made of brick and granite and inscribed with the words "Sacred to the Memory of our sailors, soldiers and citizens, who suffered and died on board British prison ships in the Wallabout during the American Revolution." But the mausoleum and park still lacked a new memorial to replace the original, which had long since been defaced and looted, and reduced to ruin.

Two more decades would pass. Then, in 1896, the Society of Old Brooklynites revived the long-standing effort to build a permanent memorial to the prison ship martyrs on the hill near the mausoleum in Washington Park.* Three years later, more bones were found during construction at the Brooklyn Navy Yard. The excavation also turned up two oak coffins, five feet in length, containing hundreds of bones. They were placed in the mausoleum on June 16, 1900. A few years later, crews digging a subway tunnel nearby uncovered more bones. This was simply the latest incident of bones' being discovered. As the historian Edwin G. Burrows described, local citizens routinely found bones of the prison ship martyrs all along the coastline of Brooklyn, oftentimes "as thick as pumpkins in an autumn cornfield."

Likewise, in October 1902, a startling discovery occurred. During an expansion of the docks at the Brooklyn Navy Yard and renovation of the warship USS *Connecticut*, work crews found artifacts believed to be from the *Jersey*. Old timbers, shards of pottery, rusted nails, and other items were collected. The location matched the descriptions of the ship's final resting place and scholars dated the artifacts uncovered to the late eighteenth century.

The discovery of so many more bones and relics of the *Jersey* as the centennial of the opening of the original tomb for the prison ship

---

* Washington Park had been renamed Fort Greene Park in honor of the famed general Nathanael Greene. The original Revolutionary-era structure, Fort Putnam, had been renamed for General Greene prior to the War of 1812.

martyrs neared sparked interest in the memorial project once again. On June 28, 1902, Congress approved a joint resolution to appropriate $100,000 to build a new memorial. New York City offered another $50,000, the state allocated $25,000, and private donors matched that last amount to raise the necessary funds for the memorial. With the funds finally secured, in 1905 the Society of Old Brooklynites and the Daughters of the American Revolution commissioned the famous architectural firm McKim, Mead and White to design a new entrance to the crypt and an appropriate monument to honor those who perished on the prison ships.

The memorial was unveiled on November 14, 1908, at the planned site—a small hill in Fort Greene Park—in time to mark the centennial of the original tomb. A grand parade attended by somewhere between twenty thousand and thirty thousand people marked the solemn occasion. As had been the case a hundred years earlier, the procession wound its way through the city, led by a trumpeter on a black horse, his helmet adorned with black and red feathers. A black silk banner was draped below the trumpet, with these words:

Mortals, avaunt!
11,500
Spirits of the martyred brave
Approach the tomb of Honor, of Glory, of
Virtuous Patriotism.

The result was impressive. The tall Doric column measured 149 feet high and stood majestically upon the hill. It was topped by a bronze lantern sculpted by the noted artist Adolph Alexander Weinman. Below, four eagles were mounted to the corners of granite posts. The base of the monument read simply, "1776 THE PRISON SHIP MARTYRS MONUMENT 1908."

The new vault sat nearby. The bones of the martyrs were interred for the fourth time, carried to the new crypt in twenty coffins. A tablet marked the entrance to the crypt, inscribed as follows:

In the name of the spirits of the departed free
Sacred to the memory of that portion of American seamen, soldiers
On board the prison ships of the British during the Revolutionary
War at the Wall About . . .

While the ghosts of Wallabout Bay can still be found at Fort Greene Park and along Wallabout Bay, history has largely forgotten the incident. Yet this was not always so. During the Revolutionary War, the Hell Ship's reputation was widely known. As she haunted the waters off Brooklyn, so too did she haunt households throughout the colonies. Stories of the old prison ship were once whispered around countless dinner tables and from pub stools. As Christopher Hawkins remembered years after his own harrowing ordeal aboard the *Jersey*, "Her fame spread far and wide, and her very name was an object of terror, for she was looked upon as nothing less than a charnel-house."*

The words of several prisoners who survived the Hell Ship bear witness to both the horrors of British prison policy and the lives lost. As one account cried out, "God grant that the record of such crimes may be opened up in heaven against our enemies, and not against us!" Late in life, Thomas Andros was still wrestling with the demons of his imprisonment aboard the *Jersey*. In his memoir, he summed up the tragedy as a "blot which a thousand ages cannot eradicate." He prayed for his British tormentors that "the pious and humane among them" would repent and see the "error in all they had done" so that the Almighty would spare humanity from such evil ever "happen[ing] again between two countries."

---

* A charnel house is a building or vault for corpses and bones; the term is often used to connote death and destruction.

Postscript

So much I suffer'd from the race I hate,
So near they show'd me to the brink of fate;
When seven long weeks in these damn'd hulks I lay,
Barr'd down by night and fainting through the day . . .
Not unreveng'd shall all the woes we bore,
Be swallow'd up inglorious as before:
The dreadful secrets of these prison caves,
Half sunk, half floating on my Hudson's waves.

—Philip Freneau, "The British Prison-Ship" (1781)

The prisoners and crew of the HMS *Jersey* met a variety of fates. Captain David Laird, commander of the prison ship, returned to Scotland after the war and worked on a merchant ship. His position required him to periodically sail to New York harbor, but on such occasions Laird chose to remain on his ship, never again stepping foot on American soil. Joshua Loring, who oversaw British prisons and prisoners, fled to England in November 1782 to reunite with his family. He never returned to America, passing in 1789 at the age of forty-five.

The vile marshal of the Provost prison, William Cunningham, remained unrepentant and malicious to the bitter end of the war.

Not surprisingly, newspapers delighted in sharing an amusing story from the waning weeks of the war. It seems that a couple who operated a tavern on Murray Street in New York City had begun their celebration early by flying the new American flag atop their establishment, something that was prohibited in British-occupied territory. Outraged by the display of patriotism and bitter about losing the war, Cunningham went to the tavern and demanded they take down the flag. With a crowd of curious onlookers watching, the woman who owned the tavern hit the hated warden over the head, presumably with a broom or stick. The blow made "the powder fly from his hair, and caused him to beat a hasty retreat, amid the jeers and laughter of some few spectators." Other similar incidents occurred as the British were abandoning the city, including one on Chapel Street: on his way out of New York, Cunningham again tried to get residents there to take down their American flags. The warden cursed and shouted threats, but was greeted by disdain and defiance. Nor were the soldiers under his command willing to try to enforce his orders. The war was over.

Cunningham evacuated the city in November 1783, sailing on a British man-of-war back to England. It is uncertain as to what became of the cruel man. An American newspaper suggested he was arrested for forgery in August 1791, sentenced to prison, and later hanged at Newgate Prison. Sources claimed he offered a dying confession, admitting that he killed and starved hundreds of Americans and even that he placed arsenic in the prisoners' food. One source recorded his final words as "I shudder to think of the murders I have been accessary to, both with and without orders from the government, especially while in New York, during which time there were more than 2000 prisoners starved in the different churches, by stopping their rations, which I sold." Yet no reliable record exists to validate the stories, and historians have questioned their veracity.

There are also conflicting accounts of what became of the infamous David Sproat, the commissary who oversaw the *Jersey*. A handful of scholars, such as Philip Ranlet and David Lenox Banks, the latter a descendant of Sproat's, have attempted to defend him, going so far as to suggest that he acted "humanely."* Ranlet points to comments made by Sproat that indicated he tried to help fellow Pennsylvanians in prison who were not being represented by the state, commissaries, or cartels. He also cites letters Sproat wrote defending his tenure as the prison ship commissary, such as one to John Dickinson, a Founding Father who served during the Revolution as both president of Delaware and president of Pennsylvania.† In it Sproat claimed, "Since my appointment, I have at all times contributed as much as it has been in my power to relieve their distress and make confinement as comfortable to them as possible." Ranlet dismisses the allegations of countless American prisoners as unreliable but accepts Sproat's defense of his own unforgivable record as credible. However, the preponderance of letters and evidence offer a far different assessment of Sproat.

Sproat was fired by Admiral Mariot Arbuthnot in September 1780, but after the admiral was replaced, Sproat was given his old job back by Lord George Rodney when he assumed control over British forces. Later, when Loring sailed for England in 1782, Sproat assumed his responsibilities as well. His cruel treatment of prisoners ran from his appointment in October 1779 to the very end of the war.

A few sources suggest Sproat moved to Philadelphia after the war, but most reliable accounts say the commissary moved back to Scotland. Shockingly, one year after the war ended, Sproat requested to be reimbursed for more than £2,000 that he claimed he spent from his own funds to care for the prisoners. Sproat claimed that he had been promised the reimbursement. Robert Morris, the Revolutionary treasurer, submitted the request along with numerous other similar petitions to the Congress, advocating payment as a gesture of goodwill to the British, who still held some Americans captive. It is not certain if he was ever paid, although it appears that Congress initially

---

* Lenox's father, Robert, was Sproat's bookkeeper and relative.
† During the Revolution, the title "president" was used rather than "governor."

rejected the petition but later reversed its position and paid the hated commissary just over £100. The rationale given was the need to ensure that prisoner exchanges continued after the war. Congress reimbursed Joshua Loring approximately £830 of his total claim of £1,050 and also repaid Abraham Skinner and other American commissaries for the funds they used to purchase food and clothing for the prisoners.

Sproat never returned to America, dying in Kirkcudbright, Scotland, in 1799.

The five former prisoners profiled in this book all lived to tell their tales. Christopher Hawkins, the young boy from Rhode Island who went to sea against the British at age thirteen, ended up moving to Fairfield, Connecticut, after the war. In 1791 he moved again, becoming one of the first settlers in the village of Newport, New York. When the village was formally incorporated in 1807, he was chosen to be the first town supervisor. Hawkins would later pen his account of his time on the *Jersey*, which opened with these words: "In the following narrative is given the adventures of one of these lucky few." Hawkins only spent a few days as a prisoner on the *Jersey*, the shortest incarceration of the five prisoners whose stories are told here. But he experienced a number of adventures, battles, captures, and a daring escape during his teenage years. Like the other four prisoners, Hawkins lived far beyond the average life expectancy for the time, dying in 1838 at age seventy. His memoir was published posthumously.

Andrew Sherburne nearly died on his way home after being released, but eventually made it back to Portsmouth and to a family that had long thought him dead. Sherburne dedicated himself to two tasks—informing families of the fate of their loved ones, and becoming an itinerant Baptist preacher. One surviving account places him in Maine as a schoolteacher; another one notes that he traveled west to the frontier. Sherburne's account of the *Jersey* is refreshingly personal and introspective, as he often confesses that he was afraid, shares with the reader his struggle with depression, and admits to breaking down in tears. It is also an important resource on British prisons, as Sherburne was caught and incarcerated three times!

Like the other survivors, Sherburne wrote his memoir late in life, when "there are yet surviving a few, and but a few, who lived, acted and suffered" on the *Jersey*. Sherburne was prompted to pen his account because "the number [of prisoners] is very fast diminishing." It was printed in 1831, in New York. Sadly, as is also the case for most of the other prisoners, there is no surviving likeness of Sherburne and, other than his memoir, no artifacts from his life remain.

Hawkins and Sherburne were barely into their teenage years when they entered the war, but Ebenezer Fox was only twelve. The native of Providence, Rhode Island, was sent away as a child by his family to work for a farmer. Unhappy and looking for "excitement," Fox and a friend ran away and joined the crew of a privateer. The young boy got more than he ever imagined. In addition to his capture and imprisonment on the *Jersey*, Fox was pressed into service with the Royal Navy and sent to Jamaica and France. Remarkably, the teenager made it home in 1783 with fantastical tales. Later in life, Fox was encouraged to write a memoir by his seven grandchildren, who begged, "Do tell us your revolutionary adventures, Grandfather." At age seventy-five he did. Fox lived to the age of eighty, passing on December 14, 1843.

Like his fellow prisoners, Thomas Andros carried the physical and emotional scars of his time on the *Jersey* for the remainder of his life. He spent those years thinking at length about his imprisonment and the nature of war, concluding late in life that "war in all its causes and forms" was only justifiable in "absolute self-defense" and when pursued with the Christian principles of trying to avoid as many casualties as possible and treating prisoners humanely. After a long and difficult convalescence at home at the end of the war, Andros fulfilled his promise to God to become a preacher. He was ordained in March 1788 and served as the pastor of the Congregationalist Church of Berkley in Massachusetts. Believing it was divine providence that saved him, Andros, like Sherburne, devoted the remainder of his life to religion.

The former prisoner found some closure to his experience on the *Jersey* by writing his memoirs, saying of the task, "Perhaps the recollection of these things will hereafter be delightful."* Andros felt that, for prisoners to cope with their harsh imprisonment, they must realize it was God's will. The prisoners, wrote Andros, needed to understand that their suffering on the *Jersey* was "good and just," and the cause "by which we were sustained and our deliverance effected, was the bestowment of a gracious and compassionate Creator." Andros closed his memoir with a prayer: "Thy thoughts of love to me surmount, the power of numbers to recount."

After fifty-seven years in the pulpit, Andros died in Berkley in December 1845 at the advanced age of eighty-six. An organization of ministers said of Andros on his passing, "He was an eminent example of self-taught men, a warm patron of education and a deeply-interested friend of the rising generation. As a preacher he held high rank; as a pastor he was affectionate, laborious and untiring in interest, both for the spiritual and temporal welfare of his people."

Thomas Dring was finally released after his five-month-long ordeal aboard the *Jersey*. He recalled of that first night on the sloop headed back home for freedom that he had nightmares of guards shouting, "Down, Rebels, down!" He and his former crewmates sat up at night enjoying, for the first time in a long time, candlelight, clean water, fruit and vegetables, fresh air, and a view of the stars overhead. The next day they ate a satisfying breakfast and sat on deck experiencing the sun as free men.

Dring later learned that his former captain of the privateer *Chance* had made it back to Providence and that it was he who arranged with

---

* Andros borrowed the line from Virgil's *Aeneid*, the epic poem written between 29 and 19 B.C.E. about Aeneas, a Trojan who comforts his tortured companions by reminding them that perhaps one day their recollections of the event would help to heal the horrors of it.

the owners of the *Chance* and John Creed, a deputy commissary of prisoners from Providence, the prisoner exchange.

The journey home was temporarily placed in jeopardy when the sloop was detained by two British warships. However, with the war ending, the Americans were let go. But their troubles were far from over. A number of the former prisoners were severely malnourished and suffering from diseases contracted on the *Jersey*. Dring worried that they might not live to see Rhode Island.

One of them was a young boy from Barrington, Rhode Island, named Bicknell, who was in the grip of a severe fever and looked as if he would die. Bicknell reminded Dring of Palmer, the twelve-year-old cabin boy from the *Chance*, who died after Dring's experimental inoculation the first day on the *Jersey*. As an officer, Dring felt responsible for both lads from his ship. As the ship neared Narragansett, Bicknell asked Dring to carry him ashore so that he might "look once more upon" his home. The boy remained remarkably stoic, bolstered by the knowledge that he would at least be buried back in Rhode Island by his family. His "sensible" courage overwhelmed Dring and affected all the men.

As the sloop anchored in the harbor, Dring agreed to take Bicknell in a rowboat to land and then by carriage to his home, which was but a short distance from the wharf. Bicknell was so weak from yellow fever that he could not sit up, collapsing on Dring's shoulder. Hearing the boy's breathing getting fainter and fainter, the officer called out to two boys in town to run to Bicknell's home and quickly fetch his family. Dring remained in the small launch near the dock, comforting Bicknell. As the two sat by the dock, Dring wrote that "God heard his prayers to be buried with his family." Only moments later, Bicknell's family arrived at the dock. But it was too late. The officer handed them their "yet warm, but lifeless" son.

After staying briefly at the boy's home, Dring returned to the sloop, which again set sail. The sloop reached Providence at eight o'clock that night. Fortunately, there were no quarantines in place to detain the former prisoners. However, because several of the men on board the sloop had the fever, the captain anchored in the middle of the river as a precaution. Word quickly spread through the town that the prisoners had arrived, and soon people were lined up waving to the sloop and hollering to them with news of loved ones. One of the officers called back that the ship had yellow fever aboard. The dock emptied immediately and the town was gripped by fear.

The former prisoners were eventually put ashore. Dring remembered the look of alarm when the people of Providence saw the ghostly figures shuffling through town. Many residents refused the men access to their homes or businesses, but a few charitable families opened up their hearts and brought the sailors food, water, and clothing. Clark and Nightingale, the owners of the *Chance*, who had helped arrange their former crewmembers' exchange, also supplied the prisoners with necessities.

Thomas Dring finally made it home. Once he fully recovered from his ordeal on the *Jersey*, he joined the crew of a merchant fleet and soon after became the commander of a ship sailing out of Providence. Captain Dring spent the rest of his life in Providence, but most of it at sea, gaining a reputation as an "able and experienced officer." Like his fellow prisoners, he often thought of the *Jersey*. He still carried a scar on his hand from his self-administered inoculation that saved his life on the ship. The sight of it, he stated, always brought back vivid memories, such as of the massacre on July 4. Yet Dring never regretted his "captivity nor my sufferings; for the recollection of them has ever taught me how to enjoy my after life, with a greater degree of contentment than I should perhaps have otherwise ever experienced."

Forty-two years later he wrote his memoir, believing he had a responsibility "to record the history of their former sufferings." At the time he was only one of three members of the crew of sixty-five still alive and the only officer. The sixty-page book was completed in 1824, less than a year before his death on August 8, 1825. In the beginning of the memoir, Dring wrote, "Hence, so little that is authentic, has ever been published upon the subject, and so scanty are the materials for information respecting it, which have as yet been given to the rising generations of our country, that it has already become a matter of doubt, even among many of the intelligent and well-informed of our young citizens, whether the tales of the Prison-Ships, such as they have been told, have not been exaggerated beyond the reality." He promised to correct the record with an accurate accounting of the struggles aboard the *Jersey* and tell the story so that those who perished would not be forgotten.

Dring noted of his feeble effort to tell the stories of the ghost ship of Brooklyn, "They have not been exaggerated . . . but not one half the detail of its horrors has ever been portrayed."

"*The Poet of the American Revolution*"

Known as "The Poet of the American Revolution," Philip Freneau was a prolific and prominent writer and newspaper editor who happened to be imprisoned on the British prison ship *Scorpion* during the Revolutionary War. Freneau spent roughly six weeks suffering aboard the disease-infested ship, and his story was not unlike those of his fellow patriots on the nearby *Jersey*.

After his release on July 12, 1780, Freneau traveled to New Jersey and then to his home in Philadelphia, recalling, "I was afflicted with such pains in my joints, I could scarcely walk, and besides, was weakened with a raging fever." Freneau was in such dire straits that he worried his "ghastly looks" would terrify his family and neighbors. Yet as soon as he arrived home Freneau began work on his book-length, first-person account of his experiences on the prison ship. It was published in 1781 as "The British Prison-Ship," the work from which the poetic lines at the beginning of each chapter in this book were taken.

Born on January 2, 1752, in New York to Pierre Freneau, a French Huguenot who sought refuge in America from the persecution of King Louis XIV, and Agnes Watson, a "most cultivated and beautiful woman" from Scotland, young Philip attended Princeton, where he was James Madison's roommate and friend.* The young man intended to become a preacher. However, he developed a passion for politics and travel while in college. Torn between an interest in the studious and sedentary life of a writer and poet and a passion for adventure, Freneau satisfied both yearnings by traveling to the West Indies in 1776, joining the New Jersey militia in 1778, and then writing about his experiences. All the while, he wrote travel essays and anti-British satire that rebelled against the work of established writers and poets, which Freneau deemed to be too culturally conservative and "holdovers of old Tory attitudes." His work soon gained fame as being written for the masses.

In addition to his political essays against the British, Freneau published commentary on the issues of the day such as the essay "The Virtue of Tobacco," which opined on slavery and the South. He also penned lighthearted works such as "The Jug of Rum," which discussed the popular West Indies drink, and even dabbled in comedic poetry, as is evident in "On a Honeybee." But his most ambitious writing centered on the British prison ships, including the memoir *Some Account of the Capture of the Ship Aurora* in 1780, which chronicles his time at sea and as a prisoner.

Freneau was not a sailor; rather, he was a passenger on the *Aurora*, which was sailing from Philadelphia to the West Indies. Unfortunately for Freneau, the *Aurora* doubled as a privateer and had captured a "small sloop" on May 25 before heading to the West Indies, seizing the stores of corn and sending their prize to Cape May. But the next day at three o'clock in the afternoon, the British brig HMS *Active* and larger frigate HMS *Iris* spotted the *Aurora* and gave chase.

The poet begged the *Aurora*'s captain, a man named Laboyteaux, to sail to Egg Harbor on the Jersey coast and run the ship aground,

---

* Huguenots were French Protestants who had been persecuted in Europe by the Catholic Church.

but Laboyteaux refused and tried to outrun the British warships. Soon the warships closed the distance and opened fire. The *Aurora* was hit "several times" by cannon fire and was leaking badly. Her small 4-pounders were but "trifles" against the powerful guns of the brig and frigate. A final blast struck on the main deck, blowing apart a row boat, and tearing through Captain Laboyteaux, who died of his wounds later that night. Freneau survived, but the deck of the *Aurora* was strewn with debris and bleeding sailors. As the *Iris* pulled alongside, a half dozen men on the sinking privateer lowered the remaining skiff and raced for the coast. The rest, including Freneau, remained on board and were captured.

Freneau remembered arguing with the British captain: "[I said to him] I was a passenger, going on my private business to the islands, and insisted that such usage was cruel, inhuman, and unjust. He asked me if I was not a colonist: I told him I was an American. Then, said he, you have no right to expect favors more than others." Freneau's fate was sealed when the British discovered Captain Laboyteaux's manifest, which listed the poet as a "gunner."

Freneau was "cruelly seized and driven down" belowdecks on the *Iris* without being allowed to get his chest with his clothing and possessions. There, the Americans were shackled along with roughly a hundred other prisoners in the fore hold. Two hundred others were crowded elsewhere on the ship. The poet remembered the ghastly experience: "so many melancholy sights, and dismal countenances . . . the stench of whom was almost intolerable." It was also so hot and crowded that Freneau believed he would suffocate. He again raised objections with his captors, but was ridiculed by the crew.

The *Iris* sailed to New York, and on June 1, 1780, Freneau was put aboard the prison ship *Scorpion*. The poet recorded the experience: "At sundown we were ordered down between the decks to the number of nearly three hundred of us. The best lodging I could procure this night was on a chest, almost suffocated with the heat and stench. I expected to die before morning, but human nature can bear more than one would at first suppose. The want of bedding and the loss of all my clothes rendered me wretched indeed . . . for who would assure me that I should not lie six or eight months in this horrid prison?"

Two nights after being imprisoned on the *Scorpion*, the "weather was very stormy and the river uncommonly rough." The old ship rolled badly, causing water to gush into the lower decks and over the prisoners lying about. In the dark, the prisoners began screaming, "The ship is sinking!" A panicked mob of prisoners raced up to the main hatch, where the guards, with swords drawn, slashed at the prisoners and beat them back into the hold.

In the days after the incident, the prisoners became increasingly desperate. A group of about thirty-five men attempted to escape. The opportunity presented itself when a schooner pulled alongside the *Scorpion*. The men on the upper deck attacked the guards, who were momentarily distracted by the arriving schooner. There were only a handful of Hessians standing sentry and the prisoners managed to overpower them. One guard was tied to the railing; the others were forced into the guardhouse and the door was sealed. The malnourished prisoners then rushed the schooner. The sailors onboard used hand-spikes and other weapons to repel what to them must have resembled ghosts and demons from Hell. It was futile. The prisoners poured over the deck and attacked the few sailors crewing the schooner. They succeeded in commandeering the ship.

As the prisoners were sailing away on the schooner, other guards on the *Scorpion* who had heard the commotion appeared on the upper deck. They quickly freed their trapped colleagues and launched a counterattack to retake the ship. In the fighting that ensued, the guards managed to beat the prisoners back down into the holds of the *Scorpion*, then fired indiscriminately into the lower deck, killing a few prisoners. The guards managed to take back the *Scorpion*, but several of the prisoners escaped.

The next morning, the deputy commissary of prisons boarded the ship to investigate the uprising. The prisoners—whether they had taken part in the coup or not—were placed in irons and forced to spend the day facedown on the deck in the hot sun without any food or water. One of the wounded prisoners died from the exposure. From that moment on, food and water rations were cut and guards became increasingly violent and cruel. Indeed, the guards on the *Scorpion* appear to have been nearly as cruel as those on the *Jersey*. Freneau remembered the daily routine of being driven belowdecks with threats of violence and screams of "Down, Yankees!" and "Damn'd dogs, descend, or by our broadswords die!" The routine mirrored that on the *Jersey*.

Freneau soon contracted one of the diseases that plagued the prison ships: "When finding myself taken with a fever, I procured myself to be put on the sick list, and the same day was sent with a number of others to the *Hunter* hospital ship, lying in the East River."

Of the hospital ship, he wrote, "She was miserably dirty and cluttered. Her decks leaked to such a degree that the sick were deluged with every shower of rain. Between decks they lay along struggling in the agonies of death, dying with putrid and bilious fevers, lamenting their hard fate to die at such a fatal distance from their friends; others totally insensible, and yielding their last breath in all the horrors of light-headed frenzy."

Freneau nearly died in early July, but survived his captivity and was released on July 12, 1780.

After the publication of his book-length poem about the prison ships and the end of the war, Freneau published additional collections of poetry. In 1790, at the urging of his friends Thomas Jefferson and James Madison, he established the *National Gazette* in Philadelphia, a newspaper that espoused Anti-Federalist views and was critical of George Washington's presidency and such politicians as John Adams and Alexander Hamilton, prompting the president to label Freneau as a "rascal." Jefferson, however, praised his friend, claiming Freneau "saved our Constitution which was galloping fast into monarchy."

Late in life, Freneau returned to sea from time to time, but retired to a farm where he wrote about a number of topics including travel, nature, Indians, warfare, and politics. He ended up revising his poetic masterpiece six times over the remaining years of his life. Freneau's poetry remains as an important contribution to early American romanticism and lyricism. It also offers a valuable glimpse into life aboard a British prison ship during the American Revolution.

List of Prison Ships

PRISON SHIPS IN WALLABOUT BAY

Year	Ship	Note
1776	*Whitby*	Held 250 prisoners
1777	*Kitty*	Held 250 prisoners (burned in 1777)
	Unknown ship I	Held 250 prisoners (burned in 1778)
1778	Unknown ship II	Held 500 prisoners (burned in 1778)
1779	*Good Hope*	Held 250 prisoners (burned in 1780)
	Unknown ship III	Held 500 prisoners
1780	*Falmouth*	Held 200 prisoners (hospital ship)
	Hope	Held 200 men (hospital ship)
	Hunter	Held 200 prisoners (hospital ship)
	Jersey	Held 400 prisoners
	Prince of Wales	Relocated from the North River
	Scorpion	Held 300 prisoners
	Strombolo	Held 200 prisoners

1781   *Jersey*   Held 850–1,000 prisoners

1782   *Jersey*   Held 1,000–1,200 prisoners

1783   *Bristol*   No records (hospital ship)
        Frederick   Unknown numbers (hospital ship)
        Jersey   Held 1,000–1,200 prisoners
        John   Held 200–300 prisoners
        Perseverance   Unknown numbers (hospital ship)

Note: A few ships were also moored in the North River and East River.

Notes

Introduction

Pericles' funeral oration: "Thucydides: Pericles' Funeral Oration." For analysis of the meaning of such military burials, see "Pericles Funeral Oration in Depth."

Lincoln's Gettysburg Address: Wills, *Lincoln at Gettysburg*; see also Lincoln, "The Gettysburg Address." For a discussion on the meaning of military burials, see Delahunty, "The Burials of Greek Warriors."

"No degree of gratitude": Taylor, *Martyrs to the Revolution*, p. iii.

Walt Whitman poems: "Brooklyniana, No. 5" (see also Walt Whitman Archive, http://whitmanarchive.org/published/periodical/journalism/tei/per.00220.html); Whitman, *Uncollected Poetry and Prose*, pp. 236–245; "Ode," July 4, 1846 (see also Walt Whitman Archive, http://whitmanarchive.org/published/periodical/poems /per.00062).

West's address: West, *Horrors*, pp. 2–3.

"All this evidence": Taylor, *Martyrs to the Revolution*, p. 33.

Stories of suffering: Ranlet, "Tory David Sproat," p. 185.

"Among the varied events of the war": Dring, *Recollections*, p. 1.

Hawkins's description and quote: Hawkins, *Life and Adventure*, p. 1.

"Temporary triumph of passions": Taylor, *Martyrs to the Revolution*, p. 5.

Descriptions of and quotes about ship: West, *Horrors*, p. 5.

The *Jersey* as a symbol and the quote "America's historical memory": Ranlet, "Tory David Sproat," p. 185.

Newspapers influencing public opinion about the war: Humphrey, "Top 10."

Chapter 1. Warship

War of Spanish Succession: Falkner, *The War of Spanish Succession*.

Anglo-Spanish War: Adams, "The Spanish Armada."

War of Jenkins' Ear: see Davis, *America's Hidden History*.

Horace Walpole quote: Hickman, "War of Jenkins' Ear"; see also Ford, *Admiral Vernon and the Navy*.

Lawrence Washington: Nolan, "Lawrence Washington."

"The braces, bowlines shot away": Willis, *Fighting at Sea*, p. 158.

Early battles of the *Jersey*: Armbruster, *Wallabout Prison Ships*, p. 16.

"At the commencement" and "Without ornament": Taylor, *Martyrs to the Revolution*, pp. 12–13.

CHAPTER 2. "THE GLORIOUS CAUSE"

Rule Britannia: Burrows, *Forgotten Patriots*, p. 31.

"Traitors": Brigham, *British Royal Proclamations*, pp. 224–230.

British expeditionary force in summer of 1776 and challenges to George Washington's command: Myers, "George Washington: Defeated."

"Tho' I am truly sensible": United States Continental Congress, *Journals*, vol. II, p. 92 (June 16, 1775).

"Without clothes and shoes": Armbruster, *Wallabout Prison Ships*, p. 7.

Challenges facing the hungry Continental Army: Allen, *Naval History of the American Revolution*, p. 212. "Every type of horse food": Jones, *History of New York*, p. 599; Force, *Archives*, 5th Series, vol. I, p. 835; and letter from George Washington to Congress, August 9, 1776, in Washington, *Writings* (ed. Ford), vol. 4, p. 337.

"The time is now near" and "Those who have committed": Washington, *Papers* (ed. Chase), vol. 5, pp. 179–182; McCullough, *1776*, p. 145.

Start of the battle: Manders, *Battle of Long Island*, p. 40; and Gallagher, *Battle of Brooklyn*, pp. 101–103.

"The Hessians and our brave": Manders, *Battle of Long Island*, pp. 43–44; Gallagher, *Battle of Brooklyn*, pp. 113–125; and Onderdonk, *Revolutionary Incidents*, pp. 137–140.

"The rebels had resolved": Myers, "George Washington: Defeated."

"I never shall forget": Stiles, *Letters from the Prisons*, pp. 3–16; see Gillet's letter dated December 2, 1776.

Attempts to surrender to the Hessians and their hanging prisoners: Johnston, *The Battle of Harlem Heights*, pp. 150–155, and Johnston, *The Campaign of 1776*. Brutality of the Hessians and surrendering Americans "massacred": Burrows, *Forgotten Patriots*, pp. 5–6.

"Good God, what brave fellows": quoted in McCullough, *1776*, p. 177.

Washington's escape from Brooklyn: Stockwell, "Battle of Long Island."

"The stench of the dead": Serle, *Journal*, pp. 79–92; Onderdonk, *Revolutionary Incidents*, p. 136; Gallagher, *Battle of Brooklyn*, pp. 135–137; and Manders, *Battle of Long Island*, p. 62.

The terrible conditions of Brooklyn after the battle: Burrows and Wallace, *Gotham*, pp. 241–242.

Howe's dilemma about prisoners: Burrows, *Forgotten Patriots*, p. 9.

CHAPTER 3. CITY OF PRISONS

The number of prisoners arrested: Taylor, *Martyrs to the Revolution*, p. 7.

"City of Prisons": "City of Prisons," pp. 461–462.

Finding jails for prisoners: Lindsey, "Treatment of American Prisoners," p. 9.

"A number of people": Cresswell, *Journal*, pp. 244–245.

Poor treatment of prisoners: Taylor, *Martyrs to the Revolution*, p. 8.

"Burning and laying waste": Starkey, "War and Culture," p. 15; and Daughan, *If by Sea*, pp. 43–46.

Same strategy in War of 1812: Watson, *America's First Crisis*.

"Rebels taken in arms": Gruber, *Howe Brothers*, p. 31, see letter by Captain MacKenzie.

"Brutal severity": Amerman, "Treatment of American Prisoners," p. 263.

"The term rebel": Graydon, *Memoirs of His Time*, pp. 205–210.

"Side arms, watches": Johnston, *Battle of Harlem Heights*, p. 198.

Treatment of Lt. Lindsay and other prisoners: Burrows, *Forgotten Patriots*, p. 45; and "The William Darlington Story," *Pennsylvania Evening Post*, May 3, 1777.

"Each morning, several frozen": Stone, "Experiences of a Prisoner," p. 527.

"The distress of the prisoners" and "Rather than experience": Force, *American Archives*, 5th Series, vol. 3, pp. 1429–1430.

Insufficient rations: Stone, "Experiences of a Prisoner," p. 528.

Lack of wood and resorting to eating shoes: Lindsey, "Treatment of American Prisoners," p. 11.

"In a confused manner" and "The next day": Stone, "Experiences of a Prisoner," p. 527.

"Loring fingered": Burrows, *Forgotten Patriots*, p. 10.

"As Cleopatra of old": Alden, *History of the American Revolution*.

Descriptions of Cunningham and Provost: O'Malley, "Provost Marshal Cunningham"; Dandridge, *American Prisoners*, ch. 5; Lossing, *Pictoral Field-Book*; and Taylor, *Martyrs to the Revolution*, p. 8. The story of Captain Birdsall: Dandridge, *American Prisoners*, ch. 21.

"Under cover of": Lossing, *Pictoral Field-Book*; and Watson, *Annals*.

"Cruelty and wickedness" and other quotes: Dandridge, *American Prisoners*, pp. 100–102, 200–202.

"Would threaten to hang" and other quotes: American Scenic and Historic Preservation Society, *Old Martyrs' Prison*; and Field, *Historic and Antiquarian Scenes*, pp. 14–16.

Account of Cunningham even beating prisoner's wife: Taylor, *Martyrs to the Revolution*, p. 30.

Nathan Hale quotes and capture: "The Execution of Nathan Hale, 1776," Eyewitness to History and the Connecticut Society of the Sons of the American Revolution (www.connecticutstar.org/patriots/hale-nathan.htm).

Quote "that many of the cruelties" and correspondence between Boudinot, Washington, and Howe: Force, *Archives*, 5th Series, vol. 3, pp. 1311, 1483. For a discussion of the concerns about Cunningham and prisoners, see also Dandridge, *American Prisoners*, ch. 5; Boudinot, "Journal of Events"; "City of Prisons," p. 461, Lindsey, "Treatment of American Prisoners," p. 14; and Stone, "Experiences of a Prisoner," p. 529.

The Royal Navy capturing ships and sailors: Watson, *America's First Crisis*.

Howe and Loring and the dilemma of the prisoners: Burrows, *Forgotten Patriots*, pp. 12–13.

"Great, however, as were": West, *Horrors*, p. 4.

CHAPTER 4. PRIVATEERS

The Royal Navy in America: see Coggins, *Ships and Seamen*.

State of the American navy and letters of marque to establish privateers: Frayler, "Privateers in the American Revolution"; Chidsey, *American Privateers*; Armbruster, *Wallabout Prison Ships*, pp. 6–7; and Maclay, *History of American Privateers*, p. 113.

CHAPTER 5. PATRIOTS

Hawkins's description of the *Eagle*: Hawkins, *Life and Adventure*, pp. 5–6. Captain Porter and *Eagle* next to the British ship: Hawkins, p. 6. Caught in the gale: Hawkins, p. 7.

Dring sailing on the *Chance*: Dring, *Recollections*, p. 7. Dring caught by the *Belisarius*: Dring, pp. 7–8.

Andros as boy: Andros, *Old Jersey Captive*, p. 3, preface. Andros fighting in the war: Andros, pp. 59–61. "A good effective Firearm" and "the first day of December": Continental Army Enlistment Form, June 1776.

Andros aboard the *Hannah*: Andros, *Old Jersey Captive*, pp. 62–63. Andros and taking a ship as a prize: Andros, pp. 6–7. Andros captured: Andros, p. 7.

Fox's youth: Fox, *Adventures*, p. 7. Apprenticed as a boy: Fox, pp. 15–17. Employment as a sailor: Fox, p. 19. The first battle and nearly being captured: Fox, p. 34. "Whistled around my head," "wet clothes," and other quotes: Fox, p. 35.

Sherburne's youth: Sherburne, *Memoirs*, pp. 2, 14. His exposure to religion: Sherburne, pp. 14–16. Quotes "I wished myself . . . " and "I was filled with anxiety": Sherburne, p. 18. Quotes "Almost a man," "Pack up their clothes," and others: Sherburne, p. 19.

CHAPTER 6. ADVENTURE ON THE HIGH SEAS

Fox discussing "largest sum": Fox, *Adventures*, p. 38. "Evil consequences": Fox, p. 42. Fox joining the war: Fox, p. 47. Being recruited to the navy: Fox, p. 56. Song the new recruits sang: Fox, p. 58. Fox's first naval battle: Fox, pp. 62–64. "Paraded the streets": Fox, p. 79. "Evil day": Fox, p. 85. Fox's capture and "damned rebels": Fox, p. 89.

Sherburne first setting sail: Sherburne, *Memoirs*, p. 20. Seeing sails by Jamaica: Sherburne, p. 21. *Ranger*'s crew capturing their first prize: Sherburne, pp. 22–24.

Fighting in Charleston: Sherburne, p. 27. Sherburne's first time being captured and trip back home: Sherburne, p. 29.

Quotes and description of Sherburne going back to sea: Sherburne, *Memoirs*, p. 35. Quotes and description of the cursed cruise to Canada: Sherburne, pp. 38–41. As a captive at Old Mill Prison: Sherburne, pp. 44, 79–81. Back home and promising not to go back to sea: Sherburne, p. 103. Quotes and description of the *Scorpion*'s being captured and the crew sent to New York: Sherburne, pp. 108–109. "Half starved, emaciated" and other quotes: Sherburne, pp. 110–111.

Reputation of the *Jersey* and sailors' fear of her: Ranlet, *New York Loyalists*, pp. 110–111; and Anderson, "Establishment of British Supremacy," pp. 81–89.

CHAPTER 7. FLOATING DUNGEONS

Crime and prisons in England: Campbell, *Intolerable Hulks*, p. 10. "The fact is": Bolton, "William Eden," p. 37. A bill to use prison ships: Bolton, "William Eden," p. 36. Prison ships in the West Indies: Campbell, *Intolerable Hulks*, p. 129.

Problems with the prison ships: Rigden, *Floating Prisons*.

Transport ships hulked in America: Dandridge, *American Prisoners*, pp. 95, 224. The Hulks Act: Campbell, *Intolerable Hulks*, pp. 5–15. For a discussion of the early prison ships, see Johnson, *English Prison Hulks*, p. 84.

Description of Wallabout Bay: Dandridge, *American Prisoners*, ch. 21.

Details on the *Whitby*: Stiles, *History of the City of Brooklyn*, vol. I, p. 333.

"Bad provisions": West, *Horrors*, p. 4.

"Soon, according to another" and Johnson's account: Dandridge, *American Prisoners*, ch. 21. "Our present situation," "Crowded promiscuously together," and other quotes: Dandridge, *American Prisoners*, ch. 21. The letter in question was written on December 9, 1776, onboard the *Whitby*, while the *Connecticut Gazette* article is from February 8, 1777; see also Force, *Archives*, 5th series, vol. 3, p. 1138.

Robert Sheffield's description: *Connecticut Gazette*, July 10, 1778, and Onderdonk, *Revolutionary Incidents*, pp. 227–228. Thorp's description: see Thorp, Revolutionary War Pension Application, file W15427, Records of the Veterans Administration, Record Group 15, National Archives. Ichabod Perry's description: Perry, *Reminiscences of the Revolution*, pp. 15–20. William Gamble's and William Sterrett's descriptions: Dandridge, *American Prisoners*, ch. 21 (article is from the *Connecticut Gazette*, February 8, 1777).

"During two months": Taylor, *Martyrs to the Revolution*, pp. 9–10.

"Dead bodies were hoisted": Little, "Revolutionary War Pension Application," Records of the Veterans Administration, Record Group 15, National Archives.

"Even by fire" and "So great was": Taylor, *Martyrs to the Revolution*, pp. 11–12.

"The prisoners, except a few": Johnson, "Notes and Observations"; Dandridge, *American Prisoners*, ch. 21; and West, "Prison Ships," p. 122. Descriptions of other ships arriving at Wallabout: Amerman, "Treatment of American Prisoners," p. 268; Lindsey, "Treatment of American Prisoners," p. 15; and West, "Prison Ships," pp. 4–5.

CHAPTER 8. DEAD RECKONING

Description of the *Jersey*: Dandridge, *American Prisoners*, p. 242; and Bushnell, *The Prison Ship "Jersey."* Early accounts of the *Jersey*: Onderdonk, *Revolutionary Incidents*, p. 229, and *Pennsylvania Packet*, August 22, 1780.

The number of prisoners on the *Jersey*: "American Prisoners of the Revolution: Names of 8000"; and Lossing, *Pictoral Field-Book*, vol. 2, p. 660.

The *Jersey* as the main prison ship: Dandridge, *American Prisoners*, p. 249.

Accounts by Captain John van Dyke and Alexander Coffin of prisoners moved to *John* in 1782: Dandridge, *American Prisoners*, p. 317.

"Incoherent ravings": Dring, *Recollections*, p. 42.

Descriptions of prisoners stealing, stumbling, and suffering: Amerman, "Treatment of American Prisoners," p. 270; and Taylor, *Martyrs to the Revolution*, p. 27.

Descriptions of the waste tub, officers' bunk, and "dismal" conditions of the "lower dungeon": Dring, *Recollections*, pp. 40, 47. Discussion of the prisoners in the gangways and on the upper deck: Dring, pp. xiv, 37–38.

A system of governance on the *Jersey*: Dring, *Recollections*, pp. 84–86. Dring's account of the rules: Dring, pp. 84, 86–87. Enforcing and violating rules: Andros, *Old Jersey Captive*, p. 13.

"Most of these," "suffered even more," "British officers," and other quotes: Dring, *Recollections*, pp. 43, 50–51; and Fox, *Adventures*, p. 108.

Accounts and quotes about European prisoners on the *Jersey*: Onderdonk, *Revolutionary Incidents*, pp. 228–232, and Fox, *Adventures*, p. 108.

Treatment of American prisoners in England: Taylor, *Martyrs to the Revolution*, p. 18, and Armbruster, *Wallabout Prison Ships*, p. 17. Fox's description and quotes such as "The inhabitants": Fox, *Adventures*, p. 108; and Dandridge, *American Prisoners*, p. 256.

CHAPTER 9. WELCOME TO HELL

"I'll soon fix you," "multitude of," and other quotes: Dring, *Recollections*, p. 9.

Information on Loring, Cunningham, and Sproat: Dring, *Recollections*, pp. 9–10.

Sproat's blaming prisoners' deaths on Washington: Amerman, "Treatment of American Prisoners," p. 269.

"Universally detested": Taylor, *Martyrs to the Revolution*, p. 15.

Sproat as a "refugee" and starting his job as commissary: Ranlet, "Tory David Sproat," pp. 187, 189, 198; and Lowenthal, *Hell on the East River*, p. 11.

"A pritty little fortune": Ranlet, "Tory David Sproat," p. 187.

Refugees: Calhoon, *Loyalist*, pp. 393–394; and Skemp, *William Franklin*, pp. 233–234.

Sproat's appointments: Ranlet, "Tory David Sproat," p. 189.

Location of *Jersey* in Wallabout Bay: Andros, *Old Jersey Captive*, pp. 7–8.

"A lamentable thing," "Death has no relish," and other descriptions of capture by the *Belisarius*: Dring, *Recollections*, pp. 12–13; and Taylor, *Martyrs to the Revolution*, p. 16.

"It was my hard fortune": Dring, *Recollections*, p. 5. The cabin boy Palmer: Dring, p. 12.

"A large proportion": Sherburne, *Memoirs*, p. 107.

"Stripped of everything": Quote by Stephen Buckland in Stiles, *Letters from the Prisons*, p. 20.

"Getting on quite" and "The yearning wish": Hawkins, *Life and Adventure*, p. 7. "An opportunity," "A fit of roaming," "Prospect of a long," and other quotes: Hawkins, pp. 7–8. Descriptions of and quotes about *Jersey*: Hawkins, pp. iv, 8–9.

"I found myself among" and other quotes about boarding *Jersey*: Dring, *Recollections*, p. 13.

Morning eating schedule on the ship: Lindsey, "Treatment of American Prisoners," p. 17.

"From every direction": Dring, *Recollections*, p. 14. "Scenes of wretchedness": Dring, p. 15. "How different": Dring, p. 18. "Motley crew of wretches": Dring, pp. 16–17. Discussion of and quotes about inoculation: Dring, p. 20. Death of young Palmer: Dring, p. 66.

Death of Dring's two crewmates: Dring, *Recollections*, p. 68.

Quotes by Andros when boarding *Jersey*: Andros, *Old Jersey Captive*, pp. 9–10. "I was so overwhelmed" and subsequent quotes from Andros about the ship: Andros, pp. 9–10. Describing the numbers of prisoners: Andros, p. 10. "The complete image and anticipation" and description of Hell: Andros, pp. 8–9. "Take heed": Andros, p. 10.

Chapter 10. The Final Voyage

Dring's description of rations and "rancid": Dring, *Recollections*, pp. 26–27.

Organization and size of mess: Lossing, *Pictoral Field-Book*, Dring, *Recollections*, p. 26; and "City of Prisons."

Information on the menu and disease: West, "Prison Ships," p. 123.

"Burgoo": Dring, *Recollections*, p. 28.

Pigs on the ship: Taylor, *Martyrs to the Revolution*, p. 25.

"The prisoners received their mess": Dandridge, *American Prisoners*, p. 294.

Butter was "so rancid": Dring, *Recollections*, p. 27.

Bread full of "living vermin": White, "Thomas Andros," p. 519.

"I do not recollect": Andros, *Old Jersey Captive*, p. 12.

"The bread had been": Sherburne, *Memoirs*, p. 107.

"There were never provisions": Wertenbaker, *Father Knickerbocker*, p. 166.

Hawkins's and others' descriptions of food: Hawkins, *Life and Adventure*, p. 8.

The great copper: Armbruster, *Wallabout Prison Ships*, p. 19.

Dring's descriptions of the food and not eating from great copper: Dring, *Recollections*, p. 29. "The most scrupulous": Dring, p. 82. Getting and cutting wood: Dring, pp. 80–83. Descriptions of "His Majesty the Cook": Dring, p. 88. Dring's getting burned by cook: Dring, pp. 31, 87–88. Cook's constant insults: Dring, p. 30.

Old marines on board ship: Dring, *Recollections*, p. 71.

Bringing water on board: Armbruster, *Wallabout Prison Ships*, p. 19.

Sherburne's getting a ration of water: Sherburne, *Memoirs*, p. 115.

"Where all the filth": Hawkins, *Life and Adventure*, p. 8.

Descriptions of the foul water: Dring, *Recollections*, pp. 72–73; and Lindsey, "Treatment of American Prisoners," p. 18.

"Little else could": Andros, *Old Jersey Captive*, p. 8.

Description of the work parties: Dring, *Recollections*, pp. 45–46.

Description of the dead boat and burials: Andros, *Old Jersey Captive*, p. 11; and Watson, *Annals*, p. 336. Dring's going ashore to bury Carver: Dring, *Recollections*, pp. 60–63.

"Not so much from": Dring, *Recollections*, p. 58. "Visit to the land": Dring, p. 65.

Isaac Gibbs and others freezing during burial detail and James Little's description: Revolutionary War Pension Application, file W8256, Records of the Veterans Administration, Record Group 15, National Archives.

"If he is not dead": Taylor, *Martyrs to the Revolution*, pp. 30–31.

Andros's description of shallow graves: Andros, *Old Jersey Captive*, p. 11.

Description of cleaning ship: Andros, *Old Jersey Captive*, p. 12.

"The privilege alone": Dring, *Recollections*, p. 46. "For a few hours": Dring, p. 48.

Sherburne's story of catching pneumonia during transfer: Sherburne, *Memoirs*, pp. 114–115. Everyone's getting wet and sick on the transport ship: Sherburne, p. 117.

Description of cleaning the latrines: Dring, *Recollections*, p. 48.

Chapter 11. Tempest

Crew of *Jersey*: Armbruster, *Wallabout Prison Ships*, p. 17.

"The crew had no": Dring, *Recollections*, p. 38.

"Rebels and traitors": Andros, *Old Jersey Captive*, p. 12.

"The soldiers in charge": Ostrander, *History of Brooklyn*, vol. II, p. 11.

Descriptions of the guards: Lossing, *Pictoral Field-Book*; Taylor, *Martyrs to the Revolution*, p. 19; and Lowenthal, *Hell on the East River*, pp. 25–26.

"Always preferred": Taylor, *Martyrs to the Revolution*, p. 24.

"Removed, and moored": Dring, *Recollections*, pp. xiii–xiv.

"Were hurled promiscuously": Andros, *Old Jersey Captive*, p. 8.

"Self preservation appeared": Taylor, *Martyrs to the Revolution*, p. 19.

"Pointed to their uniforms": Dring, *Recollections*, p. 24. "What? You alive yet?": Dring, pp. 59–60.

Quotes and descriptions of the violent "refugees": Taylor, *Martyrs to the Revolution*, p. 19; and Dring, *Recollections*, pp. 61–62, 67–71.

"Rebels! Turn out your dead!": Taylor, *Martyrs to the Revolution*, p. 31.

"Down, Rebels, down!": Taylor, *Martyrs to the Revolution*, p. 20.

"All's well!": Dring, *Recollections*, p. 49.

"The King of Terrors": Andros, *Old Jersey Captive*, p. 10.

"The whole ship": Andros, *Old Jersey Captive*, p. 12; and Taylor, *Martyrs to the Revolution*, p. 15.

"Putrid fevers": Dring, *Recollections*, p. 18.

"Mingled" together: Andros, *Old Jersey Captive*, p. 12.

"He kill'd as many": Freneau, *British Prison-Ship*, p. xxxx.

"The small pox": Hawkins, *Life and Adventure*, pp. 8–9.

Crew and guards getting diseases: Armbruster, *Wallabout Prison Ships*, p. 19.

Description of the nurses: Dring, *Recollections*, p. 53.

"When the weather": Dring, *Recollections*, p. 54.

Men who were not inoculated: Andros, *Old Jersey Captive*, p. 11.

Problems of overcrowding: Dring, *Recollections*, p. 51.

Dring's describing physical appearance and "their long hair and beards": Dring, *Recollections*, p. 40. "Though conducive to cleanliness" and "ordinary cleanliness was impossible": Dring, p. 41.

Description of and quotes about physicians: Sherburne, *Memoirs*, p. 116; and Freneau, *British Prison-Ships*.

Numbers aboard the *Jersey*: Taylor, *Martyrs to the Revolution*, p. 23; Stiles, *Letters from the Prisons*, p. 20; "letter from Capt. Stephen Buckland," April 9, 1782, letters from April 26, 1782, p. 29, and November 9, 1782, p. 33.

"Cramped up with hundreds": Hawkins, *Life and Adventure*, p. 8.

Estimates of prisoners who died per day: Ranlet, "Tory David Sproat," p. 200.

Deaths during winter: Taylor, *Martyrs to the Revolution*, p. 25.

Gen. Heath's report: Heath, *Heath's Memoirs*, pp. 388–389.

Gen. Washington's letter about overcrowded condition: "George Washington to the officer commanding His Britannic Majesty's ships of war," August 21, 1781, Washington, *Writings* (ed. Fitzpatrick), vol. XXIII, p. 24; "Captain Edmund Affleck to George Washington," August 30, 1781, Washington, *Writings* (ed. Sparks), vol. VIII, pp. 523–524.

"Keep from freezing": Taylor, *Martyrs to the Revolution*, p. 25.

"No fires warmed": "City of Prisons," p. 416.

Hospital ships: Dring, *Recollections*, pp. 51–52.

"The sick were seldome": Taylor, *Martyrs to the Revolution*, p. 14.

Dring's account that only three men returned: Dring, *Recollections*, p. 52.

"Terrible" hospitals: Dring, *Recollections*, p. 52.

Nurses' stealing prisoners' possessions: Sherburne, *Memoirs*, pp. 111–114. "The nurses took more": Taylor, *Martyrs to the Revolution*, p. 27. Sickness and death of Robert Carver: Dring, *Recollections*, p. 54. Fresh air and other conditions on hospital ships: Dring, *Recollections*, pp. 52–53; and Armbruster, *Wallabout Prison Ships*, p. 17.

Crowding on the hospital ships: Lowenthal, *Hell on the East River*, p. 22; Andros, *Old Jersey Captive*, p. 13; and Dring, *Recollections*, p. 50.

"Exceedingly fast": Sherburne, *Memoirs*, p. 112.

"I verily believe": Dandridge, *American Prisoners*, p. 318.

"Wretchedly unsanitary": Sherburne, *Memoirs*, p. 113.

Andros's describing death on hospital ship: Andros, *Old Jersey Captive*, p. 10.

"Relieve myself" and other quotes about hospital ships: Sherburne, *Memoirs*, pp. 114–115.

Ordeal of John and Abraham Fall: Taylor, *Martyrs to the Revolution*, pp. 25, 28.

"Mockery" and other quotes about hospital ships: Taylor, *Martyrs to the Revolution*, p. 14.

"The depravity of the heart": Sherburne, *Memoirs*, p. 114.

The affliction aboard the ship was "sickness of the heart": Dring, *Recollections*, p. 44. Dring's also describing that young sailors "became dismayed" and "died that most awful" and the poem he remembered: Dring, p. 44. Dring's struggles and "These loathsome creatures": Dring, p. 19.

The men had "been through the furnace": Dring, *Recollections*, p. 43. Wishing for death to "not long delay": Dring, p. 18.

Andros wishing for a preacher: Andros, *Old Jersey Captive*, p. 8.

Dring recalling another poem ("Night and day"): Dring, *Recollections*, p. 43.

CHAPTER 12. NEGOTIATIONS

The regiment of refugees "with green uniforms": Dring, *Recollections*, p. 71.

Dring's boast that "During my whole period": Dring, *Recollections*, p. 71.

Andros's also saying "no one [was] seduced": Andros, *Old Jersey Captive*, p. 13.

Ethan Allen's capture and details of arrest: Allen, *Narrative*, p. 32. Allen aboard the ship, "Those will be good": Jellison, *Ethan Allen*, p. 162; and Lindsey, "Treatment of American Prisoners," p. 24. Allen's detainment in castle and "you shall grace": Allen, *Narrative*, pp. 24, 37–38.

Howe and Washington's expressing interest in Allen's imprisonment: Haffner, "The Treatment of Prisoners," pp. 63–68, Jellison; *Ethan Allen*, pp. 171–172; and Huguenin, "Allen, Parolee on Long Island," p. 120.

Ben Franklin's interest in prisoners: Wharton, *Revolutionary Diplomatic Correspondence*, vol. 2, pp. 409–410; see also vol. 6, p. 375.

Prescott's capture and cruelty: Diman, *The Capture of General Richard Prescott*.

British viewed the Continental Army as rebels: Lindsey, "Treatment of American Prisoners," p. 23.

"Captured Americans created": Anderson, "Treatment of Prisoners of War," p. 66.

"Flour exhausted": Stiles, *History of the City of Brooklyn*, vol. I, p. 341.

Problem of feeding an army and "The known shortage": Jones, *New York During the Revolutionary War*, Vol. II, p. 425; and Force, *Archives*, 5th Series, vol. II, p. 838.

Prevailing practices of prisoner exchanges in Europe: Lindsey, "Treatment of American Prisoners," p. 24.

Prisoners taken to castles in England and the *Jersey*: Armbruster, *Wallabout Prison Ships*, p. 12; and Lindsey, "Treatment of American Prisoners," p. 5.

American prisoners did not have "claims" and "Every American soldier": Armbruster, *Wallabout Prison Ships*, p. 18.

Gen. Washington's writing to Gen. Gage in August 1775: Burrows, *Forgotten Patriots*, p. 37; letter "William Eden to Germain," September 18, 1775. Additional letters from Washington to Gage and Howe written in 1775: Force, *Archives*, 4th Series, vol. 3, pp. 245–246; Ranlet, "Tory David Sproat," p. 188; Jordan, "Colonel Elias Boudinot," pp. 460–461; Sterling, "American Prisoners of War," pp. 376–378; and Washington, *Writings* (ed. Fitzpatrick), vol. VII, pp. 4–5, "George Washington to Lord Richard Howe," January 13, 1777.

Gage's responses, "The Britons": Force, *Archives*, vol. 3, pp. 246, 328.

Gen. Washington's reaction to prisoners being murdered in 1775: Lindsey, "Treatment of American Prisoners," p. 8; Force, *Archives*, 4th Series, vol. 3, p. 712; and Washington, *Writings* (ed. Fitzpatrick), vol. 7, p. 246.

Letter to Gen. Howe, "It is hoped that the possession": Force, *Archives*, 4th Series, vol. 4, p. 903; "Lord George Germain to Sir William Howe," February 1, 1776. Additional Howe letters: Letter, "William Howe to Lord Dartmouth," December 14, 1775, in Public Record Office, London, CO 5/93-f, pp. 14–15; see also "George Washington to Thomas Jefferson," November 23, 1779, in Washington, *Writings* (ed. Fitzpatrick), vol. XVII, pp. 166–167; and Ranlet, *New York Loyalists*, pp. 108–110.

Estimates that one of every three Americans taken prisoner perished: Amerman, "Treatment of American Prisoners," p. 257.

Washington's complaining to Howe in March 1777, "Those who have lately": O'Malley, "Fortune of War"; and Taylor, *Martyrs to the Revolution*, p. 36.

"Washington to Howe," January 13, 1777, and "I am sorry": Taylor, *Martyrs to the Revolution*, pp. 35–36. Washington ended his letter of October 13, 1777, with the warning "You may call us": DeWan, "Wretched Prison Ships." "I would beg": Taylor, *Martyrs to the Revolution*, pp. 36–37.

Gen. Montgomery also complained about prisoners: Force, *Archives*, 4th Series, p. 1138.

Washington believed British cruelty was to promote enlistments, "It is preposterously": Washington, *Writings* (ed. Fitzpatrick), vol. 10, p. 65, November 14, 1777. Other letters: Washington, *Writings* (ed. Fitzpatrick), "Washington to de Grasse," October 13, 1781, "to oblige them," vol. 23, p. 255, and "Washington to Laurens," July 10, 1782, vol. 24, p. 421.

Washington's letter to Howe complaining about prisoners ("Similarly"): Taylor, *Martyrs to the Revolution*, p. 37.

Washington's letter to Digby ("if the fortune of war"): Taylor, *Martyrs to the Revolution*, p. 34.

Robert Morris's complaints: "To the Board of War," September 29, 1781, in Morris, *Papers,* vol. 2, p. 374.

"Jefferson to Demeunier," June 26, 1786, and "so long without": Jefferson, *Memoirs,* vol. 1, p. 428.

Washington's response to Howe's request for an exchange ("I shall redeem"): Force, *Archives,* 5th Series, vol. 2, p. 438; see also Howe's letter to Washington, p. 464.

Washington's meeting with Patterson, "Col. Patterson then proceeded": O'Malley, "July 20, 1776."

Howe's realization the war would be long and the details of the first large prisoner exchange in 1777: Lowenthal, *Hell on the East River,* p. 29.

"Exchanging seamen for soldiers": Armbruster, *Wallabout Prison Ships,* p. 11.

"The suffering of seamen": Onderdonk, *Revolutionary Incidents,* p. 233.

The British kept taking more prisoners: Lowenthal, *Hell on the East River,* p. 32.

"Unfit for exchange": Allen, *Naval History,* vol. 2, p. 263.

Loring and "deplorable condition": White, "Thomas Andros," p. 519; and Andros, *Old Jersey Captive,* pp. 20, 23.

One of the earliest exchanges: Stone, "Experiences of a Prisoner," p. 529.

Connecticut prisoners who died after their release: Caulkins, *History of New London,* p. 527.

Lt. Oliver Babcock story: Lindsey, "Treatment of American Prisoners," p. 11.

Congress gives Washington the right to retaliate: United States Continental Congress, *Journals,* vol. XIV, pp. 27–28.

CHAPTER 13. JULY 4

A "very corpulent old woman": Dring, *Recollections,* p. 75. Descriptions of the woman and prisoners, including "distress," "famished wretches," and "Whenever I bought": Dring, p. 76. The prisoners' awaiting Dame Grant "always faithfully" and "awaited with extreme": Dring, pp. 76–77.

The "sutler": Dring, *Recollections,* p. 79. Items brought aboard the ship: Dring, p. 79; and Sherburne, *Memoirs,* p. 113.

Andros quotes on religion: Andros, *Old Jersey Captive,* p. 13. Andros's remembering poems: Andros, p. 14.

Dring's descriptions of Cooper: Dring, *Recollections,* pp. 89–90. Cooper's sermons and the warning to him: Dring, pp. 90–92. Cooper's criticism of Sproat and quotes: Dring, pp. 90–92. Disappearance of Cooper: Dring, p. 95.

Impressment of sailors and new recruits: Watson, *America's First Crisis,* pp. 5, 15–17. Use of press gangs: P. Allen, *History of the American Revolution,* vol. II, p. 257.

Amherst plan: Letter, "Gen. James Robertson to Lord Amherst," January 25, 1782, in Klein and Howard, *Twilight of British Rule,* p. 236.

Admiral Arbuthnot and press gangs: Lowenthal, *Hell on the East River,* p. 49.

Fox's crewmates being conscripted: Fox, *Adventures*, p. 94. "The idea": Fox, pp. 94–95. "Conceived the design": Fox, p. 95. Fox quotes "A British officer" and "almost envied": Dandridge, *American Prisoners*, p. 271.

Fox, Dring, and Andros's discussing offers to join British: Dandridge, *American Prisoners*, p. 254. Fox ultimately enlists: Dandridge, *American Prisoners*, p. 277.

Blatchford's recollection of survival: Dandridge, *American Prisoners*, pp. 146–160.

"Vermin" inside "snuff box": Fox, *Adventures*, p. 145.

Descriptions and quotes about preparing for July 4 celebration: Lowenthal, *Hell on the East River*, pp. 25–26; and Dring, *Recollections*, pp. 97–98. Angry response by the guards, "triumphantly demolished" and "Down, Rebels, down": Dring, *Recollections*, pp. 98, 133; and Armbruster, *Wallabout Prison Ships*, p. 18.

Numbers on the prisoners being killed on July 4: Taylor, *Martyrs to the Revolution*, p. 20, and Dring, *Recollections*, p. 105. "The helpless prisoners": Stiles, *History of the City of Brooklyn*. Attack by guards belowdecks and quotes of it: Dring, *Recollections*, p. 100; and Taylor, *Martyrs to the Revolution*, p. 21.

Dring's recalling the evening, thirst, and the ghastly scene the next day: Dring, *Recollections*, p. 100. Dring's quote "thronged to the water": Dring, p. 103. Andros's remembering "more spiteful": Andros, *Old Jersey Captive*, p. 10, "Turn out your dead" and what happened the day after the attack: Onderdonk, *Revolutionary Incidents*, p. 237; Dring, *Recollections*, p. 105; and Taylor, *Martyrs to the Revolution*, p. 22.

The Hessians being preferable: Dring, *Recollections*, p. 104.

"For god's sake": Taylor, *Martyrs to the Revolution*, pp. 22–23.

CHAPTER 14. ESCAPE

General information on Elizabeth Burgin: see Hagist, "Elizabeth Burgin Helps the Prisoners"; and Silcox-Jarrett, *Heroines*, p. 26.

Burgin's writing to Rev. Calville: "Elizabeth Burgin to Reverend James Calville," November 19, 1779, in *Papers of the Continental Congress*, http://research.archives .gov/description/5916026. Washington's writing on behalf of Burgin: "George Washington to the President of Congress," December 25, 1779, in *Papers of the Continental Congress*, http://research.archives.gov/description/5913711. Burgin's writing to Washington: "Elizabeth Burgin to George Washington," March 16, 1780, Founders Online, National Archives, http://founders.archives.gov/documents /washington/99–01–02–01137.

Rivington Gazette article is from March 1, 1780; see Dandridge, *American Prisoners*, ch. 21.

Number of guards versus the number of prisoners on the *Jersey*: Dring, *Recollections*, p. 38.

"The physical force" and "occasionally brought back": Dandridge, *American Prisoners*, pp. 258–259.

"By having our miserable" and "hardly sufficient": Dandridge, *American Prisoners*, p. 263.

Stories of reprisal by the guards for attempted escapes: Armbruster, *Wallabout Prison Ships*, p. 19.

Stories of escapes: See Dandridge, *American Prisoners*, ch. 31; Dring, *Recollections*, p. 469, and *Connecticut Gazette*, May 25, 1780.

Ebenezer Fox's stories of escape: *New Jersey Gazette*, June 4, 1780; and Dandridge, *American Prisoners*, ch. 21. January 1780 escape to New London: Onderdonk, *Revolutionary Incidents*, p. 231, February 16, 1780.

CHAPTER 15. RUN!

Hawkins's escape: Hawkins, *Life and Adventure*. Hawkins and Waterman quotes about planning to escape: Hawkins, p. 9. The challenge of escaping and quotes about getting off the ship: Hawkins, pp. 9–10. In the water swimming: Hawkins, pp. 9–10. Coming ashore: Hawkins, p. 10. First night off the ship: Hawkins, p. 11. Eluding the Tories and Hessians: Hawkins, p. 11. Encountering young woman with a basket: Hawkins, p. 11. Sleeping in barns: Hawkins, p. 12. Meeting old woman and her son who fed him: Hawkins, pp. 12–13. Arriving home: Hawkins, pp. 13–14.

Dring's planned escape: Dring, *Recollections*, pp. 107–108. Prisoners crawling through the wall and the guards catching them: Dring, pp. 109–110. "Perverse" action by guards and prisoners panicking: Dring, pp. 111–112.

Andros escape: Andros, *Old Jersey Captive*. "While on board": Andros, p. 14. An opportunity presented itself in a prisoner exchange: Andros, p. 15. Andros in despair after not getting off *Jersey*: Andros, p. 14. Believes he must escape or die: Andros, pp. 15–16. Story about Young and Spicer: Andros, pp. 12–13. Poems and quotes about God's plan: Andros, p. 16. Quotes about going ashore on a work party: Andros, p. 17. Hiding in swamp: Andros, pp. 18–19. First night and day on the run: Andros, pp. 20–21. In woods and avoiding the dragoons: Andros, pp. 21–22. Asking for milk from a patriot: Andros, p. 23. Giving the helpful couple money: Andros, p. 25. Day of judgment: Andros, p. 26. Belief in providence and signs from God: Andros, pp. 26–27. "Sink under such trials" and sobbing: Andros, p. 32. Whaling boat back home: Andros, pp. 39–40. Arriving home: Andros, pp. 42–43.

CHAPTER 16. TURNING POINT

Ferling quote: Ferling, "Myths of the American Revolution."

Fluctuations between the number of loyalists and patriots: USHistory.org, "Loyalists, Fence-sitters, and Patriots."

"The Adams Third": "John Adams to James Lloyd," in Adams, *Works*, vol. X, pp. 108–111.

Academic debate over "Adams Third": Smith, *A New Age*, vol. I, p. 656; Marina, "Only 1/3 of Americans"; Aptheker, *American Revolution*, pp. 54–55; Alden,

American Revolution, p. 87; Palmer, *Age of the Democratic Revolution*, vol. I, p. 200; Schellhammer, "John Adams's Rule of Thirds"; Rutman, *Morning of America*, p. 178; Greene, *Comparative Revolutionary Movements*, p. 47.

McKean's response to Adams: Schellhammer, "John Adams's Rule of Thirds."

Studies that estimate the number of patriots and loyalists: Calhoon, *Loyalist;* Fleming, *Liberty*; and Smith, *A New Age.*

Loyalists in different colonies: Middlekauff, *Glorious Cause*, p. 550.

The number of British loyalists in uniform: Schellhammer, "John Adams's Rule of Thirds"; Smith, *A New Age*, pp. 264–267; and Calhoon, *Loyalist*, p. 502.

George Washington's comment about the number of countrymen who support cause: Aptheker, *American Revolution*, pp. 54–55.

Adams's "Divided" quote: Schellhammer, "John Adams's Rule of Thirds."

Hawkins's commenting on escapes: Hawkins, *Life and Adventure*, p. iv.

The *Freeman's Journal*: Dandridge, *American Prisoners*, ch. 21; and *Freeman's Journal*, January 19, 1777.

Holt's New York Journal and the king's intention: Lossing, *Pictoral Field-Book*; Dandridge, *American Prisoners*, ch. 21 (article from October 19, 1775, which was reprinted from a London newspaper on August 5, 1775).

"Associations of intense horror": Lossing, *Pictoral Field-Book*, 1850.

Quotes about the "Old Jersey" "striking terror": Dring, *Recollections*, p. 5.

Hawkins's getting help from a woman: Hawkins, *Life and Adventure*, pp. 12–13.

Dring's quote about yellow fever: Dring, *Recollections*, p. 142.

The *Connecticut Journal* report on Captain Calhoon: Dandridge, *American Prisoners*, ch. 21; see also *Connecticut Journal*, March 22, 1781. *Connecticut Gazette* story about 200 prisoners: *Connecticut Gazette*, January 8, 1777. 130 prisoners' arriving near New London: article is from January 4, 1782.

Report on the prisons for Connecticut Legislature and the Babcock, Trumbull, and Washington letters about Connecticut prisoners: letters "Babcock to Trumbull," January 7, 1777, and "Trumbull to Washington," December 12, 1776, in Washington, *Papers* (ed. Chase), vol. 7, pp. 322–324, "Washington to Trumbull," December 21, 1776, in vol. 7, p. 406, "Trumbull to Washington," January 12, 1777, in vol. 8, pp. 53–54, and "Trumbull to Washington," January 14, 1777, in vol. 8, pp. 70–71.

Pennsylvania Council of Safety report: letter, "Pennsylvania Council of Safety to Washington," January 15, 1777, in Washington, *Papers* (ed. Chase), vol. 8, pp. 74–76.

Reports on how many prisoners died in winter: Amerman, "Treatment of American Prisoners," pp. 267–268.

Disturbing reports of the guard's behavior toward prisoners: Taylor, *Martyrs to the Revolution*, pp. 34, 38–40, 42.

George Batterman's allegations in the newspaper and David Sproat's reply: *Philadelphia Journal*, January 17, 1781; see also "Batterman's Declaration" in Banks, *David Sproat*, pp. 34–37. The Sproat letter is from January 29, 1781; see Banks, pp. 39–43.

"It is painful to repeat": *New Hampshire Gazette*, February 4, 1779; see also Dandridge, *American Prisoners*, ch. 21.

Christopher Vail story: DeWan, "Wretched Prison Ships."

Robert Sheffield story: Dandridge, *American Prisoners*.

The lengthy report in the *Connecticut Journal*: see *Connecticut Journal*, January 30, 1777; see also Dandridge, *American Prisoners*, ch. 21; Taylor, *Martyrs to the Revolution*, p. 39; and *Thatcher's Journal*, p. 76.

"I am now a prisoner": Dandridge, *American Prisoners*, ch. 21.

Pennsylvania Packet story: letter from August 10, 1781, published in the *Pennsylvania Packet*, September 4, 1781.

The Tory newspaper: the paper was run by James Rivington and allegedly quoted an American prisoner named John Cooper. See "John Cooper to James Rivington," June 11, 1782, in Banks, *David Sproat*, pp. 72, 78. The newspaper article was "Cooper and Others to Friends and Fellow Countrymen of America."

Cunningham's propaganda: Lossing, *Pictoral Field-Book*. British telling Americans that their country did not care for them: Taylor, *Martyrs to the Revolution*, p. 38. Captain Dawson's report: Amerman, "Treatment of American Prisoners," p. 257; see also Brumbaugh, "Report," pp. 237–238; and "Report of an Enquiry on Board His Majesty's Prison Ship *Jersey*," February 2, 1781, in Banks, *David Sproat*, pp. 50–53. Sproat's reports: "Captains' Report," June 22, 1782, in Banks, pp. 82–84; and Morris, *Papers*, vol. V, pp. 583–584, July 15, 1782.

The letters between Dawson and Washington: "Captain Dawson to General Washington," February 2, 1781, in Banks, *David Sproat*, pp. 49–50. "Washington to Skinner," February 18, 1781, in Washington, *Writings* (ed. Fitzpatrick), vol. XXI, pp. 243–244. "Arbuthnot to Washington," April 21, 1781, in Washington, *Writings* (ed. Sparks), vol. VII, p. 384; see also reports in *New York Mercury*, February 5, 1781, and *Boston Gazette*, May 28, 1781.

"I was refused permission": Taylor, *Martyrs to the Revolution*, p. 37, letter "Skinner to David Sproat."

British papers criticizing Americans as "outlaws": Burrows, *Forgotten Patriots*, p. 36; and Lutnick, *American Revolution and the British Press*, pp. 80–85.

"There are now 5000 prisoners": Dandridge, *American Prisoners*, ch. 21.

British were not able to restore order by force alone: Marina, "Only 1/3 of Americans"; and Shy, "The American Revolution," pp. 130–139.

Concerns by General Gage and quote "Americans lose 600": Kuhn, *Structure of Scientific Revolutions*, p. 148; and Marina, "Only 1/3 of Americans."

Historian John Shy: Shy, "The American Revolution," p. 148. "Constant skirmish": Marina, "Only 1/3 of Americans."

Nathanael Greene's motto: Thayer, "Nathanael Greene." "A war of ravage and destruction": Shy, "The American Revolution," p. 146; and Marina, "Only 1/3 of Americans."

CHAPTER 17. FREEDOM

Continental Congress approves prisoner exchanges: *Journal of the Continental Congress*, vol. 3, p. 400.

Reports in the *Virginia Gazette* and Gen. Washington's letter to Gen. Gage: *Virginia Gazette*, Issue 1, July 1775; and Ramsay, *History of the American Revolution*.

"A sufficient supply": *Connecticut Gazette*, April 30, 1777, and *Connecticut Gazette*, January 4, 1782.

Gov. Trumbull to Washington, "In New York": Force, *Archives*, 5th Series, vol. 3, p. 1193.

Corrupt negotiations by British commissaries: Jones, *History of New York*, p. 304.

Gov. Clinton's pushing for exchanges: Lowenthal, *Hell on the East River*, p. 46.

New London paper report on 500–600 prisoners: see letters of August 18, 1779, and September 29, 1779, in the *Connecticut Gazette*; see also Onderdonk, *Revolutionary Incidents*, pp. 228–232. Their "countenances indicate": the article is from September 2, 1779.

Early newspaper reports: Onderdonk, *Revolutionary Incidents*, p. 240. "The prisoners, instead": Dandridge, *American Prisoners*, ch. 21.

Washington's difficult decision on exchanges: Armbruster, *Wallabout Prison Ships*, p. 8.

Admirals Rodney and Arbuthnot and the exchanges: Ranlet, "Tory David Sproat," pp. 191–192; "Rodney to Stephens," October 28, 1780, and "Rodney to Navy Board," November 13, 1780, in Rodney, *Letter-Books*, vol. I, pp. 55–56, 76.

Washington and Digby on exchanges: "George Washington to Robert Morris," December 11, 1782, in Morris, *Papers*, vol. VII, pp. 193–194. Adm. Digby's concerns and intentions: "David Sproat to Abraham Skinner," January 25, 1782, in *Papers of the Continental Congress,* Item 169, Reel 188, pp. 292–293; see also "Abraham Skinner to George Washington," February 18, 1782, in *Papers of the Continental Congress*, Item 169, Reel 188, p. 284. Adm. Digby's playing games and Washington's anger: "George Washington to Tench Tilghman," July 10, 1782, in Washington, *Writings* (ed. Fitzpatrick), vol. XXIV, p. 423, "George Washington to President of Congress," February 18, 1782, in Washington, *Writings* (ed. Fitzpatrick), vol. XXIV, pp. 5–6; and "Abraham Skinner to David Sproat," June 24, 1782, in Banks, *David Sproat*, pp. 88–93.

Ben Franklin letter: April 24, 1782, in Wharton, *Revolutionary Diplomatic Correspondence*, vol. 5, pp. 326–327.

Sherburne's learning he would be exchanged: Sherburne, *Memoirs*, p. 118. Worrying about "lice and vermin": Sherburne, pp. 119–120. Being rescued by the captain of the small boat: Sherburne, p. 121. Meeting the family of a former crewmate: Sherburne, p. 122. Arriving home: Sherburne, p. 127.

Dring still on the *Jersey*: Dring, *Recollections*, p. 117.

Washington, Clinton, and Digby's ongoing efforts for an exchange: "General Washington to Admiral Digby," June 5, 1782, in Washington, *Writings* (ed. Fitzpatrick), vol. XXIV, pp. 315–316.

Sproat and Skinner letters: Onderdonk, *Revolutionary Incidents*, p. 240, "David Sproat to Abraham Skinner," June 1, 1782.

Washington agrees to meet with three prisoners: "Admiral Digby to General Washington," June 10, 1782, in Banks, *David Sproat*, p. 87. "Abraham Skinner to David Sproat," June 9, 1782, in Banks, pp. 75–77. "Abraham Skinner to George Washington," June 11, 1782, in Banks, pp. 79–80. Washington gets minor improvements on the *Jersey*: Armbruster, *Wallabout Prison Ships*, pp. 18–19.

Three prisoners meet Washington: Stiles, *History of the City of Brooklyn*, vol. I, p. 356; and Dring, *Recollections*, p. 119. Washington explains the dilemma to the three prisoners: Dring, *Recollections*, pp. 122–123. Dring reads Washington letter to *Jersey* prisoners: Dring, p. 121.

Capt. Aborn arrives back at the *Jersey*: Dring, *Recollections*, p. 127. Prisoners are told the mission was a failure: "David Sproat to Prisoners on *Jersey*," June 11, 1782, in Banks, *David Sproat*, p. 73.

The sloop arrives: Dring, *Recollections*, p. 128. Prisoners learn that there is an exchange from a cartel: Dring, p. 169. Dring's quotes on his thoughts and feelings about exchange: Dring, pp. 129–130. Prisoners are called to board sloop: Dring, p. 130. Dring's apprehension on board sloop: Dring, p. 131. Dring is finally free: Dring, p. 132.

CHAPTER 18. DEATH AND DEMISE

Gen. Carleton and change of command at the end of the war: Lowenthal, *Hell on the East River*, p. 53; and Onderdonk, *Revolutionary Incidents*, p. 244, letters from New London paper, June 21, 1782.

British "paroles" at the end of the war: Schaukirk, *Occupation of New York City*, p. 26.

Descriptions from a New London paper of the ship at the end of the war: *Connecticut Gazette*, February 14, 1783.

Final releases at the end of the war: Sherburne, *Memoirs*, p. 116; see also Wertenbaker, *Father Knickerbocker*, p. 170.

Sproat's announcement: "Sproat to Major MacKinzey," May 10, 1783, in British Headquarters Papers, No. 7660, New York Public Library.

Drowne's fate: Dandridge, *American Prisoners*, p. 432.

"The old hulk" quote: West, *Horrors*, p. 7.

The *Jersey*'s finally sinking: Dring, *Recollections*, p. 145; and Armbruster, *Wallabout Prison Ships*, p. 22.

"The thousands" quote: West, "Prison Ships," p. 123.

Sherburne's visiting the sunken *Jersey*: Sherburne, *Memoirs*, pp. 151, 247.

Additional accounts of seeing the *Jersey*: Stokes, *Iconography*, vol. 5, p. 1319. (The account on April 18, 1795, was by Dr. Alexander Anderson.) See also Dandridge, *American Prisoners*, p. 306; and the letter from Silas Talbot in Onderdonk, *Revolutionary Incidents*, p. 236. The letter from Captain Roswell Palmer's son to Henry Drowne in 1856 is in Dandridge, *American Prisoners*, p. 306.

George Washington's farewell at Fraunces Tavern: "Memoirs of Col. Benjamin Tallmidge," 1820, available at Fraunces Tavern Museum in New York City.

Heath's account of the *Jersey*: Heath, *Heath's Memoirs*, pp. 388–389. Sproat's meticulous records: Ranlet, "Tory David Sproat," p. 198.

Accounts by West and Taylor: West, "Prison Ships," p. 123; and Taylor, *Martyrs to the Revolution*, p. 32.

Onderdonk's version: Newspaper article from May 8, 1783, in Onderdonk, *Revolutionary Incidents*, p. 245.

Town of Fishkill and Samuel Loudon: Lowenthal, *Hell on the East River*, p. 58. (The *Connecticut Gazette*, April 25, and the *Pennsylvania Packet*, April 29.) See also Stokes, *Iconography*, vol. 5, p. 1044. "Baseless conjecture": Lowenthal, *Hell on the East River*, p. 60.

Jefferson's deposition: letter "Thomas Jefferson to William Phillips," July 22, 1779, in Jefferson, *Papers*, vol. II, p. 45; "Jefferson to Jean Nicolas Demeunier," June 26, 1786, vol. X, pp. 61–62; "Deposition of Richard Riddy," August 17, 1786, vol. X, p. 269.

Remsen's account: Malone, *Jefferson*, pp. 232–233. Remsen on the Riddy deposition: Jefferson, *Papers*, vol. X, p. 269. See also West, "Prison Ships," p. 123; and Lowenthal, *Hell on the East River*, p. 65.

Elias Boudinot's account: Dandridge, *American Prisoners*, p. 445. Dring "has never been": Dring, *Recollections*, p. 5. "Three to eight per day": Webb, *Correspondence and Journals*, vol. II, pp. 191–193. Henry Laurens's estimate: Letter "Henry Laurens to John Burnett," July 24, 1778, in Smith, *Letters of Delegates*, vol. X, p. 345.

George Washington letter: "George Washington to Rear Admiral Robert Digby," June 5, 1782, in Washington, *Writings* (ed. Fitzpatrick), vol. 24, p. 316.

Lowenthal: Lowenthal, *Hell on the East River*, p. 10.

Peckham: Peckham, *Toll of Independence*, p. 132.

Lemisch: Lemisch, "Listening."

Report that listed 8,000 names: Society of Old Brooklynites, *A Christmas Reminder*, p. 3; "American Prisoners of the Revolution: Names of 8000 Men."

Peckham's study: Peckham, *Toll of Independence*, pp. 130–133.

Lowenthal on the relative population: Lowenthal, *Hell on the East River*, p. 67.

Lossing quote and Andros quote: Lossing, *Pictoral Field-Book*; and Andros, *Old Jersey Captive*, p. 8.

Scholars have weighed in on the issue: Lowenthal, *Hell on the East River*, p. 60; Armbruster, *Wallabout Prison Ships*, pp. 24–28; Ranlet, *New York Loyalists*, pp. 186, 199; and Burrows, "Prisoners of New York," p. 2.

CHAPTER 19. REDISCOVERY

Jackson procuring the land at Wallabout Bay: West, *Horrors*, p. 9.

The involvement of Tammany Hall: Cray, "Commemorating," pp. 576–578.

Effort to build a memorial: Lossing, *Pictoral Field-Book*; and Cray, "Commemorating," pp. 578–579.

The politics of Jefferson, the Anti-Federalists, and impressment: Watson, *America's First Crisis*.

Dewitt's oration and the ceremony: West, *Horrors*, p. 13.

The nickname "Tomb of the Patriots": West, *Horrors*, pp. 11–12.

Details and quotes on the dedication in 1808: Dring, *Recollections*, p. 146; and West, *Horrors*, pp. 10–13.

Romaine's role and passing: Armbruster, *Wallabout Prison Ships*, p. 22.

The Martyr Monument Association of 1855: Taylor, *Martyrs to the Revolution*, p. 45.

"The Orator": Dring, *Recollections*, p. 94.

Developments in 1873: West, *Horrors*, p. 19; see also *New York Times*, June 9, 1783, p. 2.

One of the stories of boys' stealing the bones from the crypt was told by A. J. Spooner late in life. He recalled watching boys vandalize the memorial as a thirteen-year-old. The account is in Stiles, *History of the City of Brooklyn*, vol. I, pp. 372–373.

Looting at the mausoleum and memorial: "Huge Bronze Eagle Stolen from Park," *New York Times*, February 2, 1914, and "Smashed Bronze Door to Martyrs' Tomb," *New York Times*, May 12, 1923.

The Burrows quote about developing the memorial: Burrows, *Forgotten Patriots*. Developments in the early 1900s: Coggins, *Ships and Seamen*, p. 79; and West, "Prison Ships," p. 123. Discovery of bones in the early 1900s: Wisner, "The HMS *Jersey*." Architectural plans and artifacts are held at the old Navy Yard: Wisner, "The HMS *Jersey*." The DAR and Brooklyn Historical Society have found items that they believe to be from the HMS *Jersey*. They are held at the Brooklyn Historical Society.

Walt Whitman and others' complaining of the neglect: McCullough, *Brooklyn*, p. 109.

Quotes and details from 1908 ceremony: "Taft and Hughes at Martyrs' Shaft," *New York Times*, November, 15, 1908.

Hawkins's quote: Hawkins, *Life and Adventure*, p. iv. "God grant that": Taylor, *Martyrs to the Revolution*, p. 33. Andros quote: Andros, *Old Jersey Captive*, p. 14.

POSTSCRIPT

Laird: Dandridge, *American Prisoners*, p. 292.

Loring: Ranlet, "Tory David Sproat," p. 198.

Cunningham's evacuating city: Lossing, *Pictoral Field-Book*, vol. 2, p. 632, *Connecticut Journal*, December 3, 1783; Onderdonk, *Revolutionary Incidents*, pp.

247–248; and Stiles, *History of the City of Brooklyn*, vol. I, p. 332. End of Cunningham's life: Bruce, *Romance of the Revolution*; Onderdonk, *Revolutionary Incidents*, pp. 245–247; and Lowenthal, *Hell on the East River*, p. 105.

In defense of Sproat: Ranlet, "Tory David Sproat," p. 189; see the letter "Sproat to Abraham Skinner," January 29, 1781, in Banks, *David Sproat*, pp. 41–42; and "Sproat to John Dickinson," July 5, 1783, in Hazard, *Pennsylvania Archives, 1st Series*, vol. 10, p. 68. Sproat's cruelty to prisoners until the end of the war: Hannay, *Rodney*, pp. 144–146. See also "Rodney Letters to Commissioners for Sick and Hurt Seamen," October 28, 1780, in Rodney, *Letter-Books*, vol. I, pp. 63–64; and Brown, *Valentine's Manual*, p. 211.

Sproat's being reimbursed: Letter, "David Sproat to Robert Morris," December 10, 1783, in Banks, *David Sproat*, pp. 107–110, and "Robert Morris to the President of Congress," January 16, 1784, in Banks, p. 112. Congress and the repayment of Sproat: Ranlet, "Tory David Sproat," p. 201. See also United States Continental Congress, *Journals*, vol. XXVI, pp. 337–338. End of his life: Lowenthal, *Hell on the East River*, p. 104; McKinney, *Pennsylvania Archives, 9th Series*, "May 14, 1791"; and Sabine, *Biographical Sketches*.

Hawkins: Hawkins, *Life and Adventures*, p. iv.

Sherburne: Sherburne, *Memoirs*, pp. v, 123.

Andros after the *Jersey*: Andros, *Old Jersey Captive*, pp. 46, 49. Andros's reflecting on imprisonment: Andros, p. 61. Andros's memoir: Andros, p. 46. Description of Andros: Andros, pp. 3–4, preface.

Dring's being exchanged: Dring, *Recollections*, pp. 134, 138. Story of Bicknell: Dring, pp. 139–140. Yellow fever scare on way home and charity of residents: Dring, pp. 142–143. Descriptions of Dring: Dring, p. iv. "Captivity nor my feelings": Dring, p. 105. "To record the history": Dring, p. 2. "They have not been exaggerated": Dring, pp. 2–3.

APPENDIX I

Freneau's early life and legacy: Bowden, "In Search of," pp. 174–192.

Stories of sailing and capture: Freneau, *Some Account*.

Stories of the Scorpion and imprisonment: Freneau, "British Prison-Ship."

Bibliography

HISTORICAL DOCUMENTS

Note: Numerous newspapers and letters from the Revolutionary War period were used. They are cited in the notes section of the book.

Adams, John. *The Works of John Adams, Second President of the United States: with a Life of the Author, Notes, and Illustrations, by His Grandson Charles Francis Adams.* 10 vols. Boston: Little, Brown, 1850–1856.

Allen, Ethan. *Narrative of Colonel Ethan Allen's Captivity; Containing His Voyages and Travels.* Philadelphia: Robert Bell, 1779. Reprint: New York: Georgian Press/Fort Ticonderoga Museum, 1930.

Allen, Paul. *A History of the American Revolution: Comprehending All the Principal Events Both in the Field and in the Cabinet.* First published 1819. Baltimore: William Wooddy, 1822.

American Scenic and Historic Preservation Society. *The Old Martyrs' Prison, New York: An Historical Sketch of the Oldest Municipal Building in New York City.* [Pamphlet.] N.p.: n.p., n.d.

Andros, Thomas. *The Old Jersey Captive; or a Narrative of the Captivity of Thomas Andros, on Board the Old Jersey Prison Ship at New York, 1781.* Boston: William Peirce, 1833.

Association for Erecting a Monument to the 11,500 Martyrs of the British Prison Ships: Bylaws and Minutes, 1852–1855. Lot 1977.048, box A0030. Brooklyn Historical Society, Brooklyn, NY.

Boudinot, Elias. "Letters of Elias Boudinot." *Pennsylvania Magazine of History and Biography* 43 (1919): 283–287.

Brooklyn Bicentennial Commission Medals, 1976. Lot 2011.024, Box A0135. Brooklyn Historical Society, Brooklyn, NY.

Brown, Henry Collins, ed. *Valentine's Manual of Old New York for 1916–1917*. New York: Valentine, 1916.

Bruce, Oliver Bell. *The Romance of the Revolution: A History of Personal Adventures, Romantic Incidents, and Exploits*. New York: H. Dayton, 1853.

Bushnell, Charles. *The Prison Ship "Jersey."* [Pamphlet.] Brooklyn, NY: Brooklyn Historical Society, n.d.

Butterfield, L. H., ed. *Adams Family Correspondence*. Cambridge, MA: Harvard University Press, 1963.

Caulkins, Frances Manwaring. *History of New London, Connecticut, from the First Survey of the Coast in 1612 to 1860*. New London, CT: Frances M. Caulkins, 1852.

"A City of Prisons." *Harper's Weekly*, July 17, 1880, pp. 461–462.

Clark, William Bell, and William James Morgan, eds. *Naval Documents of the American Revolution*. Washington, DC: GPO, 1964.

Continental Army Enlistment Form. Printed by Benjamin Edes, Watertown, Massachusetts, June 1776. Library of Congress, Rare Book and Special Collections Division—Broadsides and Printed Ephemera Collection.

Cresswell, Nicholas. *The Journal of Nicholas Cresswell, 1774–1777*. New York: Dial Press, 1924.

Dandridge, Danske. *American Prisoners of the Revolution*. Charlottesville, VA: Michie, 1911. Reprint: New York: Three Rivers Press, 1998.

Diman, J. Lewis. *The Capture of General Richard Prescott by Lt. Col. William Barton: An Address Delivered at the Centennial Celebration of the Exploit at Portsmouth, Rhode Island, July 10, 1877*. Providence: S. S. Rider, 1877.

Dring, Thomas. *Recollections of the Jersey Prison Ship; Taken and Prepared for Publication from the Original Manuscript of the Late Captain Thomas Dring of Providence, R.I., One of the Prisoners*. Edited by Albert Greene. Providence: H. H. Brown, 1829.

Field, Thomas W. *Historic and Antiquarian Scenes in Brooklyn and Its Vicinity*. Brooklyn, 1868.

Force, Peter, ed. *American Archives*. 1st–5th Series. Washington, DC: Clarke and Force, 1837–1853.

Ford, Worthington Chauncy, comp. and ed. *Prisoners of War (British and American), 1778*. Philadelphia, 1893.

Founders Online. Washington, DC: National Archives and Records Administration. http://founders.archives.gov/documents.

Fox, Ebenezer. *The Adventures of Ebenezer Fox in the Revolutionary War*. Boston: Charles Fox, 1833.

Freneau, Philip. "The British Prison-Ship: A Poem in Four Cantoes." Philadelphia: F. Bailey, 1781. Reprint: Washington, DC: America in Class/National Humanities Center, 2010.

———. *Some Account of the Capture of the Ship Aurora.* New York: M. F. Mansfield & A. Wessels, 1899.

Geismar, Joan H. *Monument Lot Archaeological Dig Report.* 2003. Lot 2007.036, Box 2007.036. Brooklyn Historical Society, Brooklyn, NY.

Graydon, Alexander. *Memoirs of His Time, with Reminiscences of the Men and Events of the Revolution.* Philadelphia: Lindsay and Blakiston, 1846.

Hawkins, Christopher. *The Life and Adventure of Christopher Hawkins, a Prisoner on Board the "Old Jersey" Prison Ship During the War of the Revolution.* New York: Holland Club, 1858. Reprint: London: Forgotten Books, 2015.

Hazard, Samuel, ed. *Pennsylvania Archives, 1st Series.* 12 vols. Philadelphia: J. Severns, 1852–1856.

Heath, William. *Heath's Memoirs of the American War.* Edited by Rufus Rockwell Wilson. New York: A. Wessels, 1904.

Hopkinson, Francis. *The Miscellaneous Essays and Occasional Writings of Francis Hopkinson, Esq.* Philadelphia: T. Dobson, 1792.

Jefferson, Thomas. *Memoirs, Correspondence, and Private Papers of Thomas Jefferson.* Edited by Thomas Jefferson Randolph. London: Colburn and Bentley, 1829.

———. *The Papers of Thomas Jefferson.* 42 vols. Edited by Julian P. Boyd et al. Princeton: Princeton University Press, 1950–2014.

Johnston, Henry P. *The Battle of Harlem Heights: September 16, 1776.* London: Macmillan, 1897.

———. *The Campaign of 1776 Around New York and Brooklyn.* London: Macmillan, 1878.

Jones, Thomas. *History of New York During the Revolutionary War.* New York: New York Historical Society, 1879. Reprint: New York: Arno Press, 1968.

Lossing, Benson J. *Pictoral Field-Book of the Revolution,* supp. IV, vol. II, *British Prisons and Prison Ships.* New York: Harper Brothers, 1859–1860.

McKinney, Gertrude, ed. *Pennsylvania Archives, 9th Series.* 10 vols. Pennsylvania: Department of Property and Supplies, 1931–1935.

Morris, Robert. *The Papers of Robert Morris, 1781–1784.* Edited by E. James Ferguson et al. Pittsburgh: University of Pittsburgh Press, 1973–1975.

Onderdonk, Henry, Jr. *Revolutionary Incidents of Suffolk and Kings Counties: With an Account of the Battle of Long Island, and the British Prisons and Prison-Ships at New York.* New York: Leavitt, 1849.

Papers of the Continental Congress. Washington, DC: National Archives and Records Administration.

Perry, Ichabod. *Reminiscences of the Revolution.* Lima, NY, 1915.

Prison Ship Martyrs' Monument Association. *Dedication of the Monument and Other Proceedings.* New York: Macgowan & Slipper, 1913.

———. *Secretary's Report of the Obsequies of the Prison Ship Martyrs at Plymouth Church, Brooklyn, N.Y.* New York: Macgowan & Slipper, 1901.

Ramsay, David. *The History of the American Revolution.* 2 vols. Edited by Lester H. Cohen. Indianapolis: Liberty Fund, 1990. The citation is from volume 1.

Roberts, James A. *New York in the Revolution as Colony and State.* Hudson, NY: Three Rivers, 1898.

Rodney, George Brydges. *Letter-Books and Order Book of George, Lord Rodney, Admiral of the White Squadron, 1780–1782.* Edited by Dorothy C. Barck. 2 vols. Collections of the New York Historical Society, vols. 65 and 66. New York, 1932.

Russell, Charles Theodore. *Mr. Russell's Oration: Delivered Before the Municipal Authorities of the City of Boston, July 4, 1851.* Boston: J. H. Eastburn, 1851.

Sabine, Lorenzo. *Biographical Sketches of Loyalists of the American Revolution.* First published 1864. Reprint: Port Washington, NY: Kennikat, 1966.

Schaukirk, Ewald Gustav. *Occupation of New York City by the British.* New York: Arno Press, 1969.

Serle, Ambrose. *The American Journal of Ambrose Serle: Secretary to Lord Howe, 1776–1778.* Edited by Edward H. Tatum Jr. San Marino, CA: Huntington Library, 1940.

Sherburne, Andrew. *Memoirs of Andrew Sherburne: A Pensioner of the Navy of the Revolution.* Providence: H. H. Brown, 1831.

Smith, Paul H., ed. *Letters of Delegates to Congress, 1774–1789.* Washington, DC: GPO, 1976.

Society of Old Brooklynites. *A Christmas Reminder; Being the Names of About Eight Thousand Persons, A Small Portion of the Number Confined on Board the British Prison Ships During the War of the Revolution.* Brooklyn, NY: Eagle, 1888.

———. *An Appeal to the Congress of the United States from the Society of Old Brooklynites; for the Erection of a Monument over the Remains of 11,500 Prisoners Who Died on Board the British Prison Ships During the Revolutionary War.* Brooklyn: G. Tremlett, 1890.

Stiles, Henry Reed. *A History of the City of Brooklyn; Including the Old Town and Village of Brooklyn, the Town of Bushwick, and the Village and City of Williamsburg.* New York, 1867.

———, ed. *Letters from the Prisons and Prison-Ships of the Revolution.* New York, 1865. Reprint: Farmington Hills, MI: Thomson Gale, 1969.

Taylor, George. *Martyrs to the Revolution; in the British Prison-Ship in the Wallabout Bay.* New York: W. H. Arthur, 1855.

United States Continental Congress. *Journals of the Continental Congress, 1774–1789.* Edited by Worthington Chauncy Ford. 34 vols. Washington, DC: GPO, 1904–1937.

Washington, George. *The Diaries of George Washington, 1748–1799.* Edited by John C. Fitzpatrick. 4 vols. Boston: Houghton Mifflin, 1925.

———. George Washington Papers, Series 4: General Correspondence, 1697–1799. Library of Congress, Washington, DC.

———. "George Washington to Continental Army: Farewell Orders, November 2, 1783." In George Washington Papers, Series 6: Military Papers, 1755–1798. Library of Congress, Washington, DC.

———. *The Papers of George Washington: Revolutionary War Series.* 24 vols. Edited by Philander D. Chase et al. Charlottesville: University of Virginia Press, 1985–2008.

———. *The Writings of George Washington.* Collected and edited by Worthington Chauncey Ford. 14 vols. New York: G. P. Putnam's Sons, 1889–1893.

———. *The Writings of George Washington; Being His Correspondence, Addresses, Messages and Other Papers.* Edited by Jared Sparks. Boston: American Stationers' Company, 1834–1840.

———. *The Writings of George Washington from the Original Manuscript Sources, 1745–1799.* Edited by John C. Fitzpatrick. 39 vols. Washington, DC: GPO, 1931–1944.

Watson, John F. *Annals and Occurrences of New York City and State, in the Older Time.* Philadelphia: H. F. Arnes, 1846.

Webb, Samuel Blachley. *The Correspondence and Journals of Samuel Blachley Webb.* Edited by Worthington Chauncy Ford. Lancaster, PA: Wickersham Press, 1893–1894.

West, Charles E. *Horrors of the Prison Ships: Dr. West's Description of the Wallabout Floating Dungeons; How Captive Patriots Fared.* New York: Eagle, 1895.

———. "Prison Ships in the American Revolution." *Journal of American History* 5 (1911): 120–125.

Wharton, Francis, ed. *The Revolutionary Diplomatic Correspondence.* Washington, DC: GPO, 1889.

Whitman, Walt. "Brooklyniana, No. 5." *Brooklyn Standard*, January 4, 1862.

———. "Ode: To Be Sung on Fort Greene; 4th of July 1846." *Brooklyn Daily Eagle*, July 2, 1846.

Books

Alden, John R. *A History of the American Revolution.* New York, 1954. Reprint: Boston: Da Capo Press, 1989.

Allen, Gardner W. *A Naval History of the American Revolution.* Boston: Houghton Mifflin, 1913.

Aptheker, Herbert. *The American Revolution: 1763–1783.* New York: International Publishers, 1960.

Armbruster, Eugene L. *The Wallabout Prison Ships: 1776–1783.* New York, 1920.

Banks, James Lenox. *David Sproat and Naval Prisoners in the War of the Revolution, with Mention of William Lenox, of Charlestown.* New York: Knickerbocker Press, 1909.

———. *Prison Ships in the Revolution: New Facts in Regard to Their Management.* New York, 1903.

Brigham, Clarence S., ed. *British Royal Proclamations Relating to America.* First published 1911. New York: Franklin, 1968.

Burrows, Edwin G. *Forgotten Patriots: The Untold Story of American Prisoners During the Revolutionary War*. New York: Basic Books, 2008.

Burrows, Edwin G., and Mike Wallace. *Gotham: A History of New York City to 1898*. New York: Oxford University Press, 2000.

Calhoon, Robert McCluer. *The Loyalist in Revolutionary America, 1760–1781*. New York: Harcourt Brace Jovanovich, 1973.

Campbell, Charles F. *The Intolerable Hulks: British Shipboard Confinement, 1776–1857*. Bowie, MD: Heritage Books, 1993. Reprint: Tucson: University of Arizona Press, 2001.

Chidsey, Donald Barr. *The American Privateers*. New York: Dodd, Mead, 1962.

Coggins, Jack. *Ships and Seamen of the American Revolution*. Harrisburg, PA: Stackpole Books, 1969.

Daughan, George C. *If by Sea: The Forging of the American Navy from the American Revolution to the War of 1812*. New York: Basic Books, 2008.

Davidson, Philip G. *Propaganda and the American Revolution, 1763–1783*. Chapel Hill: University of North Carolina Press, 1941.

Davis, Kenneth C. *America's Hidden History: Untold Tales of the First Pilgrims, Fighting Women, and Forgotten Founders Who Shaped a Nation*. New York: Smithsonian Books, 2008.

Falkner, James. *The War of Spanish Succession, 1701–1714*. South Yorkshire, UK: Pen and Sword, 2015.

Fleming, Thomas. *Liberty: The American Revolution*. New York: Viking, 1997.

Ford, Douglas. *Admiral Vernon and the Navy: A Memoir and Vindication*. Ann Arbor: University of Michigan Library, 1907.

Gallagher, John J. *The Battle of Brooklyn*. Boston: Da Capo Press, 2001.

Greene, Thomas H. *Comparative Revolutionary Movements*. Englewood Cliffs, NJ: Prentice Hall, 1974.

Gruber, Ira D. *The Howe Brothers and the American Revolution*. Chapel Hill: University of North Carolina Press, 1972.

Haffner, Gerald O. "The Treatment of Prisoners of War by the Americans During the War of Independence." Ph.D. dissertation, Indiana University, 1952.

Hannay, David. *Rodney*. London: Macmillan, 1910. Reprint: Ann Arbor, MI: Gregg Press, 1972.

Jellison, Charles A. *Ethan Allen: Frontier Rebel*. Syracuse, NY: Syracuse University Press, 1983.

Jensen, Merrill. *The Founding of a Nation: The History of the American Revolution*. New York: Oxford University Press, 1968.

Johnson, William Branch. *The English Prison Hulks*. London: Phillimore, 1957.

Klein, Milton M., and Ronald W. Howard, eds. *The Twilight of British Rule in Revolutionary America*. Cooperstown: New York State Historical Association, 1983.

Kuhn, Thomas S. *The Structure of Scientific Revolutions*. Chicago: University of Chicago Press, 1970.

Lang, Patrick J. *The Horrors of the English Prison Ships, 1776 to 1783, and the Barbarous Treatment of the American Patriots Imprisoned on Them*. Philadelphia: Society of the Friendly Sons of Saint Patrick, 1939.

Lowenthal, Larry. *Hell on the East River: British Prison Ships in the American Revolution*. Fleischmanns, NY: Purple Mountain Press, 2009.

Lutnick, Solomon. *The American Revolution and the British Press, 1775–1783*. Columbia: University of Missouri Press, 1967.

Maclay, Edgar Stanton. *A History of American Privateers*. New York: Appleton, 1899.

Malone. Dumas. *Jefferson and the Ordeal of Liberty*. Boston: Little, Brown, 1962.

Manders, Eric I. *The Battle of Long Island*. Monmouth Beach, NJ: Philip Freneau Press, 1978.

McCullough, David. *1776*. New York: Simon and Schuster, 2006.

———. *Brooklyn, and How It Got That Way*. New York: Dial Press, 1983.

Metzger, Charles H. *The Prisoner in the American Revolution*. Chicago: Loyola University Press, 1971.

Middlekauff, Robert. *The Glorious Cause: The American Revolution, 1763–1789*. New York: Oxford University Press, 1985.

Morison, Samuel Eliot. *John Paul Jones: A Sailor's Biography*. Boston: Little, Brown, 1959.

Palmer, R. R. *The Age of the Democratic Revolution*. Princeton, NJ: Princeton University Press, 1959.

Peckham, Howard H. *The Toll of Independence: Engagements and Battle Casualties of the American Revolution*. Chicago: University of Chicago Press, 1974.

Ranlet, Philip. *The New York Loyalists*. Knoxville: University of Tennessee Press, 1986.

Rigden, Reg. *The Floating Prisons of Woolwich and Deptford*. London: Borough of Greenwich, 1976.

Rutman, Darrett B. *The Morning of America: 1607–1789*. New York: Houghton Mifflin, 1971.

Silcox-Jarrett, Diane. *Heroines of the American Revolution: America's Founding Mothers*. Chapel Hill, NC: Green Angel Press, 1998.

Skemp, Sheila L. *William Franklin: Son of a Patriot, Servant of a King*. New York: Oxford University Press, 1990.

Smith, Page. *A New Age Now Begins: A People's History*. New York: McGraw-Hill, 1976.

Stokes, I. N. Phelps. *The Iconography of Manhattan Island, 1498–1909*. 6 vols. New York: R. H. Dodd, 1915–28. Reprint: New York: Arno Press, 1967.

Watson, Robert P. *America's First Crisis: The War of 1812*. Albany: SUNY Press, 2014.

Wertenbaker, Thomas J. *Father Knickerbocker Rebels*. New York: Scribner's, 1948.

Whitman, Walt. *The Uncollected Poetry and Prose of Walt Whitman*. Edited by Emory Holloway. New York: Doubleday, 1921.

Willis, Sam. *Fighting at Sea in the Eighteenth Century: The Art of Sailing Warfare*. London: Boydell Press, 2008.

Wills, Garry. *Lincoln at Gettysburg: The Words That Remade America*. New York: Simon & Schuster, 2006.

ARTICLES AND ONLINE SOURCES

Adams, Simon. "The Spanish Armada." BBC Online. February 17, 2011. www.bbc .co.uk/history/british/tudors/adams_armada_01.shtml.

"Admiral Edward 'Old Grog' Vernon." http://www.geni.com/people/admiral -edward-old-grog-vernon/6000000001599759655.

"American Prisoners of the Revolution: Names of 8000 Men." American Merchant Marine at War. http://www.usmm.org/revdead.html.

Amerman, Richard H. "Treatment of American Prisoners During the Revolution." *Proceedings of the New Jersey Historical Society* 78 (1960): 260–267.

Anderson, Olive. "The Establishment of British Supremacy at Sea and the Exchange of Naval Prisoners of War, 1689–1783." *English Historical Review* 75 (January 1960): 81–89.

———. "The Treatment of Prisoners of War in Britain During the American War for Independence." *Bulletin of the Institute of Historical Research* 28 (May 1955): 62–82.

Bolton, G. C. "William Eden and the Convicts." *Australian Journal of Politics and History* 26, no. 1 (1980): 30–40.

Bowden, Mary Weatherspoon. "In Search of Freneau's Prison Ships." *Early American Literature* 14, no. 2 (Fall 1979): 174–192.

Brumbaugh, Catherine B. "Report on the British Prison Ship *Jersey*, February 2, 1781." *Daughters of the American Revolution Magazine* 44 (1914): 237–238.

Burrows, Edwin. "Prisoners of New York." *Long Island History Journal* 22 (2011): 1–10.

Calhoon, Robert M. "Loyalism and Neutrality." In *The Blackwell Encyclopedia of the American Revolution*, edited by Jack P. Greene and J. R. Pole. New York: Blackwell, 1991.

Cray, Robert E., Jr. "Commemorating the Prison Ship Dead: Revolutionary Memory and the Politics of Sepulture in the Early Republic, 1776–1808." *William and Mary Quarterly* 56, no. 3 (July 1999): 565–590.

Delahunty, Robert J. "The Burials of Greek Warriors." Law and Religion Forum (blog), Center for Law and Religious Freedom, St. John's University School of Law, October 22, 2015. https://clrforum.org/2015/10/22/the-burials-of-greek -warriors.

DeWan, George. "The Wretched Prison Ships." The Dear Surprise (blog), May 2, 2011. http://www.thedearsurprise.com/the-wretched-prison-ships.

"Elizabeth Burgin." National Women's History Museum. https://www.nwhm.org
/education-resources/biography/biographies/elizabeth-burgin.

Elliott, Emory B., Jr. "Freneau, Philip [Morin]." In *A Princeton Companion*, edited
by Alexander Leitch. Princeton, NJ: Princeton University Press, 1978.

Ferling, John. "Myths of the American Revolution; A Noted Historian Debunks
the Conventional Wisdom About America's War for Independence." *Smithsonian Magazine*, January 2010.

Frayler, John. "Privateers in the American Revolution." The American Revolution:
Lighting Freedom's Flame, December 4, 2008. National Park Service. https://
www.nps.gov/revwar/about_the_revolution/privateers.html.

Furman, Robert. "The Prison Ship Martyrs: A History of Commemoration." 2014.
http://gaz.jrshelby.com/Furman%20-%20The%20Prison%20Ship%20Martyrs
%20(c).pdf.

Hagist, Don N. "Elizabeth Burgin Helps the Prisoners . . . Somehow." *Journal of the American Revolution*, September 11, 2014. https://allthingsliberty
.com/2014/09/elizabeth-burgin-helps-the-prisoners-somehow.

Hickman, Kennedy. "Seven Years' War: Admiral Edward Boscawen." About
.com, December 14, 2014. http://militaryhistory.about.com/od/naval/p/Seven
-Years-War-Admiral-Edward-Boscawen.htm.

———. "War of Jenkins' Ear: Admiral Edward Vernon." About.com, August
12, 2015. http://militaryhistory.about.com/od/naval/p/War-Of-Jenkins-Ear
-Admiral-Edward-Vernon.htm.

———. "War of Jenkins' Ear: Prelude to a Greater Conflict." About.com, January
14, 2016. http://militaryhistory.about.com/od/battleswars16011800/p/jenkins
ear.htm.

History Channel. "The HMS *Jersey*." 2010. http://www.history.com/topics
/american-revolution/the-hms-jersey.

Huguenin, Charles A. "Ethan Allen, Parolee on Long Island." *Vermont History* 25
(1957): 105–111.

Humphrey, Carol Sue. "Top 10 Revolutionary War Newspapers." *Journal of the American Revolution*, February 26, 2015. https://allthingsliberty.com/2015/02
/top-10-revolutionary-war-newspapers.

"Jenkins' Ear, War of (1739–1742)." *Europe, 1450 to 1789: Encyclopedia of the Early Modern World*. Encyclopedia.com. http://www.encyclopedia.com/history
/modern-europe/wars-and-battles/war-jenkinss-ear.

Jordan, Helen. "Colonel Elias Boudinot in New York City, February, 1778." *Pennsylvania Magazine of History and Biography* 24 (1900): 460–461.

Keith. "The Prison Ship Martyrs' Monument: More Americans Died Emprisoned
[*sic*] in New York Harbor Than in All Revolutionary War Battles Combined."
Keith York City (blog), November 3, 2012. https://keithyorkcity.wordpress
.com/2012/11/03/the-prison-ships-martyrs-monument-more-americans-died
-emprisoned-in-new-york-harbor-than-in-all-revolutionary-war-battles-combined.

Knight, Betsy. "Prisoner Exchange and Parole in the American Revolution." *William and Mary Quarterly* 38 (April 1991): 219–225.

Lemisch, Jesse. "Listening to the 'Inarticulate': William Widger's Dream and the Loyalty of American Revolutionary Seamen in British Prisons." *Journal of Social History* 3, no. 1 (Fall 1969).

Lincoln, Abraham. "The Gettysburg Address." Abraham Lincoln Online. www .abrahamlincolnonline.org/lincoln/speeches/gettysburg.htm.

Lindsey, William R. "Treatment of American Prisoners of War During the Revolution." *Emporia State Research Studies* 22, no. 1 (Summer 1973): 5–32.

Marina, William. F. "Only 1/3rd of Americans Supported the American Revolution?" History News Network, August 8, 2005. http://historynewsnetwork.org /article/5641.

———. "The American Revolution and the Minority Myth." Independent Institute, January 1, 1975. http://www.independent.org/publications/article .asp?id=1398.

Moran, Don N. "Casualties During the American Revolution." *Liberty Tree Newsletter*, March 2006. http://www.revolutionarywararchives.org/warstats.html.

Myers, J. Jay. "George Washington: Defeated at the Battle of Long Island." *American History*, June 2001.

"Newly Discovered Eyewitness Accounts of the War for Independence." *American Heritage* 31, no. 3 (April/May 1980).

Nolan, Kiera E. "Lawrence Washington." *The Digital Encyclopedia of George Washington*. http://www.mountvernon.org/digital-encyclopedia/article/lawrence -washington.

O'Malley, Brian Patrick. "Fortune of War." Prisoners of the Revolution (blog), March 2, 2016. http://brianomalley1776.blogspot.com/2016/03/fortune-of-war .html.

———. "July 20, 1776." Prisoners of the Revolution (blog), July 20, 2012. http:// brianomalley1776.blogspot.com/2012/07/july-20–1776.html.

———. "November 21, 1777." Prisoners of the Revolution (blog), November 20, 2009. http://brianomalley1776.blogspot.com/2009/11/november-27–1777.html.

———. "Provost Marshal Cunningham." Prisoners of the Revolution (blog), March 15, 2013. http://brianomalley1776.blogspot.com/2013/03/provost -marshal-cunningham.html.

"Pericles' Funeral Oration from the Peloponnesian War." *Ancient History Sourcebook*, Fordham University. http://legacy.fordham.edu/halsall/ancient/pericles -funeralspeech.asp.

"Philip Freneau." *Revolutionary Writers in American History: From Revolution to Reconstruction and Beyond*. University of Groningen. http://www.let.rug.nl /usa/outlines/literature-1991/authors/philip-freneau.php.

"Privateers and Mariners in the Revolutionary War." American Merchant Marine at War. http://www.usmm.org/revolution.html.

Ranlet, Philip. "In the Hands of the British: The Treatment of American POWs During the War of Independence." *The Historian* 62, no. 4 (Summer 2000): 731–757.

———. "Tory David Sproat and the Death of American POWs." *Pennsylvania History* 61, no. 2 (1994): pp. 185–205.

Schellhammer, Michael. "John Adams's Rule of Thirds," *Journal of the American Revolution*, February 11, 2013. http://allthingsliberty.com/2013/02/john-adamss-rule-of-thirds.

Shy, John. "The American Revolution: The Military Conflict Considered as a Revolutionary War." In *Essays on the American Revolution*, edited by S. G. Kurtz and J. H. Hutson, 121–156. Chapel Hill: University of North Carolina Press, 1973.

Smith, Paul H. "The American Loyalists: Notes on Their Organization and Numerical Strength." *William and Mary Quarterly* 25 (1968): 259–277.

Starkey, Armstrong. "War and Culture: A Case Study: The Enlightenment and the Conduct of the British Army in America." *War and Society* 8 (May 1990): 1–28.

Sterling, David L. "American Prisoners of War in New York: A Report by Elias Boudinot." *William and Mary Quarterly* 13 (July 1956): 376–378.

Stockwell, Mary. "Battle of Long Island: Moving Around." *Digital Encyclopedia of George Washington*. http://www.mountvernon.org/digital-encyclopedia/article/battle-of-long-island.

Stone, Hiram. "The Experiences of a Prisoner in the American Revolution." *Journal of American History* 2 (1908): 520–530.

Thayer, Theodore. "Nathanael Greene." In *George Washington's Generals*, edited by George A. Billias, 109–136. New York: William Morrow, 1964.

"Thucydides: Pericles Funeral Oration in Depth." Background to the PBS documentary *The Greeks: Crucible of Civilization*. www.pbs.org/empires/thegreeks/background/36.html.

USHistory.org. "Loyalists, Fence-sitters, and Patriots." *U.S. History Online Textbook*. http://www.ushistory.org/us/11b.asp.

White, Joseph. "Thomas Andros: Captive." *New England Quarterly* 10 (1937): 510–520.

Wilford, John Noble. "Bones May Be Those of Ancient Athenians in Pericles' Funeral Oration." *New York Times*, February 17, 2000.

Wisner, Meredith. "The HMS *Jersey*, Is She or Isn't She?" BNY Blog, Building 92: Brooklyn Navy Yard Center, May 2012. http://bldg92.org/blog/hms-jersey.

Index